CW01022711

Children and Separation

Childhood separation and loss have become virtually a way of life for a large number of children throughout the world. Children separated from their genetic parent(s) and consequently their genealogical, social and cultural roots due to processes such as adoption, parental divorce/separation, donor insemination, single parenthood by choice and child trafficking can face social, emotional and psychological difficulties.

This book explores the premise that a proper understanding of the complex inner world of modern day separated children and their psycho-social development requires a shift in focus or emphasis. It presents the notion of *socio-genealogical connectedness* as a new theoretical framework for studying and promoting these children's growth and development. This new theory simultaneously challenges and complements existing notions of psycho-social development, including attachment theory and Erikson's psycho-social theory of personality development. Owusu-Bempah proposes that this sense of socio-genealogical connectedness is an essential factor in children's adjustment to separation, and their emotional and mental health; much like those adopted, separated children suffer a loss of genealogical continuity, and hence, loss of 'self'. This hypothesis is discussed and ultimately supported through both the author's own research and a broad selection of theoretical and empirical material from other areas.

The book further considers the implications of this notion of socio-genealogical connectedness for childcare policy and practice, as well as directions for future research in this and related fields. *Children and Separation* is an invaluable resource for academics, students and childcare professionals. The accessible style of the book ensures that it will also be useful to parents and anybody affected by childhood separation.

Kwame Owusu-Bempah, Chartered Psychologist, Chartered Scientist and Associate Fellow of the British Psychological Society, is Reader in Psychology at the University of Leicester. He has published extensively on topics in several areas of his discipline. His current research interests are in the areas of racial justice and the psychological well-being of separated children.

Children and Separation

Socio-Genealogical Connectedness Perspective

Kwame Owusu-Bempah

Routledge
Taylor & Francis Group

LONDON AND NEW YORK

First published 2007 by Routledge
27 Church Road, Hove, East Sussex, BN3 2FA

Simultaneously published in the USA and Canada
by Routledge
270 Madison Avenue, New York, NY 10016

*Routledge is an imprint of the Taylor & Francis Group, an
Informa business*

© 2007 Psychology Press

Typeset in Times by RefineCatch Limited, Bungay, Suffolk
Printed and bound in Great Britain by TJ International Ltd,
Padstow, Cornwall
Cover design by Design Deluxe

All rights reserved. No part of this book may be reprinted or
reproduced or utilized in any form or by any electronic,
mechanical, or other means, now known or hereafter
invented, including photocopying and recording, or in any
information storage or retrieval system, without permission in
writing from the publishers.

British Library Cataloguing in Publication Data
A catalogue record for this book is available from the British Library

Library of Congress Cataloging-in-Publication Data
Owusu-Bempah, Kwame.
  Children and separation : socio-genealogical connectedness
  perspective / Kwame Owusu-Bempah.
     p. cm.
  Includes bibliographical references and index.
  ISBN-13: 978–0–415–34212–4 (hardback)
  ISBN-10: 0–415–34212–0 (hardback)
  1. Parental deprivation. 2. Loss (Psychology) in children.
  3. Attachment behavior in children. 4. Personality development.
  I. Title.
BF723.P255O98 2007
155.4′18–dc22   2006101418

ISBN: 978–0–415–34212–4

In memory of my parents and my late 'adoptive' sister, friend and colleague, Pauline Hardiker.

To my children, Akwasi and Abenaa, and 'adoptive' grandchildren, Hiten and Maree Roupari (Jessica); to *all* separated children of the world, listening to and reading about your experiences provided the fuel that propelled and sustained me to embark upon and complete this project. I hope that this book, in some way, represents your collective experiences; I wish you all well.

Contents

Preface

Throughout human history, the growing human being and, hence, the nature, quality and purpose of life have been viewed through a variety of lenses, through mythological, metaphysical, religious, sociological and psychological lenses. In modern times, since Sigmund Freud's time, however, the psychological account of human development has dominated other explanations or propositions in the western world, and, as a consequence of the global dominance of western values, notably 'science', in the rest of the world. Psychological theories, especially Freud's psychosexual theory and learning theory have, however, tended to present human development in terms which suggest that the developing child is destined to grow into a self-reliant, atomic adult, to be independent of their social and spiritual environments or relationships with other human beings for meeting their needs or attaining their wishes. In other words, these explanations presume a person who has priority over the community in which they live or its members with whom they interact.

Psychological assumptions regarding child development have not always gone unquestioned or unchallenged. Individually, they fail to do full justice to the complexity of human nature and development. At best, each theory provides but a partial understanding of human growth and development. Many of these theories ignore not only the universally held belief that a human being, whether a child, young person, adult or elderly, is innately a communal being who naturally seeks relationships with other human beings, particularly their kith and kin or, indeed, clan. This book takes full cognisance of this universal belief. Taking into account the cultural setting in which development occurs, it proposes the idea of socio-genealogical connectedness as a theoretical (as well as therapeutic) framework for a better understanding of psycho-social development.

The term socio-genealogical connectedness refers to the degree of our knowledge about our hereditary origins and the extent to which one assimilates that knowledge into one's inner world. With specific regard to children, it refers to the extent to which they integrate their biological parents' genetic, cultural/ethnic and social backgrounds. It is from this perspective that this book examines the implications of separation and loss for children who are separated from not only their genetic parent(s), but also from their genealogical, social and cultural roots.

This book argues that a proper understanding of the inner world of these children and their psycho-social developmental needs requires not just a synthesis, amalgamation or fusion of established perspectives, whatever word or term one chooses to describe the outcome of the process; it requires added viewpoints as well. Thus, it presents the notion of socio-genealogical connectedness as an additional perspective on child psycho-social development; its emphasis, though, is on separated children. The author presents his own research and a wide range of theoretical and empirical material from other areas, adoption (domestic as well as cross-country), divorce, and assisted conception, to support his hypotheses. In brief, the book defines the concept of socio-genealogical connectedness, develops and elaborates its significance and helpfulness in understanding the psycho-social development difficulties facing separated children. It also seeks to answer implicit questions and anomalies in traditional theories, for instance, attachment theory, and at the same time to add to them.

The book also raises questions about culture and identity. It acknowledges that definitions of who we are as children are not wholly dependent on our relations with our parents. Thus, the thesis it presents can act as a theoretically unifying catalyst. For example, it builds upon the author's own empirical data, interlaces with and analyses other theoretical constructs. However, readers may find that there is sometimes a lack of current literature, especially regarding current approaches to the classic theories examined, attachment theory, for example. This must by no means detract from the potential contribution of the work to knowledge, to our understanding of separated children's developmental needs and how best we may meet those needs, and to childcare policy and practice. One of the principal purposes of the book is to bring together generations of important theories on child development in a radical and new synthesis. In other words, the work is essentially a new synthesis of research into child development spanning many decades. It pays careful attention to the thoughts and ideas of pioneering writers on children's identity development. Yet, it is not history in any real sense, but an attempt to draw together significant ideas into a new synthesis of major practical importance to psychologists, psychiatrists, family therapists, social workers, and many other professions working with children.

The book's approach is extraordinarily modern in that, as well as bringing classic psychological ideas on child development into a coherent synthesis, it takes up major issues in the handling of policy in relation to separated children, including those produced with the help of medical technology such as in the case of sperm or gamete donation. It also offers key ideas to help understand the circumstances in which the children of lone parents may prosper or may become problems.

Besides considering the implications of the notion of socio-genealogical connectedness and research built upon it for childcare policy and practice, the book signposts directions for future research in this and related fields. It is therefore highly relevant to the activities of academics, such as attachment and identity writers and researchers and those concerned with the effects of assisted conception. These topics cut across disciplines of sociology, social policy, psychology and psychiatry. It is also an invaluable resource to teachers, students and childcare professionals.

In summary, the book offers plenty of food to provoke thought and stimulate discussion. It also raises a number of issues which some readers may find controversial. Nonetheless, that is an inherent feature of new ideas. So, the author believes that it is a risk worthy of taking, and he has taken it; and, in one's view, the more the issues with which this book deals perturb our 'comfort zones' the better.

Acknowledgements

First and foremost, I must express my special gratitude to Dennis Howitt of Loughborough University. Dennis, metaphorically speaking, assiduously encouraged and facilitated my courtship with this 'strange' idea of socio-genealogical connectedness. He has never tired of my going on and on about the idea and its development, whatever the situation we were in. Thanks a lot for your friendship, patience and the numerous occasions you provided and continue to provide valuable suggestions for developing the idea to this stage.

I am equally indebted to Jane Aldgate, my second 'adoptive sister', friend and colleague. Jane has, in various ways, enthusiastically and untiringly nourished the idea which forms the basis of this book right from its embryonic stage, since 1993. Many thanks, Jane. I am sure that you are, naturally, 'over the moon' to hold your 'niece/nephew' in your hands.

My special thanks also go to Peter Stratton of the University of Leeds, Sandy Fraser of the Open University, and my colleague, Sandra Dwyer of the University of Leicester for their valuable and encouraging feedback on the manuscript. Tribute is also due to the University of Leicester and Leicestershire Social Services Department for awarding me grants of £2000 and £400 respectively to start the research which has culminated in this book. University of Leicester also granted me a special study leave of one semester during the preparation of this book. Finally, I am grateful to Psychology Press for not only being bold enough to commission this book, but also for their extraordinary patience over delay, for various reasons, in submitting the manuscript.

1 Theories of childhood separation

An overview

For a long time the infant's sense of self includes too much, since it also encompasses those close to him in a literal sense. To be separated from his mother is to lose a part of himself as much as to be separated from a hand or foot.

(Burns, 1979, p. 148)

Roman mythology has it that we owe the city of Rome, and hence the Roman civilization, to twin brothers Romulus and Remus. According to the legend, they were the sons of Mars, the god of war, and Reha Silvia, daughter of King Numitor. King Numitor's brother, Amulius, dethroned him. Having deposed Numitor, Amulius forced Rhea Silvia to become a vestal virgin so that she would not marry or have children. This made Romulus and Remus unwanted children because not only were they born out of wedlock, but also because they were a threat to Amulius; that is, Amulius feared that they would grow up and reclaim the throne. To dispense with the brothers, when the River Tiber broke its banks, he had them placed in a trough and thrown into it, expecting them to drown. When the flood abated, the trough, still containing the two boys, came ashore. They were then found by a she-wolf who, instead of eating them, suckled them and protected them from predators. The wolf was assisted in her maternal duties by a woodpecker who also brought them food. As the story goes, both creatures were sacred to Mars.

Fortuitously, one of the King's shepherds, Faustulus, later found them. He took them home and he and his wife adopted them. Unaware of their origins, they named one Romulus and the other Remus. The twin brothers soon grew up as strong and daring young men who led a bellicose band of shepherds. The brothers killed Amulius and reinstated Numitor, their grandfather, as King of Alba Longa. In furtherance of their achievements, they decided to found a town of their own. Naturally, Romulus and Remus chose the site where the she-wolf had nursed and protected them as the ideal place to locate it. They soon began building walls around the town for protection against invasion or disturbances from neighbouring tribes. The twin brothers got into a minor dispute over the construction of the walls; until then there had been no rivalry between them. This dispute soon escalated into a ferocious fight. Remus died in the fight, leaving Romulus the sole ruler of the town whose initial citizens comprised a gang of outlaws and fugitives. Romulus eventually developed the town into a new city which he named Roma (Rome) after himself. Apart from a short period when he shared the governance of Roma with Titus Tatius, Romulus remained supreme ruler of the city.

According to his subjects, Romulus was immortal; that is, he did not die, but rather disappeared one day in a tempest. Believing that the storm had transported him to paradise, where they hoped to reunite with him in the future, they continued to worship him under the name of Quirinus. Today, the term 'Quirinal' may be seen as signifying the legend's enduring influence on the Italian psyche.

CHILDHOOD SEPARATION

The moral of this ancient story, in the context of the present work, is that the phenomenon of childhood separation has been an aspect of the animal kingdom since creation. In the Christian scriptures, for example, Romulus and Remus' story reminds one of the circumstances of the birth, childhood experiences and adult lives of Moses and Jesus Christ. Every culture in the world has a similar legend which continues to be narrated either orally or in writing by one generation to the next generation. Human babies as well as animal young are every day abandoned by their parents or separated from them for various reasons. In modern times in the human world, the accompanying sense of loss and its emotional and psychological consequences have been a major concern for developmental theorists and child welfare practitioners for many years. Today, due not only to social changes but also to global political, economic and ecological changes, a large number of children are each day separated from one or both birth parents. In other words, childhood separation continues to be a major concern for society at large. In many cases, the extent of loss inherent in childhood separation extends beyond the biological parent(s). It also entails disconnection from genealogical, social and cultural heritage.

In modern times, initial theoretical concerns for separated children were mainly about those reared in total institutions or orphanages, and those who experienced short-term separation from their mothers (Bowlby, 1944, 1951, 1969, 1973, 1980; Goldfarb, 1943; Spitz, 1945). For example, Spitz expressed grave concern about children who, when deprived of maternal care and stimulation, would curl up, refuse food and literally die, although they had access to resources – adequate food, clothing and shelter – to meet their basic needs. Spitz used the phrase 'marasmus and hospitalisation' to epitomize this bizarre phenomenon. Harlow's early 1960s experiments with rhesus monkeys supported Spitz's clinical observations regarding children raised in total institutions. Since then, general concern has been for a much wider range of children: children of parental divorce/separation; those involved in domestic and cross-country adoption; displaced/unaccompanied children; children of lone mothers by choice; and the offspring of donor insemination.

Historically, in efforts to understand the effects of separation on the social, emotional and psychological functioning of these children and youngsters, researchers and childcare professionals have presented adopted children as a case in point. In these presentations, the children either 'sink or swim'. Those who 'swim' tend to be presented as heroes and heroines, while little is heard of those who 'sink'. Today, while some highlight the case of those who 'swim', others tend to emphasize the experiences of the children who 'sink' or who are rescued from 'sinking' through, for instance, adoption. Many of those rescued are seen as among the lucky ones. However, they are rescued at great loss to themselves, the loss of their biological parents and socio-genealogical roots. This is mainly because, in the western world particularly, the effects of an adoption order have historically been to legally and irreversibly sever a child's link to their birth and extended family and, consequently, from their genealogical roots, ostensibly to foster a 'healthy' relationship with their adoptive family. As we will see in this book, this practice has been shown to have detrimental effects on the children. Today, children involved in cross-country adoption are at particular risk of losing not only their birth parents and siblings, but also, and equally importantly, their genealogical and cultural heritage.

CAUSES OF CHILDHOOD SEPARATION

Children are separated from their birth parents and socio-genealogical roots for reasons other than adoption (Kaplan, 1995). Indeed, in modern times, apart from domestic and cross-country adoption and child trafficking, disasters, both natural and man-made, are major causes of childhood separation. Disasters very often leave in their trail devastation and deaths; they destroy life and ravage whole communities; they may desolate villages, towns and even cities. Civil wars and international conflicts often result in severe damage to communities. Similarly, natural occurrences such as earthquakes, hurricanes, floods or droughts invariably cause timeless anguish. Whether caused by nature or man-made, infants and children are always among the casualties. In these circumstances, communities are often dispersed. In fleeing from drowning (floods) or famine (drought), bombing and killings, or pestilence, families are often split, following different routes to safety. In this process of flight and scattering, large numbers of children become permanently separated from their families and often end up far away from home and their ancestral roots, in a foreign land, oftentimes on another continent. These occurrences have been a part of human history. Today, many children escaping from their countries for safety or other reasons continue to be dispersed around western Europe and North America.

In more recent memory, Bonnerjea (1994), for example, reported that in the early 1990s, apart from the number of Romanian and Russian children who found themselves in western European nations and North America through adoption, many other children were separated in the battles of Angola and Rwanda, in Thai provinces children were bonded, sold or kidnapped into the sex trade, and ever-increasing numbers of separated children were to be found on the streets of South America. During this period, many children were also separated during the Bosnian conflict, in the Indian earthquake and in Peruvian battles. Bonnerjea estimated that in 1994 the UK received a number of Somali and Sudanese children who fled experiences as child soldiers or whose parents sent them to avoid forced conscription; in the Netherlands, nearly 20 per cent of asylum seekers were unaccompanied/separated children, the largest numbers coming from Angola and China. Bonnerjea estimated that in the USA, many of the unaccompanied/separated children, largely from Central America, who entered the country had been abducted or kidnapped and trafficked, or had travelled independently in search of better life chances. Ressler and colleagues (1988) take a more retrospective look and record the Red Cross's estimate of around 13 million children who were separated from their kith and kin, taken from their ancestral roots at the end of World War II, including children deported as slave labourers and illegitimate children of labourers who were not allowed to keep them. In the year 2005 alone, thousands of children lost their birth families through natural disasters – the Indian Ocean tsunami, hurricane Katrina in New Orleans, and the Pakistani earthquake. The exact number of these children most probably may never be known.

In times of peace and plenty, children's need for their birth family is hardly ever questioned. In times of disaster, however, we quickly lose sight of the importance of the family and cultural identity to the child. In these circumstances, Ressler and colleagues (1988) have noted that the physical survival of children takes precedence over all other concerns, such as their emotional and psychological needs, including their need to be close to their kith and kin. Hence, both local and international intervention programmes routinely separate them from their families in order to concentrate rescue resources and efforts on them. Such measures remind us of the programmes and efforts that were mounted to transport en masse children from Vietnam to the USA and western Europe for adoption in the 1970s. Although obviously well meaning, such measures disregard the long-established mass of research evidence showing that, in most cases, children's emotional and social needs are best served by their own families; that meeting best the needs of infants and children requires the continuity, stability and sensitive responsiveness of family members. Ressler and colleagues argue that during emergencies adult kith and kin remain the primary source of security, protection and comfort for children, so that family attachments and bonding which take on heightened importance in emergencies need to be preserved. Simply put, in most circumstances the best interests of the children are served and protected by the birth family. Notwithstanding, measures taken in times of disaster very frequently result in a large number of children losing their birth families through both domestic and cross-country adoption, refugeeism and child trafficking; and, in many cases, institutional adoption (i.e. orphanages).

CHILDREN OF LONE PARENTS

Other groups of children separated from their birth parent(s) and extended family include children of parental divorce/separation, children resulting from donor insemination, and children of lone mothers by choice or by default. In today's western world particularly, a large number of children are separated from one biological parent for these reasons. Globally, the USA is at the top of the league table, as in many aspects of life, for having the largest number of these children – dependent children living with only one parent. In the European Union (EU), the UK tops the league. For example, the Statistical Office of the European Community (EuroStat) in Luxembourg reported that in 1996, EU-wide, 10.7 million dependent children lived with one parent. This represents 13 per cent of all dependent children in the EU in that year. Of these, 1.8 per cent were under 5 and a further 5.9 per cent were aged 5 to 15. The UK has by far the highest proportion (23 per cent) of families with dependent children. In absolute terms, between 2001 and 2004, 599,275 children under 16 years of age in England and Wales alone were living with only one of their birth parents (Office for National Statistics, 2005a). At the other extreme, as discerned from the EuroStat report, Greece and Italy had 7 per cent each and Spain 8 per cent. EU-wide, 84 per cent of lone parents were women. The report concluded that the rise in lone parenthood has been one of the most striking demographic and social trends in recent years.

Today, the two main routes of entry into lone parenthood are marriage or relationship breakdown and the birth of a child outside marriage or a stable relationship. Both have increased since the early 1960s. In the UK, according to the Office for National Statistics (2005a), the number of divorces recorded increased from 27,224 in 1961 to 153,399 in 2004. EU-wide, the UK is reported to take the lead here – with the highest divorce rate and the largest number of children born outside marriage. In this respect, the UK comes second only to the USA which has 40 per cent of dependent children living in lone-parent families. Anderson (2002) contrasts these data with those of Italy where practically every child is born within marriage and has a much lower probability (7 per cent of all dependent children) of experiencing family disruption due to parental divorce or separation before the age of 15 (*http.// europa.eu.int/en/comm/eurostat/compres/en/9798/6309798a.htm, accessed 18/ 04/2005*).

Yet another group of children (and adults) disconnected in many ways from one or even both parents' biological, social and cultural roots are those who resulted from donor insemination. Worldwide, this group comprises a significant number. In a keynote address to the Annual Conference of the Human Fertilisation and Embryology Authority in 2004, the then

Parliamentary Under Secretary of State for Public Health reported that since 1991 (when the Human Fertilisation and Embryology Act came into force), over 73,000 babies had been born in the UK alone as a result of treatment procedures regulated under the Act. This is consistent with Blyth's (1999) estimate that in 1995 alone 7510 children were born following treatment using donated gametes. Blyth and colleagues (2001) estimated that 1612 of the 2143 donor-conceived births were recorded in the UK in one year, between 1 April 1998 and 31 August 1999 – the most recent period for which data were available. These figures, however, did not take into account the births resulting from self-insemination.

There is a consensus amongst researchers that because donor insemination, by and large, requires minimum medical intervention or none at all, it has been practised for considerably longer than either egg or embryo donation, and remains the most prevalent form of assisted conception. As we will see in later chapters, in the UK, as in many other western nations, until very recently, the offspring of donor insemination have been, de jure as well as de facto, denied any information that would lead them to the donor. Thus, they have no means of contact with that person, their genetic parent. In the less extreme case of parental divorce or separation, research consistently shows that a substantial proportion of the children involved also lose contact with the non-resident parent, usually the father.

DEVELOPMENTAL IMPLICATIONS

Review of the clinical literature clearly indicates that one of the major features which all groups of separated children share in common is their negative psycho-social developmental outcomes. From this literature (which will be reviewed in later chapters) these problems seem virtually endless. In childhood, the symptoms range from emotional problems such as enuresis to physical growth problems such as dwarfism; in adolescence and adulthood these range from psychiatric problems such as depression to affectionless personality (or psychopathy). Psychologically, these individuals are characteristically associated with identity confusion, especially in adolescence. Furthermore, not only are many of these difficulties manifest in adulthood and old age, but some of them, including social and marital relationships, mental health, and maladaptive parenting skills, are also claimed to be generationally transmitted. Thus, in the past century, particularly since the 1940s onwards, psychologists and clinicians have endeavoured to find explanations for these problems and also to design intervention programmes for solving or, at least, ameliorating them.

EXPLANATIONS

The thesis about to be presented agrees with many traditional as well as contemporary theories that human need for connection to other human beings is innate. Prior to Bowlby's (1969, 1973, 1980) attachment theory, popularly termed 'maternal deprivation', theorists explained this need in terms of drive. The favourite theories, then, were psychoanalytic and learning theories. Both attributed the development of a feeling of human connectededness, particularly the bond between infants/children and their mothers, the proto-type of human connection, to the pairing of nutritional or physiological needs and to the ability and preparedness of a specific person to meet these needs. According to these theories, the extent and manner in which the child's physiological needs are met, by and large, determine the degree or strength of the child's attachment, bond or connectedness to that person and other human beings. The following section summarizes the central tenets of those theories.

PSYCHOANALYTIC THEORY

Orthodox Freudian theory sought to explain human psycho-social develop-ment in terms of the infant's or child's psychic libido. Libido refers to the urges that gather momentum in us and demand release or gratification with-out delay. Libinal needs are akin to physiological needs, such as hunger and thirst, that cause tensions or disequilibrium within the body. In the case of babies and infants, the need to establish homeostasis or physiological equi-librium, to feed or be comforted, pulls the baby into close physical proximity and profound emotional relationship with the person, usually the mother, who meets this need. This is because the mother, if able and willing, can fulfil the baby's libidinal needs or appease the psychic force within it by (breast)feeding the child. In psychoanalytic terms, any delay in meeting these needs gives rise to a threat to survival which, in turn, results in tensions or anxiety (a feeling of insecurity). Psychoanalytic theory postulated that the mother's ability and readiness to feed and, thereby, satisfy her infant's libidinal needs formed the basis of the baby's enduring love for her and the unique bond between them. This explanation, however, does not provide a full account of the human need for connection to others, in that it does not generalize this relationship beyond the mother to other human beings. It is predominantly concerned with the dyadic relationship between the infant and its primary carer.

The notion of 'fixation' derived from this explanation may be viewed as Freud's attempt to take psychoanalytic proposition regarding personality development to its logical conclusion. Freud termed the first stage of person-ality development (the first year of life) the 'oral stage'. Fixation implies that if the infant's efforts to gratify its libidinal needs are thwarted or those needs are not fully met, its psychological development becomes arrested, so that it cannot progress to the next stage of development, the 'anal stage'. That is, the child develops an oral personality which it carries into adulthood. Such behaviours as over-eating, smoking and alcohol or substance abuse are manifestations of oral personality, according to psychoanalytic theory. With regard to interpersonal relationships, it may therefore not be implausible to speculate that individuals with oral personality will tend towards instrumental relationships. In other words, they are likely to enter relationships with people who either meet their libidinal needs, or at least contribute in some way towards meeting those needs. This has been suggested as one of the characteristics of children and adults who have experienced certain forms of separation and loss, for example, rejection or neglect.

LEARNING THEORY

Early learning theories similarly located the genesis of human connection in the infant–mother relationship, in the contiguous relationship between the infant's physiological needs and the meeting of those needs. In other words, early learning theories presented (breast)feeding as the major factor in developing a sense of connectedness. Dollard and Miller (1950), for example, put forward the 'secondary drive hypothesis' to account for this phenomenon. Primary drives are our essential physiological needs, such as air, food, water and bodily comfort or homeostasis. The human infant, like most infants in the animal world, relies on others to satisfy these needs; and it does not seem to matter who meets the needs (as exemplified by the legendary Romulus and Remus). As postulated by the secondary drive hypothesis, the infant comes to associate the 'feeder' with the satisfaction derived from meeting these basic needs. It is the primary caregiver, usually the mother, who fulfils these needs, and so very soon becomes associated with the primary reward of feeding, warmth and relief from physical discomfort. Consequently, in learning theory terms, the mother attains the status of a positive (secondary) reinforcer.

One of the main features distinguishing learning theories from psychoanalytic theory is that the latter generally maintains that much of the parent–child relationship is an ascribed one; that is, it depends on the experiences of each other. This is in stark contrast to the former which attribute it to psychic or instinctual forces. Learning theories have their own inherent limitations, however. One of these is the evidence from studies, such as Schaffer and Emerson's (1964), which indicated that infants can become attached to people who are not responsible for meeting their essential requirements, for example, feeding. In fact, other researchers have found that many children become attached to parents who neglect or abuse them. Animal studies have reported similar findings (e.g. Harlow, 1962; Harlow and Harlow, 1965).

In summary, early theories of human bonding, attachment or connectedness postulated that infant–mother bonding resulted from the fact that the mother was the source of food and water, two of the infant's most basic needs. For example, Freud claimed that object relations developed on the basis of feeding, and Dollard and Miller postulated that infant–mother bonding was the product of feeding. Later research findings failed to tally with these theories. Konrad Lorenz (1935), for example, showed that precocial birds such as ducklings and goslings are independent of their mother in meeting their basic physiological needs – feeding themselves – from the moment of hatching, yet they seek proximity to their mother – hence, his notion of imprinting. Harlow and co-workers' studies showed that infant rhesus monkeys sought safety and comfort from inanimate terry cloth covered surrogate mothers who had no capacity to feed them. These observations demonstrated to the investigators that the unique infant and primary caregiver relationship does not stem from such primary behaviours as feeding: geese demonstrate bonding without feeding; rhesus monkeys show feeding without bonding. In brief, a closer examination of psychoanalytic and learning theories and studies based upon them clearly suggested to researchers that an alternative explanation was required. The observations and findings of the studies indicated that a different mechanism was involved in the infant's proclivity to relate to a mother figure, whether or not she supplied food.

BOWLBY'S ATTACHMENT THEORY

Bowlby (1969) provided the alternative explanation; he perceived the need for alternative explanations to the above theories. He therefore proposed an attachment behaviour system unrelated to feeding. The concept of attachment which adopted a biological approach, separate from psychoanalysis, made sound evolutionary sense to Bowlby (Holmes, 1993). He saw attachment as a class of behaviours distinct from feeding behaviour and sexual behaviour. Because of its clinical origins, attachment theory has been firmly located in the area of 'abnormal' development, and so has been closely associated with psychopathology. For example, attachment disorders have been described in the psychological and psychiatric literature for over 60 years now.

It must be pointed out that long before Bowlby fully hatched his theory of human attachment, the importance of human connectedness to the developing child had been alluded to in the psychological and psychiatric literature by other clinicians. For example, Spitz (1945) concluded from his observations of institutionalized children that providing only for a child's physical needs is not sufficient for normal development. We must, nonetheless, acknowledge Bowlby for bringing this to the fore.

In spite of his training and background in psychoanalysis, Bowlby tried to distance himself, as far as possible, from a psychoanalytic account of human development, at least as propounded by Freud. In terms of personality, he was particularly disenchanted with Freud's proposition that development proceeds in five stages – (1) oral (birth–1 yr); (2) anal (1–3 yrs); (3) phallic (3–6 yrs); (4) latency (7–12 yrs); (5) genital (13 yrs–sexual maturity) – and that the developing child may become fixated or regress at any of these stages. Fixation at any of these stages carries characteristic personality problems. Bowlby found this account of personality development inadequate and so rejected it. He later reinforced his objection: 'although psychoanalysis is avowedly a developmental discipline it is nowhere weaker . . . than in its concepts of development' (Bowlby, 1988, p. 66).

In rejecting the psychoanalytic model of personality development, he proposed 'attachment' to account for the close infant–mother relationship as the genesis of personality. Not only did he regard attachment as the proto-type of human relationships, but also as innate, a biological imperative. In other words, he saw the need for proximity to and comfort, love and attention from others (especially the mother) as, in every respect, basic as the need for food, water and warmth. Thus, in his report to the World Health Organization, Bowlby (1951) averred:

> What is believed to be essential for mental health is that the infant and young child should experience a warm, intimate and continuous relation-ship with his mother (or permanent mother substitute) in which both find satisfaction and enjoyment.
>
> (quoted in Bowlby, 1973, p. 11)

To support this dictum, he presented evidence, including his previous obser-vations (e.g. 1944), that maternal deprivation (lack of maternal care) or dis-ruptions in child–mother (mother figure) relationship were key factors in many forms of neurosis and psychopathology, including psychopathy.

Howe (1995) has noted that many, especially Bowlby's critics, have tended to ignore or overlook the phrase 'in which both find satisfaction and enjoy-ment' contained in the above quotation. This aspect of attachment implies that the infant–mother relationship is a reciprocal one. On the infant's part, however, Bowlby portrayed it as biologically programmed to seek proximity or relate to particular human beings, especially the mother or primary care-giver. He saw the young child's hunger for his or her mother's love and presence to be as great as the hunger for food. Howe claims that Bowlby saw attachment as a primary motivational system with its own workings and interface with other motivational systems.

Kreamer (1992) has suggested that Bowlby (1969, 1973) concurred with Erikson's (1950) proposition that a person develops in relation to an accom-modation between internal needs or motivations and external reality. In other words, unlike psychoanalysis and learning theory which concerned them-selves more with the individual out of context, out of their wider environ-ment, Bowlby took a wider perspective on personality development, in the sense that he recognized the profound influence of social relationships on the developing human child's psycho-social functioning. He recognized that personality is a product of the interaction between the developing infant's biological make-up and its social and cultural milieux. In *Attachment and Loss: II*, Bowlby (1973) quotes Waddington (1957) to demonstrate his belief:

> Organism and environment are not two separate things, each having its own character in its own right, which come together with little essen-tial interrelation as a sieve and a shovelful of pebbles thrown on to it. The fundamental characteristics of the organism are time-extended

properties, which can be envisaged as a set of alternative pathways of development.

(Bowlby, 1973, p. 411)

Namely, there exists a symbiotic relationship between the infant and its environment, especially the family; the individual develops his or her identity or uniqueness in relation to the socio-cultural milieu. An individual's inability to reconcile their needs or internal motivations with those of the environment, the external reality, jeopardizes this relationship, with adverse consequences for themselves.

Many investigators (e.g. Bretherton and Munholland, 1999; Howe, 1995) agree with Bowlby's (1969, 1973, 1980) claim that attachment theory underscores the central role of relationships in personality development. He saw the role of 'mother love' in infancy and childhood in the infant/child's emotional and mental health to be equivalent to vitamins and proteins for physical health (Bowlby, 1951). Much later, Bowlby (1969) went further to suggest that individuals suffering from any type of psychiatric disorder *always* show an impairment of capacity for affectional bonding. He attributed this to negative experiences, a disturbance of bonding, in childhood which he regarded as the cause of psychiatric disorders, and so recommended it as a guideline for the routine management of individuals with psychiatric or mental health needs. This suggests that, beginning in infancy and throughout the life cycle, an individual's mental health is intractably linked to their attachment relationships. That is, it is dependent upon the attachment figure's ability and preparedness to provide not just physical sustenance but also psychological sustenance, to provide emotional support and protection to the infant/child.

Bowlby (1969, 1973, 1980) and his colleagues (e.g. Ainsworth, 1967; Ainsworth and Eichberg, 1991; Ainsworth *et al.*, 1971; Robertson and Robertson, 1971), employed the term 'attachment' to refer to a set of behaviours and associated emotions that are observable in humans from the first six months of life onwards. One of the earliest manifestations of attachment is the child's predisposition to seek proximity to the attachment figure. Attachment theory postulates that humans, particularly infants and young children, need proximity to others for their survival. It proposes attachment formation as the process of becoming a social being. For the child to achieve this, in Bowlby's initial formulations of attachment theory, he claimed that certain 'mothering' or caregiving conditions must be met. The infant/child must experience a loving, warm relationship; an unbroken relationship which provides adequate stimulation where the mothering is provided by one person (usually the mother) and occurs in the child's own home. 'An unbroken relationship' and 'mothering in own home' imply temporal continuity and spatial continuity respectively. Together, they may be conceived of as genealogical, cultural and ethnic continuity or connection, as opposed to the narrow meaning traditionally attached to these concepts.

The above conditions mean that attachment develops through being cared for and responded to continuously, consistently and positively by the attachment figure. This is believed to afford the child the conviction that a caregiver is and will always be available to appease and comfort. Bowlby (1973) outlined the prerequisites for optimal attachment:

1   Loving, unbroken relationship, typified by continuous availability and preparedness of the mother or primary caregiver (i.e. attachment figure) to respond sensitively to the child's needs.
2   The child's confidence in the availability of the attachment figure must be established during a critical period (infancy to early adolescence) – whatever expectations developed during these stages tend to persist relatively unaffected throughout the rest of the child's life.
3   The varied expectations or experiences of the availability and responsiveness of attachment figures.

Internal working models

> Just as there is a strong case for believing that gnawing uncertainty about the accessibility and responsiveness of attachment figures is a principal condition for the development of unstable and anxious personality so there is a strong case for believing that an unthinking confidence in the unfailing accessibility and support of attachment figures is the bedrock on which stable and self-reliant personality is built.
>
> (Bowlby, 1973, p. 366)

This is what Bowlby's notion of 'internal working models' or mental representation of attachment relationships is about and forms the kernel of attachment theory. Bowlby described the main function of these models as to enable the person to develop foresight and plan their life and to organize their behaviour accordingly. These internal working models of relationships are built from the child's early attachment experiences. The child's internal working model gives him an idea of who his attachment figure is, of her availability and reliability – how the child may expect her to respond to his needs. Bretherton (1991) and Howe (1995) argue that the models help children to understand how others view them, how they view themselves, how they might view others, and how the relationship between self and others might best be interpreted. 'Once the inner working models become established, they are increasingly likely to define social experience rather than be defined by social experience' (Howe, 1995, p. 71). This means that the type of internal working model, stable or shaky, that a child develops in infancy and childhood forms the template for later relationships, and how they may be maintained or modified. Namely, one's internal working model shapes one's expectations about new relationships and, consequently, one's behaviour within them. In other words, the child generalizes her or his early experiences to later relationships and social situations.

The type and quality of the working models which children develop of their attachment figures are believed to exercise a profound and lasting influence on their relationships throughout the rest of their lives. These models reflect parents' patterns of behaviour towards their children. Bowlby (1973) claimed that because children unwittingly internalize these patterns of behaviour, when they become parents they show the same behaviour patterns towards their children as they experienced during their own childhoods; that is, these behaviour patterns are more or less faithfully transmitted, undiluted, from one generation to another. Put more plainly, parents' childhood experiences largely influence how they relate to and interact with their own children. The next section briefly considers attachment theory in relation to other notions of personality development.

Attachment theory versus psychoanalytic theory and learning theories

Attachment

Rutter and O'Connor (1999) provide a brief account of the history of attachment theory in relation to childcare policy. They make a number of observations. They suggest that in order to appreciate not just the past or present, but also the enduring impact of attachment theory on research, childcare policies and professional childcare as well as child-rearing practices, it is necessary to distinguish between its initial postulates (when it was first introduced) and other theories of personality development and psychopathology, such as psychoanalytic theory and learning theories, notably behaviourism. First of all, they delineate the importance that attachment theory placed upon both continuity and sensitive responsiveness early in caregiving relationships and the key features of the environment of upbringing. They further contrast this with learning theory's (behaviourism) narrow focus on the immediate aspects or measurable contingencies governing the child's behaviour. They also compare attachment theory with traditional psychoanalysis which focused chiefly on the child's psyche or internal thought processes without paying due attention to the real life experiences or the wider socio-cultural context that provides the raw material for the child's thought processes. In other words, Rutter and O'Connor claim that the essence of the theory lies in its integration of an innate disposition and the role of nurture, its recognition of the interaction between nature and nurture with regard to personality development. In other words, they argue that attachment theory has remained distinctive insofar as it locates the parent–child relationship within a broader context than other theories do.

A further distinctive feature of attachment theory which they highlight is that it distinguished between attachment and other components of relationships. Main (1999) draws our special attention to this. That is to say, they acknowledge that attachment does not constitute the whole of relationships.

This aspect of the theory, they point out, later became overlooked or neglected owing to the theory's success and its unquestioning adoption by enthusiasts or zealots. They highlight other concepts of attachment theory, especially the psychological loss associated with both separation and rejection. Rutter and O'Connor (1999) rightly stress that these are not peculiar to attachment theory, but were most clearly articulated by attachment theory and incorporated into models of personality development and psychopathology. According to these authors, what is special about attachment theory in this respect is that it offered a compelling explanation for the feelings associated with the ' "trauma" of separation and loss – fear, anxiety, anger, sadness, and despair – and for their disruptive effects on personality development' (pp. 824–825). This aspect of attachment theory, its emphasis on separation and loss, is particularly pertinent to the theme of this book.

Summary

Earlier and contemporary theories of psycho-social development directly and indirectly influenced Bowlby's notion of attachment, notably psycho-analysis, ethology and learning theory and research, principally Lorenz's work on imprinting and Harlow's studies with rhesus monkeys. Nonetheless, like all novel ideas, attachment theory experienced its fair share of turbulence in its historical journey to global popularity. In spite of its acceptance and profound influence on almost every aspect of childcare today, attachment theory and studies derived from it continue to be scrutinized on theoretical, empirical and ideological grounds. Some of the critiques and criticisms of attachment theory will be highlighted in this book. For the most comprehensive, incisive and most cited critique of Bowlby's early formulations of the theory, see Rutter's *Maternal Deprivation Reassessed* (1981). See also Holmes (1993) for a discussion of the history of attachment theory and its continuing influence; for a feminist perspective see Oakley (1981).

Discussion of attachment theory's enduring and pervasive influence on clinical research and practice, notably psychiatry and psychotherapy, is beyond the scope of this book. Suffice it to say that literature in this area is replete with suggestions that childhood separation or maladaptive attachment or maladaptive working models are implicated in almost every mental disorder. Both the *Diagnostic and Statistical Manual of Mental Disorders* (*DSM-IV*, American Psychiatric Association, 1994) and the *International Classification of Disease* (*ICD-10*, WHO, 1992) include attachment disorders of childhood in their classification systems. Consequently, since its inception, it has influenced child-rearing practice, research, childcare policy and professional practice worldwide. See, for example, Cassidy and Shaver (1999) and Parkes and Stevenson-Hinde (1991) for detailed discussion of clinical applications of attachment theory.

ERIK ERIKSON'S PSYCHOSOCIAL THEORY

Erikson, a neo-Freudian, is another influential theorist whose ideas regarding childhood experiences and their profound influence on our psychological integrity are relevant to this book. His ideas concerning identity are still the most widely used in accounts of lifespan development. In terms of personality development and psychological functioning, unlike Freud who saw human beings as propelled by libidinal or psychic energy, Erikson saw the individual as the product of both biology and culture. Hence, instead of studying human development from a psycho-sexual perspective, he did so from a psycho-social perspective. That is, he took a more holistic or ecological approach to the study of human growth and development. He saw a 'fit' between the developing child and their culture. In this sense, Erikson depicted psychosocial development as culturally relative. He pointed out that, although children in all cultures go through the same sequence of stages, each culture has its own way of not only protecting but also monitoring and guiding children's development and behaviour at each stage.

In a similar vein, Bronfenbrenner (1992) has challenged the attachment theorists' claim that the less diluted the bond between child and primary carer, the better for the child's development and ability to cope with stress in the future. He argues that different societies have different sorts of stress, so that the type of upbringing children need to become 'well adjusted' in Russia, for example, is different from that required in the USA. That is to say, societies set children developmental tasks. Some are basic, like learning to walk; others are more variable, like intellectual development, particularly skills, and the sort of emotional development which reconciles with the society's values: 'People who live in crowded housing and work co-operatively had better not want to be alone' (Bronfenbrenner, 1992, quoted in Vesta, 1992, p. 187). Whiting and Edwards (1988) describe these cultural variations succinctly:

> Although the caretakers of young children do have goals that are universal (e.g. protection, socialisation), there are societal differences in the behaviours of caretakers that are related to the community's ecology, basic economy, social organisation, and value systems.
>
> (p. 89)

Also, unlike Freud, Erikson (1968) saw development as a lifelong process taking place throughout one's life. In his early formulations of the theory of human growth, development occurs in eight stages or phases. These stages refer to eight critical periods in which various lifelong ego concerns reach a peak. Each stage is marked by conflict. How well or badly a person resolves this conflict or crisis has implications, favourable or unfavourable, for their personality and outlook towards others and life generally. These phases and their accompanying crises are as follows:

- *Stage 1*: basic trust versus basic mistrust (birth to 1 yr).
- *Stage 2*: autonomy versus shame and doubt (2 to 3 yrs).
- *Stage 3*: initiative versus guilt (4 to 5 yrs).
- *Stage 4*: industry versus inferiority (6 yrs to puberty).
- *Stage 5*: identity and repudiation versus identity diffusion (adolescence).
- *Stage 6*: intimacy and solidarity versus isolation (young adulthood).
- *Stage 7*: generativity versus stagnation and self-absorption (mid-adulthood).
- *Stage 8*: integrity versus despair (late adulthood).

Erikson later suggested a ninth stage (1997). He described each stage in terms of a polarity with both positive and negative outcomes possible, for example, autonomy versus shame and doubt. Ideally, the child develops a favourable ratio in which the positive aspect prevails over the negative: for example, a person needs to know when to trust and when to mistrust, but generally should have a trusting outlook toward life. The following section presents a brief sketch of the core features of three of these stages. They are selected because of their particular pertinence to the subject matter of this book.

Stage 1: basic trust versus basic mistrust

The main task at this stage of development (infancy) is not necessarily a total resolution of the accompanying crisis, but rather to acquire a favourable ratio of trust or mistrust. If the scale tilts towards trust, the child has a better chance of withstanding later crises than if it leans towards mistrust. Erikson saw basic trust as an essential trustfulness of the dependability of others as well as a basic sense of one's own trustworthiness, and the essence that there is some meeting between one's needs and wishes and one's world (Stevens, 1983). According to Erikson, trusting infants can rely on their primary carer to feed and nourish them when they are hungry, and comfort them when they are anxious, in pain or in distress. They are generally accepting of their carer's temporary absence, for example, being out of sight, because they believe in his or her return. They also acquire a sense of when trust or mistrust is appropriate.

This is very much akin to Bowlby's (1969, 1973) notion of the internal working model of the primary caregiver. In short, the crucial task at this stage is to achieve an adaptive ratio, a healthy balance, between trust and mistrust, to know when it is appropriate for the child to drop their guard, to relax, and to be aware when danger looms. The positive outcome of this phase is hope, which, according to Erikson, is the enduring conviction that one's wishes are attainable. The obverse of this outcome is an inability to trust others or self, an undesirable state involving excessive caution and withdrawal in relation to the world. As we will see in later chapters, many separated children experience problems of trust because they feel abandoned or let down by their birth parent(s).

Stage 2: autonomy versus shame and doubt

Anxiety over separation from parents or primary caregivers marks this stage. The positive outcome of this stage is a sense of autonomy, a feeling of personal control, of being in charge of events that affect one's well-being; and the negative outcomes are shame and doubt. Shame implies uncertainty about one's efficacy, one's attempts to succeed in a given task, in a nutshell, one's sense of self-worth. A sense of autonomy results if the child has developed basic trust during the first stage. Shame and doubt result from the development of an unfavourable ratio between basic trust and mistrust.

Stage 5: identity and repudiation versus identity diffusion

This is the major concern of Erikson's theory of human growth and development. He believed the establishment of a healthy sense of identity to be the driving force behind human activities. He firmly believed that the quest for identity permeates all of the eight stages of development. He also maintained that trust, autonomy, initiative and industry all contribute to the child's identity. In the fifth stage, however, this concern reaches a peak. The basic task at this phase of the life cycle, according to him, is to integrate the various identifications that adolescents bring from childhood into a whole, more integrated identity. If adolescents fail to achieve this, then they are at risk of what he termed 'identity diffusion'. This means that their personality is disjointed, disorganized, lacking a hub. This may account for the frequently reported identity problems in adopted children and those in the public care system, for example.

Lewis (1990, quoted in Durkin, 1995, p. 290) agrees with Erikson when he suggests that achieving identity, in the sense of acquiring a set of beliefs about oneself, is one of the core developmental tasks of a social being. In other words, it is not an instantaneous achievement, but one which progresses through several layers of complexity and continues to develop throughout the lifespan. Erikson himself conceptualized and defined identity in a multifactorial way: biological endowment, personal organization of experience, and continuity of one's unique experience. These factors interact in a complex way to result in a unique and idiosyncratic personality:

> The process of identity formation depends on the interplay of what young persons at the end of childhood have come to mean to themselves and what they now appear to mean to those who become significant to them.
>
> (Erikson, 1977, p. 196, quoted by Kroger, 1989, p. 15)

Put differently, this means that identity is a product of not only a sociocultural process, but also a cognitive process involving self-perception and external (social) stimuli or experiences, an outcome of the interaction between how young persons see themselves – what they perceive themselves to be – and how they are seen by (significant) others: '. . . experience is not what happens to you but rather what you do with what happens to you' (Kroger, 1989, p. 140).

What all this amounts to is that understanding of human growth and development requires a broad perspective. It requires adopting such approaches as Bronfenbrenner's eco-systems perspective:

> Human development is the scientific study of the progressive, mutual accommodation, *throughout the life course*, between an active growing human being and the changing properties of the immediate settings in which the developing person lives, as this process is affected by the relations between these settings, and by the larger contexts in which the settings are embedded.
>
> (Bronfenbrenner, 1992, p. 187)

Accepting this proposition leads us to appreciate Erikson's further suggestion that the task of achieving a coherent sense of identity or self-worth may be intensified or compounded by such extra factors as minority group status, uncertainty about one's minority group status, uncertainty about one's sexual orientation, and overly strong identification with a parent, being overwhelmed by several competing occupational roles from which to choose. In the context of this book, we may add to the list uncertainty about one's cultural and genealogical roots. Failure to achieve a strong sense of self by accomplishing these tasks leads to what Erikson termed identity confusion: doubt about who you are, what you want to be, and what you want to do.

Stevens (1983) claims that Erikson had to contend with many of these factors and their accompanying developmental difficulties in both his childhood and adolescence. In Stevens' brief sketch of Erikson's biography, he was born to two Danish parents in Germany. His father separated from his mother before his birth. As a toddler, his mother remarried a German-Jewish paediatrician who adopted him and raised him as his own biological son. Throughout his life, he lacked knowledge of who his real father was. Presumably, his insistence that young people who are confused about themselves have 'identity hunger' may well be a projection of his own hunger for socio-genealogical connectedness, for knowledge about his genetic father, the other part of himself, in order to complete his sense of identity.

Despite the apparent intensity of this yearning need, Erikson appears to have maintained a positive outlook. This is perceptible in another aspect of his description of the fifth stage of development (adolescence). Although he saw this as the stage during which identity formation is most crucial, he did not regard a failure to accomplish this task at this stage of development as the end of the road for the adolescent. Rather, he optimistically suggested that unresolved crises at any phase of development can be resolved later in life. He was, in fact, reassuring in his conviction that it is never too late to resolve any of these crises. As we will see in later chapters, a number of commentators (e.g. Stevens, 1983) agree with him that many adults, for various reasons such as adoption, are still striving to establish a sense of identity or psychological integrity. This markedly conflicts with the deterministic view of attachment theory and Freud's notion of fixation.

Stevens (1983) and Miller (1999) opine that, besides his own background, childhood experiences and minority status, there are several reasons why personal identity assumed so much importance for Erikson. Drawing on his own background and childhood experiences, as well as the society in which he lived and operated, Erikson predicted that the nature of a given society will be reflected in the psychological problems typically experienced by members of that society. He argued, for example, that while sexual inhibition and repression were predominant concerns in Freud's time, the complexity, mechanization and rootlessness of contemporary industrial society have led to a shift in emphasis (Miller, 1999). Add to these factors childhood separation for various reasons – parental divorce/separation, disaster – and the unrelenting force of globalization, 'McDonaldization' and 'Microsoftization', in order to comprehend the magnitude of psychological problems facing youngsters today and the potential for them to experience a sense of rootlessness and therefore identity confusion. This book concerns a lack of socio-genealogical connectedness resulting from childhood separation that is a major psychological difficulty facing modern-day children.

2 Socio-genealogical connectedness

In theoretical context

I would like to know the names of my parents . . . where and when I was born and their occupations. Also what kind of people my mother and father were, what hobbies they had, whether they were friendly people and what likes and dislikes they had . . .

(Female adoptee, quoted by Triseliotis, 1973, p. 142)

Now at the age of thirty, I . . . feel diminished and inadequate because half of myself is unknown and will never be knowable. I don't think it's fair.

(Donor insemination offspring, quoted by Baran and Pannor, 1993, p. 59)

This book considers the developmental difficulties facing not only adopted children and children living with only one parent, but also other groups of separated children. It does so from a different perspective to the theories discussed in the preceding chapter. The following groups of separated children are a relatively new phenomenon compared to those with whom attachment theory, psychoanalysis and learning theories were originally concerned: children of cross-country adoption, those resulting from donor insemination, those involved in parental divorce/separation, and unaccompanied or displaced minors. One of the common and principal characteristics of these groups of children is the severance of their genealogical ties or roots. Encompassing as its aim is, it must be acknowledged from the outset that the theory about to be presented cannot be expected to provide all the answers. Indeed, no one developmental theory can provide a complete understanding of child psycho-social development.

Today, no discussion of human psychological, social and emotional development and functioning can avoid granting John Bowlby his enduring contribution. His influence in this area spans several generations of theorists and investigators. Although his published seminal work was 'The Forty-Four Juvenile Thieves: Their Characters and Home-life' (Bowlby, 1944), his World Health Organization monograph (1951) has dominated his other contributions, especially regarding policy and practice, in terms of attachment theory's ubiquitous influence. In this monograph, he stated that it was essential for mental health that the infant and young child should experience a warm, intimate and continuous relationship with the mother. He laid particular stress on the adverse effects of separation and loss, and so strongly advocated for continuity of care. It must, however, be borne in mind that this assertion reflected the times and society in which he lived and worked. It focused on the childcare problems that some children and their families typically experienced during that particular era – an era when divorce, for example, was comparatively rare. Compared to the period in which attachment theory was initially formulated (shortly after World War II), a much higher proportion of children, in the western world particularly, face separation and loss of one or both birth parents not only through divorce or death, but also through fostering and adoption – domestic and cross-country – assisted reproduction, especially donor insemination, and so forth.

Understanding the complexity of the developmental needs of modern-day children, therefore, requires a shift of focus or emphasis. Shifting focus, as Miller (1999) has suggested, does not necessarily absolve us, as theorists and investigators, from bias.

Miller claims that any developmental theory implicitly takes for granted the essence of human nature, what it is or ought to be; that is, what human needs are or ought to be. Namely, our thoughts and actions are largely influenced by our cultural, social, spiritual, economic and political environments. We must therefore be constantly mindful that our thoughts and activities – the contents of our thoughts and how we go about doing what we do – are subtly but heavily influenced by these ubiquitous factors. Scarr (1985) succinctly articulated this: 'We pose questions to fit our place and time; we get answers to fit our theoretical niches' (quoted in Miller, 1999, p. 16). Scarr took the argument further and recommended that we change our theoretical lenses as our culture changes. According to Miller, Scarr noted that in the 1950s and 1960s, and much later, social scientists expected and thus looked for evidence to support the assumption that boys in 'broken homes' were affected negatively by the lack of a father. The finding that these boys, when young, were observed to be low in aggression was taken to support the hypothesis that boys in female-headed homes experience poor sex-role development. As we will see in the following chapter, the present thesis presents a new theoretical approach to understanding the psycho-social developmental difficulties facing a large number of children today.

Following Bowlby, many works – books and both published and unpublished research and reports – have focused predominantly on social relationships, particularly on childhood or early relationships and their role not only in child development, but also in general well-being in adulthood. This book accepts many of the key tenets of attachment theory as propounded by Bowlby and further developed by other theorists and investigators. However, its focus is on children disconnected from their biological and/or cultural roots. Thus, it transcends social relationships by examining the part that a sense of human connectedness, social and genealogical linkage, plays in our psychological development, social competence and general well-being. Many aspects of our personality form during childhood as we experience close relationships with not only our birth parents, but also our kith and kin in general. Attachment theory and Erikson's theory of psycho-social development, for example, propose that the kind of adult a child grows into is a product of the interaction between their innate endowment and those around them during their formative years. The notion of socio-genealogical connectedness, presented in the next section, goes beyond our immediate social environment. It proposes that the process of personality development also involves the interactions, through narratives and symbols, that a child has with their biological parents, extended family and forebears. This applies not only during childhood or adolescence, but equally in adulthood and even in old age.

SOCIO-GENEALOGICAL CONNECTEDNESS: WHAT IS IT?

The rest of this chapter introduces the notion of socio-genealogical connectedness. It describes its basic tenets and how it develops in different socio-cultural settings. In this endeavour, note is taken of Greenberg's (1999) argument that it is necessary for the analysis to cross and recross the successive levels of social and cultural complexity, and to take cognisance both of the influence of cultural and societal forces on the developing child and the genesis of those cultural forces themselves. This is reminiscent of Bronfenbrenner's (1979, 1992) eco-systems approach to the study of human development and behaviour. With this in mind, the present thesis proposes that a sense of socio-genealogical connectedness is an essential factor in children's adjustment to separation, and forms the basis of one's emotional and mental health. More specifically, socio-genealogical connectedness refers to our ability and willingness to integrate our biological, social, cultural and ethnic roots. In other words, the notion relates to the extent of our knowledge about our hereditary origins and the degree to which we assimilate that knowledge into our inner world. It concerns one's knowledge and belief in one's genetic and cultural heritage, and the role this knowledge plays in one's overall emotional, psychological and mental well-being. It postulates that our psychological integrity depends very much upon the degree to which we identify with our origins; the extent to which we feel linked to our genealogical roots.

As such, it seeks to address questions related to our self-concept or personal identity. It tries to deal with such important theoretical questions as those raised by Tizard and Phoenix (1989) in relation to adoption, such as whether adopted children's internal representations of their social parents are affected by the knowledge that they are not their biological parents; and, if so, how this, in turn, affects the meaning of their relationship with the biological parents they have never seen. A further issue it attempts to address concerns the implications of adopted children's and other separated children's desire or, indeed, need to seek out their biological parents or hereditary roots.

Hypotheses

With respect to children generally, socio-genealogical connectedness is about the extent to which they integrate into their inner world their parents' biological, cultural and social backgrounds. It relates to the degree to which children see themselves as offshoots of their birth parents' backgrounds and its basic tenets are the following:

1   The amount and/or quality of information children possess about their birth parents determines the degree to which they integrate the parents' backgrounds and ancestral roots.
2   Children who possess adequate and favourable information about their birth parents have a deep sense of connectedness.
3   Conversely, children who possess no, or inadequate, or damaging information about their parents are less likely to integrate it and, therefore, have a shallow sense of connectedness.
4   Children who have a deep sense of connectedness are better adjusted than those who have no or a shallow sense of connectedness.

These assumptions suggest that socio-genealogical connectedness is about one's self-identity, one's self-worth, one's sense of psychological wholeness and one's mental health.

It is obvious that the first two assumptions are not entirely contingent upon face-to-face contact or interaction with the biological parents. Socio-genealogical knowledge, the amount or quality of it, does not have to be provided directly by the parents themselves. For example, in an extended family or small-scale collective community where linkage is often to the whole group or clan rather than to birth parents alone, the information required to achieve a sense of connectedness is public property. It is readily available through the extended family and the community. In such a context, the child's interpersonal relationships extend beyond the immediate family. The child's sense of continuity is nourished by the whole community rather than the biological parent or family. As such, it can be argued that the theory of socio-genealogical connectedness is contextual; that is, it takes into account cultural and societal influences. In this respect, it addresses the criticism levelled at attachment theory and other developmental theories that they are Euro-centric. It can also be seen as dealing, to an extent, with Miller's (1999) and Bronfenbrenner's (1992) general criticism concerning what they regard as the paucity of mainstream developmental theories in helping us in our efforts towards a better understanding of children and their developmental needs. In other words, these theories approach child development and developmental outcomes out of context. Bronfenbrenner articulates his misgivings in the following terms:

> In examining scientific conceptions of the developing person from an ecological perspective, one is struck by a curious fact: the overwhelming majority of these conceptions are context-free; i.e. the characteristics of the person are defined, both conceptually and operationally, without any reference to the environment, and are presumed to have the same meaning irrespective of the culture, class, or setting in which they are observed, or in which the person lives.
>
> (1992, p. 202)

Socio-genealogical connectedness is one of the new perspectives for which Bronfenbrenner and Miller are calling, in that it is applicable in any given cultural context, although there exist cultural variations in its mode of acquisition and expression. A key feature of the idea is that the process of identity or personality development transcends proximal relations; it also involves one's relationships with others outside one's proximal physical and social environments. Attachment theorists (e.g. Sroufe *et al.*, 1999) and social learning theorists (e.g. Bandura, 1992) suggest that a person should be conceived as embodying attitudes, feelings, expectations, aspirations and meanings which emanate from the primary caregiving setting or the child's immediate social milieu. That is, it is the individual's history of relationships that defines the entity which we vaguely refer to as the self or personality. The notion of socio-genealogical connectedness endorses the idea that a person's history is an important factor in their psychological make-up. It postulates, nonetheless, that this history or biography must not be conceived as starting and ending with one's biological parents. Our knowledge of and relationships with our grandparents and ancestors play an equally, or perhaps more important, influential role in our emotional and psychological functioning.

Over 20 years ago, Rutter (1981) argued that since Bowlby researchers, writers and practitioners have frequently been too mechanical in equating separation with bond disruption; too restricted in regarding the mother or primary caregiver as the all-important person in a child's life; and too narrow in considering love, 'maternal tender and loving care', as the only important element in the caregiving relationship. Furthermore, he stated that in most cases researchers, policymakers and practitioners had failed to give due consideration to the important role that fathers and relatives (and ancestors) play in a child's personality development. This myopic view of attachment has led to the spurious belief that these people who 'penetrate' the child's life are virtually insignificant, emotionally and psychologically. Things have not changed much in this regard. Today, the idea of 'mother love' is still received wisdom among politicians and the general public, in spite of the seemingly general acceptance amongst theorists and practitioners regarding the importance of significant others to a child's welfare. In the area of donor insemination, for instance, the following exemplifies the strong hold of the idea of 'maternal love' on the public. It also shows that Rutter's (1981) concerns remain valid:

Most of the participants (lesbian DI families) did not define the donor as a father. Therefore, the question of whether their child has, let alone needs, a father was not easily answered partly because interviewees questioned the definition of the term 'father' and . . . giving the donor such a status. Rather, they were clear about the child's need for a parent or parents who would provide long-term care, stability and love and they were confident of their abilities to provide these.

(Haimes and Weiner, 2000, p. 489)

This spurious conviction may hold in the case of infants and young children, but hardly in the case of adolescents and adults.

We will see in later chapters that many people who were adopted as babies or infants by wealthy and caring parents who never denied them long-term care, love or economic stability will still search for their birth parents and genetic roots at some stage in their lives. The above view obviously pays no heed to the stark fact that the child is made up of two sets of genetic material, and that as the child grows older their other side, the genetic father and his family, becomes increasingly important. It is in disregard of the growing recognition of the child's need for knowledge about and, where possible, relationships with the genetic father and his extended family in order to complete their biography or to establish a sense of wholeness.

CULTURE, EXPERIENCE AND SOCIO-GENEALOGICAL CONNECTEDNESS

One of the implicit assumptions of socio-genealogical connectedness is that human need for genetic linkage is a universal phenomenon. It accepts, however, that cultural variations exist regarding the means through which this human need is met. In other words, how this need is met in childhood depends, in large measure, on the belief and value systems of a given society. A family's attitude towards babies is a reflection of a given society's perception of children; it is a reflection of the value which that society attaches to children and its future generations. In societies where having babies is seen as entailing long-term economic hardship or personal sacrifice, matters are different. The pleasure principle – narcissism and hedonism – forms the pivot and the lubricant of society; every whim demands instant gratification. For example, students are not prepared to wait until the end of a class and motorists are not willing to stop in order to make social telephone calls; parents sacrifice time that might be spent preparing a balanced diet for their children for leisure pursuits; some parents seem to have no qualms about abandoning their children in pursuit of exotic, romantic holidays. So, couples tend to be less enthusiastic about starting a family or having more than one or one point five children. In these societies, children are born into a nuclear family and are expected to form attachment or bonds exclusively with their parents.

In cultures where babies are seen as an investment, as future workers and supporters of the extended family and the community, as extensions and carriers of the clan into the future, couples have more favourable attitudes towards children. In these cultures, children are treasured and treated as valuable members of the kinship system and the community as a whole. Hence, the meaning of attachment or bonding is very different from that which is held by societies where bonding is believed to be dyadic (a parent–child relationship), and seen predominantly as something that develops between children and their birth parent(s).

This view has, of course, not gone unchallenged (e.g. Bronfenbrenner, 1979, 1991, 1992; David and New, 1985; Rutter, 1981; Schaffer and Emerson, 1964). Rutter (1981/1991), for example, has pointed out that Bowlby himself recognized the fact that attachment encompasses only one dimension of this relationship. Bronfenbrenner (1979, 1992) explains how misleading it is to concentrate on relationships between two people (mother and child) while ignoring the social context. He points out that the nuclear family does not usually consist of only two people. He stresses that the developmental setting depends on the extent to which third parties present in the setting support or undermine the activities of those actually engaged in interaction with the developing child (Bronfenbrenner, 1992).

In societies where babies are not born into a nuclear family but rather are welcomed into an extended family and kinship, bonding is seen as taking place between a child and multiple members of the extended family, and oftentimes beyond. Moyo (1979) presents Ndebele culture to exemplify this type of developmental setting:

> Amongst the Ndebele people of Southern Rhodesia [Zimbabwe] 'mother' does not necessarily mean the woman who gave birth to you. Mother, in the Western sense, plus all her sisters go under the term of mother. The oldest of the female members of the household adopts the title 'big mother'.
> (Moyo, 1979, p. 180, quoted in David and New, 1985, pp. 174–175)

In traditional Ndebele land, the child's biological mother and her female siblings are all 'little mothers', and the revered 'big mother' is often the child's grandmother or some other older relation or even friend. As in other so-called Third World cultures, if a child is orphaned 'big mother' and 'little mothers' are assigned from a cohesive and caring family. The 'big mother', not the biological mother, bears the overall responsibility for the child's upbringing, although the 'little mothers' share the day-to-day childcare duties with her. In a Ndebele traditional household, no child is treated differently by their birth mother or any adult female:

> It is thought unnatural for the biological mother to show more interest in her child than in those of her sisters and cousins . . . you do not find a term which means 'child, my own biological child', and a different one

meaning 'child, my cousin's child', the same term is used for both, 'my child' . . . If a mother showed more interest in her 'own' children she would be badly thought of by the family and when her turn comes to be 'big mother' she would be passed by. She would be regarded as a very selfish person.

(Moyo, 1979, quoted in David and New, 1985, p. 175)

In this type of cultural setting, both 'big mother' and 'little mothers', 'big father' and 'little fathers' all possess the genealogical information with which to nurture a child's sense of connectedness or belonging, their identity and self-worth.

SELF-CONCEPT

It was stated previously that, as a theory of psycho-social development, one of the main concerns of the concept of socio-genealogical connectedness is identity development. It involves our biological, cultural, ethnic and social identity and, essentially, our personal identity. What then is self-concept or self-identity? Questions related to self-identity or self-concept are often posed not just out of philosophical, theological or epistemological interest. The self, however and whatever we conceive it to be, is also of psychological and practical significance. The answer within socio-genealogical connectedness to the question of what self-identity is may, therefore, be sought in Taylor's (1989) assertion that 'in order to have a sense of who we are, we have to have a notion of how we have become, and where we are going' (quoted in Giddens, 1991, p. 55). Owusu-Bempah and Howitt (2000b) have made a similar claim.

  This obviously presents us with a paradox: that is, in order to know who and what one's identity is, one requires a sense of 'self' or personhood. This is made even more complex by the simple fact that one's answers to these questions largely depend on one's cultural, ethnic or religious background (e.g. Foster, 1998; Holdstock, 2000; Kakar, 1979; Landrine, 1992; Owusu-Bempah and Howitt, 2000b). In turn, this renders any attempt at a precise or universal definition of the term self-identity or self-concept, to a greater or lesser degree, difficult if not futile. This is a long-acknowledged fact. For example, Milner (1975) described it as a repository or receptacle for the 'unexplainable' about a person. Owusu-Bempah (1994) has argued that it is a nebulous concept. Giddens (1991, p. 52) likewise claims that it is a proteus and therefore 'cannot refer simply to its consistency or persistence over time in the same way as philosophers might speak of the invariability of physical objects or entities'. In this respect, these authors are in agreement with Erikson (1968) that self-identity is not just a given, but rather an outcome of the continuities of the individual's action system; something that has to be routinely crafted and recrafted spatially and temporally in the introspective activities of the individual. Hence, Giddens describes self-identity as 'the self

as reflexively understood by the individual in terms of his or her biography'
(1991, p. 244).

Giddens' description of the self requires elaboration. In other words, a
person's biography is incomplete without its biological, social and cultural
components – the sum is always greater than its constituent parts. In seeing
the self as a product of a process of introspection or self-evaluation, he is in
agreement with such historically influential theorists of the self-concept as
William James (1890), Charles H. Cooley (1902) and George H. Mead (1934).
These theorists conceptualized the self as ultimately subjective; as subjectively understood by the person in terms of their biography. Brinich and
Shelley trace this idea back to the philosopher Kant. According to these
writers, Kant declared: 'I have no knowledge of myself as I am but merely as I
appear to myself (i.e. through others' lenses). The consciousness of myself is
thus very far from being a knowledge of myself' (quoted in Brinich and
Shelley, 2002, p. 7).

Both Cooley and Mead recognized, from their interactionist perspective,
the fluidity of the self. Indeed, Mead claimed that a person possesses as many
'selfs' as there are individuals who are significant to them, whose opinions are
valued, whether these individuals are present or not (alive or dead). Who has
never asked themselves: 'What would my mother say, if she were to see me
now . . .?' or said to themselves: 'My dad would kill me, if he knew . . .', or
'My grandmother would turn in her grave, if . . .'? This, then, is what constitutes the essence of Mead's notion of internalized expectations and his
conceptualization of symbolic interactionism. It also constitutes Hinde's
(1979) idea of 'penetration', and to an extent the notion of socio-genealogical
connectedness. However, according to Burns (1979), it was Cooley rather
than Mead who first underscored the importance of subjectively processed
feedback from others as a main source of information about the self.

Cooley introduced the metaphor 'social looking-glass self' to show that
one's self-concept is constructed and profoundly influenced by what the individual believes others think of them. The social looking-glass reflects the
imagined evaluation of others about oneself. In this scenario, a sort of mirroring takes place in these interactions. Seeing social interactions as analo-
gous to an ordinary mirror led Cooley to postulate the 'looking-glass self':
'Each to each a looking glass, Reflects the other that doth pass' (p. 184). He
elaborated on this famous dictum:

> As we see our face, figure, and dress in the glass, and pleased or otherwise
> with them according as they do or do not answer what we should like
> them to be; so in imagination we perceive in another's mind some
> thought of our appearance, manners, aims, deeds, character, friends, and
> so on, are variously affected by it.
>
> (Cooley, 1902, p. 184)

Bear with me. The relevance of these quotations and the discussion so far will soon become clear. In the meantime, in Cooley's formulation, this looking-glass self emerges from symbolic or imagined interactions or communications, verbal and non-verbal, between a person and their various primary groups or significant others. One's face-to-face interactions with significant others and members of one's community or group serve as an undistorted mirror providing feedback for the individual to evaluate, reflect and relate to their own person. Through this process the concept of the self is formed and shaped, and values, attitudes, roles and identities are accepted and integrated or repudiated (Burns, 1979).

Cooley provided an account of how the self-concept is developed in relation to the individual's perception or interpretation of the reality of the physical and social worlds: 'The objects within this reality include the physical body, opinions, purposes, possessions, ambitions, in fact, any idea or system of ideas drawn from the communicative life that the mind cherishes as it's own' (1902, p. 68). He saw the objects and ideas taken to oneself as one's own as social in two senses. First, their meaning is furnished by the common language and culture. Second, self-conceptions and their associated evaluations and meanings are derived from intrasubjective construction of significant others' evaluation or judgements of one's attributes and conduct: 'Self and society mutually define each other, acting as points of reference one for the other, so that "self and society are twin born"' (Cooley, 1902, p. 5).

Cooley and Mead, in different eras, hybridized James's concept of the self and made it the centrepiece of the notion of symbolic interactionism. In so doing, they emphasized the social or interpersonal aspects of the self. In separate conceptualizations, they both saw the self as a social construction based upon symbolic interactions, as expressed in social intercourse or discourse between members of a group (Burns, 1979). Following his predecessors' footsteps, Mead saw society or social interactions as the genesis and domicile of the self. According to him, like Cooley and James before him, any individual's self-concept is constructed from their relations to the process of social intercourse, activity and experience, and participants within those social interactions. He firmly believed in the inseparability or mutuality of self and society, with the latter serving as the vehicle via which a person receives their statement of account, with its ticks and crosses, its credits and debits (Burns, 1979). Mead laid special emphasis on the idea that it is society that moulds and gives meaning to individual self-concept. Put in a different way, it is the community which communicates to one who and what one is; that is, it is one's community which conveys to one the meaning of one's self-concept.

In the tradition of Cartesian dualism, Mead dichotomized the self into the 'I' and the 'Me'. Although these elements of the self are practically inseparable, he conceptualized the 'Me' as the known part of the self comprising a person's material possessions (and sources of possessions). He claimed that the 'Me' and the 'I' are dialectical. Namely, they have a quid pro quo relationship which characterizes the self. He argued that there would not be an 'I', at least not in the sense in which we use the pronoun in everyday parlance, nor could there be a 'Me' without a response in the form of the 'I'; that these elements of the self, as they appear in our experience, constitute the personality. Eric Fromm elaborated on the inseparability or mutuality of these elements of the self:

> The statement '*I* [subject] have *O* [object]' expresses a definition of *I* through my possession of *O*. The subject is not *myself* but *I am what I have*. My property constitutes myself and my identity.
>
> (Fromm, 1998, quoted in Brinich and Shelley, 2002, p. 63)

What a paradox (or paralogism)! To be I must possess and to possess I must be. Or is it a 'Catch 22'? However one may see it, for Fromm, Cooley and Mead the value of one's possessions is determined by one's culture, so that the power of cultural backdrop in shaping human subjects overrides biological determinism. Therefore, one has to grant that in western societies today many may regard the above statement as a truism rather than a paradox. It may explain why adoptive parents believe, and are legally encouraged to believe, that their adopted children are, de jure, their possession.

Symbolic interactionism portrays the self as a social construct, as a product of imagined social interactions, a kind of mirroring which takes place in social interactions. Conceiving self-identity in this way led Cooley to postulate the 'looking-glass self' to represent one's interiorization or introjection of other persons' attitudes and values. It is this view which presumably later led Mead to propose the notion of internalized expectations. According to symbolic interactionism, the extent to which one's relationship to others reflects one's self-esteem points to the social and cultural values accorded to this construct. Put in another way, *esse est percipi* (to be is to be perceived) – one is what one is perceived by others to be. The crucial factor in symbolic interactionism, therefore, is what we believe others, particularly significant others, perceive us to be. That is to say, our sense of being is dependent upon not just being perceived but rather how we think we are perceived.

It is in this respect that Giddens (1991) appears to part company with these historical theorists when he claims that a person's identity does not reside in their behaviour, nor in others' reactions towards them, but rather in their capacity to maintain a particular and consistent narrative or life story: 'The existential question of self-identity is bound up with the fragile nature of the biography which the individual supplies about herself' (1991, p. 54). Giddens suggests that the best way to analyse or understand self-identity in general is by contrast with individuals whose sense of self is fractured or disabled. He cites Laing (1965) to illustrate the ramifications of fractured or disintegrated self for the individual. These include a loss or lack of a stable sense of biographical continuity. He portrays a person with a reasonably stable sense of self-identity, on the other hand, as one who has a feeling of biographical continuity which they are able to grasp reflexively and, to a greater or lesser extent, communicate in some way to others. Such a person, according to Giddens, also through trust relations in infancy and childhood, has established a protective mechanism which enables them to ward off or compartmentalize day-to-day negative interactions or events which are potentially inimical to the integrity of the self. Through this psychological mechanism, the individual is able to foster and maintain a sense of self-worth. Many writers not only accept this proposition, but also argue further that some victims of negative expectations may actually be motivated or energized by them to defy their inherent self-fulfilling prophecy (e.g. Baldwin, 1979; Howitt and Owusu-Bempah 1994; Owusu-Bempah and Howitt, 1999). In terms of the relationship between childhood experiences and personality development, Giddens is more inclined towards Erikson's (1968) ideas of 'basic trust versus basic mistrust' and 'identity repudiation versus identity diffusion' than the ideas of the other theorists discussed in the preceding chapter.

CULTURE, SOCIO-GENEALOGICAL CONNECTEDNESS AND SELF-IDENTITY

> We are individuals born into a certain nationality, located at a certain spot geographically, with such and such family relations, and such and such political relations . . . The self is not something that exists first and enters into relationships with others, but it is . . . an eddy in the social current and so still part of the current. It is a process in which the individual is continually adjusting himself in advance to the situation to which he belongs, and reacting back on it.
>
> (Mead, 1934, p. 182)

We have seen that there is a consensus amongst social scientists, social anthropologists and cross-cultural psychologists in particular that culture provides the raw materials from which the self is constructed. In other words, the contents of the self, the contents of a person's biography or life history vary from one culture to another and, even in a given society, from one social or ethnic group to another, giving rise to identifiable social, cultural, ethnic and religious groupings. Giddens (1991) cites a person's name as an obvious example. This is apt, since a person's name conveys primary biographical details about them: for instance, their family, kin relations, sex, ethnicity, religion, social status, occupation, and so forth. These biographical data differ between cultures and ethnic as well as religious groups. Cultural variation in naming systems is a clear case in point. For example, in some cultures a person's first name does not signify their sex. Also in some cultures a person's surname is formally or officially documented in the reverse order to the western system.

That the contents of the self, as well as the mechanism through which they are transmitted and acquired, reflect one's cultural background may be illustrated by traditional African cultures' conceptions of the self and hence personhood. Gbadegsin (1998) describes the African context in which a sense of self-worth is instilled in the individual from birth:

> The process of socialisation begins right from birth. The mother constantly communicates to the baby by tracing the [extended] family tree from the beginning, reminding him/her of the nobility of his/her birth and the uniqueness of the family. Co-wives [i.e. co-mothers] are on hand to tease the growing child, chanting the family praise-names and demanding gratification on return. All these raise the consciousness of the child as a member of a family and he/she begins to internalise its norms.
>
> (p. 293)

Gbadegsin describes the structure of the traditional family compound (or household) as especially congenial to this process. It facilitates the process because members of the extended household of several related families who belong to a common ancestor occupy the same compound or live in close proximity. They also co-operate in their day-to-day economic and other activities. Wiredu (1998) provides a more elaborate portrait of the African context:

> Akan society is of the type in which the greatest value is attached to communal belonging. And the way in which a sense of communal belonging is fostered in the individual is through the concentrated stress on kinship identity. Not only is there what might perhaps be called an ontological basis for this identity in terms of the constituents of personhood, but there is a distinct layer of a profound social significance in that concept. Thus conceived, a human person is essentially the centre of a thick set of concentric circles of obligations and responsibilities matched by rights and privileges revolving round levels of relationships irradiating from the *consanguinity of household kith and kin, through the 'blood' ties of lineage and clan,* to the wider circumference of human familyhood based on the common possession of the divine spark.
>
> (p. 311, emphasis added)

What the above quotations simply signify is that, in African cultures, as in many other cultures beyond western frontiers, the basis of the self is relational. Namely, a person's sense of identity or self-worth derives from and is nourished by social and spiritual relations, including the 'living dead' (e.g. Holdstock, 2000; Owusu-Bempah, 1995; Owusu-Bempah and Howitt, 2000b; Witte, 2001). This contrasts markedly with western philosophy in which the genesis of the self or personhood is assumed to be essentially epistemological and psychological, in which the individual is presumed to have sole possession of self-knowledge and is seen and sees himself as unique and autonomous (Teffo and Roux, 1998).

Many writers (e.g. Berry, 1983; Enriquez, 1993; Foster, 1998; Kagitcibasi, 1984; Kakar, 1979; Owusu-Bempah and Howitt, 1995, 2000b; Roland, 1988; Triandis, 1995) have highlighted some of the implications of such assumptions for the application of western models across cultural boundaries, not just in terms of developmental models but also in terms of other models such as therapeutic models. Regarding human development, Owusu-Bempah and Howitt (2000b) have pointed out that the major traditions in developmental psychology are based on widely different historical, philosophical, economic and political orientations; that they are the products of the different geographical locations and physical and economic conditions of the western countries in which they originated; that they are by no means universal. In other words, these models were developed in a particular culture (western) with particular needs, in a particular era and particular political and economic circumstances. In brief, they are time and space-specific. Thus, they are limited in their application in providing a complete understanding of the developmental processes and needs of the diverse groups within even western societies. In psychotherapy, for example, Foster (1998) presents these scenarios to epitomize these limitations:

> How do we evaluate the impulse management of an anxious, encopretic immigrant boy ... whose early toilet training did not include indoor toilets? Would the vicissitudes of anal cathexes and its implications for character formation as delineated by Freudian drive position apply for a child who was not reared in the bathroom habits of western culture?
>
> And how do we figure out the deep self-experience of a Middle Eastern man from a religious sect, who feels that without the tribe he was trained to lead, his self-esteem is unformed, non-existent? Do we view this client through the American self-psychological terms of a narcissistically derailed self, through the Ego Psychology lens of a poorly differentiated self? Or rather, as a person centred in the ensembled self-experience of his Eastern culture, where bonding to family and group kinship renders individuals who throughout life are deeply identified with others?
>
> (Foster, 1998, pp. 259–260)

The idea of socio-genealogical connectedness circumvents these difficulties and limitations inherent in traditional developmental models for understanding children's psychological, emotional and mental health needs today. In both theoretical and practical terms, its approach is culturally contextual.

In the context of the present thesis, we may coin the term 'socio-genealogization' to represent the process described above by Gbadegsin and Wiredu, in that it refers to the process whereby a child acquires a sense of family, kinship or clan identity or a sense of belonging. Two of the central tenets of the concept of socio-genealogical connectedness are that the formation of the self or personality transcends an individual's proximal relations; that the depth and quality of the relationship one has with one's origins, including one's ancestors or remote past, form the core of our sense of being; that one's origins exercise profound influence on how one copes with the vicissitudes of life.

Both attachment theory and socio-genealogical connectedness suggest that a person should be conceived as an inner organization of attitudes, feelings, expectations and meanings, which arise in the caregiving environment. That is to say, it is the individual's history of relationships that results in the organization that the self is, however it is conceived to be. Symbolic interactionism also suggests that the self arises out of the child's proximal interactions. The present thesis endorses the idea that a person's history is an important factor in their psychological make-up. Notwithstanding, it argues that this history is not provided solely by one's birth parents. Instead, it proposes that our knowledge of and relationships (real or symbolic) with our forebears play as significant a role in our sense of self-worth and emotional and psychological functioning. As we will see in later chapters, studies involving separated individuals, such as children of divorce, adopted persons and the offspring of donor insemination, lend firm support to this proposition; it postulates a link between knowledge about hereditary background and self-worth.

Ainsworth (1989) draws a distinction between attachment behaviour and attachment bond. She sees the former as behaviour that promotes physical proximity to the attachment figure, and the attachment behaviour system as the integration of attachment behaviours within the individual. She uses the term attachment bond, on the other hand, to refer to an affectional tie. She stresses that an attachment bond is not restricted to any two specific individuals, but rather a characteristic of the individual 'entailing representation in the internal organization of the individual' (p. 711). This implies that a person can be attached to another person who is not in turn attached to them. It indicates that the existence of bonds cannot be inferred from the presence or absence of attachment behaviour (Fahlberg, 1991). Therefore, two conceptual distinctions may be made. First, there is a difference between attachment behaviour and persisting bonds: attachment bond is considered to exist consistently over time, whether or not attachment behaviour is present (Ainsworth, 1989; Baran and Pannor, 1993; Fahlberg, 1991; Mishen, 1984). Hinde's (1979) notion of 'penetration', as opposed to notions of either strength or intensity of attachment, may provide a more useful framework for characterizing an attachment bond. Hinde defines 'penetration' as a dimension of relationships that describes the centrality of one person to another's life (often unconsciously); it symbolizes the extent to which a person infiltrates a variety of aspects of another person's life. Accepting this proposition and Ainsworth's definition of attachment bond invites the conclusion that children can feel consistently and over time psychologically or emotionally close to and part of a person, even a parent from whom they are separated through death. This then suggests that there may be other dimensions, a higher level cognitive mechanism, missing in our understanding of the process of identity development and maintenance. The present thesis proposes socio-genealogical connectedness as a possible missing dimension.

Attachment theory would hypothesize that if specific attachments are to develop with respect to individual persons, those persons must have actual or face-to-face contact with the child over a prolonged period of time on the grounds that the development of attachment is a long-term process. Still, in the initial stages of attachment theory's development, researchers (e.g. Schaffer and Emerson, 1964; Schaffer, 1971) demonstrated that the absolute amount of time in the company of the child does not seem to affect the development of a child's attachment to another person. In support of the present thesis is one of their findings that the quality of the parent's interaction with the child is probably a crucial factor in attachment and presumably bonding. This is one of the obvious differences between the notion of socio-genealogical connectedness and attachment theory. Socio-genealogical connectedness does not construe actual contact as a prerequisite for one's sense of being linked to one's biological parents or relatives (Owusu-Bempah, 1993, 1995, 2006; Owusu-Bempah and Howitt, 1997, 2000a).

This is in keeping with Rutter's (1981) suggestion that separation need not involve bond disruption, so that the two should not be regarded as synonymous. He laments the fact that this assumption has led to a misguided, taken for granted belief that separation per se has detrimental effects, and that this belief has for a long time distracted researchers from other factors which may be intrinsic in separation. He stresses that separation may or may not be harmful according to its effects on bonds and attachment behaviour. Thus, he claims that it is the relationship itself which needs to be studied. Playing the devil's advocate, he poses the question:

> If bonds can be maintained during separation, then obviously bonds cannot be equated with attachment behaviour. But in that case how should one measure the strength of a bond (or even its presence) when the person with whom bonds have developed is absent?
>
> (Rutter, 1981, p. 126)

He urges researchers to strive to elucidate the bonding process in a move towards resolution of that difficulty. Acknowledging the complexity of the psycho-social mechanisms involved in children's adjustment to separation and loss, it is one of the major aims of this book to shed some light on this question. It seeks to address this apparent paradox of bonding or affectional tie that a child may have not only to an abusive parent or parent from whom they are separated, but even to one they have never actually met, such as a father or grandparent who died before the child was born. To sum all this up, it is a sound hypothesis that the strength of the bond between child and parent may weaken over a long period of separation. Nevertheless, it would be a moot point to conclude from this that the psychological importance of the parent to the child fades away completely. Hinde's idea of 'penetration' and the notion of socio-genealogical connectedness clearly support this argument.

BOND OR CONNECTEDNESS?

In pursuing further clarification of the distinction between attachment and bond, Rutter (1981) posed an exploratory but crisp question: 'Failure to form bonds or disruption of bonds?' (p. 102). He regards this question as of great theoretical interest and practical importance. Using studies carried out in the early 1960s by Pringle and her colleagues (Pringle and Bossio, 1960; Pringle and Clifford, 1962), he tried to address this question. The investigations concerned the reasons for the differences in emotional functioning often observed between stable and maladjusted children in long-term institutional care. They found that, most of the time, the stable children had remained with their mothers until well after the first year and so had had the opportunity of forming bonds prior to admission into institutional care. The emotionally stable children also had more often experienced a dependable and lasting relationship with a parent or parent substitute after going into care.

In contrast, the maladjusted children had not had the same opportunity to establish or maintain stable bonds. One of these children's outstanding characteristics was an inability to form relationships with adults or other children. The investigators reported that regular visits by parents were often sufficient to maintain relationships while the children were in institutions. Rutter interpreted these findings to mean that failure to form bonds was the most likely explanation for emotional instability. Subsequent studies during the same era tended to support Rutter's interpretation of those findings. In more recent times, studies supporting this interpretation abound. However, socio-genealogical connectedness may easily be seen as providing an alternative explanation. In the absence of further details of the studies, socio-genealogical connectedness would hypothesize that the former group of children had not been separated to the extent of losing a sense of connectedness to their biological parents. The maladjusted children, on the other hand, were not just physically separated from their parents but in actuality had not had an opportunity to establish a sense of connectedness to them in the first place.

A further crucial question that Rutter raised was whether the harm was due to disruption or distortion of relationships that separation entails (1981/ 1991). Again, he tried to deal with this question by analysing studies which compared the adjustment of three distinct groups of children: (a) those separated through death; (b) those separated through parental divorce or separation; (c) children who were living with both parents. The analysis involved a number of independent studies (Brown, 1966; Gibson, 1969; Glueck and Glueck, 1950, 1962). In each study, Rutter found that the delinquency rate was about double (compared to that of boys living with both parents) for boys whose parents had divorced or separated, whereas the delinquency rate was only slightly (and non-significantly) raised for those who had lost a parent by death.

In each of these studies, delinquency was less associated with parental death, in spite of its concomitant irreversible loss of actual contact with the lost parent, than it was with parental divorce where bonds may still be maintained by intermittent contact after separation. Investigators today have reported similar findings. Rutter concluded that it was distortion of relationship rather than bond disruption as such which caused the damage. He employed the parental conflict hypothesis to account for the negative developmental outcomes for the children in divorced and separated families. Here too, socio-genealogical connectedness offers an alternative explanation. The chapters to follow present the findings of studies based upon this idea. Concluding his painstaking review, Rutter averred:

> We may now take for granted the extensive evidence that there is an association between delinquency and broken homes; that affectionless psychopathy sometimes follows multiple separation experiences; and that dwarfism is particularly seen in children from rejecting and affectionless homes.
>
> (Rutter, 1981, pp. 123–124)

He therefore further suggested that because this is widely accepted we must now 'focus on the very important question of *why* and *how* children are adversely affected by those experiences included under the term "maternal deprivation", rather than spend time on *whether* they are affected' (pp. 123–124). He acknowledged that the average child must separate from their parents at some time during their lives if they are to develop independent personalities. For him, therefore, the question is not whether children should separate from their parents, but rather when and how separation should occur. He reinforced this by drawing attention to research findings showing that certain sorts of happy separation may actually protect young children from the adverse effects of later stressful separation. The notion of socio-genealogical connectedness takes these suggestions into account. It is concerned principally with the effects of not mere separation, but rather the type of separation which disconnects children from their genealogical roots; it is concerned with the sort of separation that results in what Shants (1946) dubbed 'genealogical bewilderment'.

Rutter also raised the question of bonding, an aspect that is very much at the heart of attachment theory and emphasized by attachment theorists. He asked whether the emotional and behavioural difficulties that separated children experience are attributable to failure to form bonds or, rather, to disruption of bonds. He finds the whole notion of bonding equally problematic. He argues that separation need not involve bond disruption and so the two should not be regarded as synonymous. To him, it is the relationship itself which must be the subject of study. He is right also to raise the important question of whether bonds can be maintained during separation. As previously alluded to, and as we will see in the following chapters, the idea of socio-genealogical connectedness would hypothesize this indeed to be the case. This obviously implies that bonds and attachment behaviour are not the same thing, however interlinked they may be. In other words, in terms of proximity seeking, for instance, attachment refers more or less to primary interpersonal relationships, albeit of a unique quality. Socio-genealogical connectedness, on the other hand, relates to biological-cum-psychological relationships. Thus, from a socio-genealogical connectedness perspective, Rutter's question – 'Failure to form bonds or failure to form bonds with mother?' (p. 106) – needs to be rephrased: Failure to form bonds or failure to feel connected to socio-genealogical roots?

Miller (1999) has argued that in addition to giving meaning to facts a theory serves a second function. She also claims that a theory is a heuristic device, a tool to guide observation and generate new information. From a Popperian position, she asserts that a theory predicts that certain empirical statements should be true; that these statements or hypotheses must be tested. Furthermore, she argues that theories not only stimulate new observations, but must also inspire us to re-examine familiar behaviour and give greater consideration to variables we have slighted. The following three chapters present empirical studies and analyses that have examined the assumptions of socio-genealogical connectedness. These studies also examined an aspect of the process of the development of a sense of socio-genealogical connectedness that has so far not received due attention.

3 Socio-genealogical knowledge

A missing dimension in Bowlby's 'Forty-Four Juvenile Thieves' study?

> My experience has shown me again and again that if these factors are not looked for they are not found.
>
> (Bowlby, 1944, p. 20)

Since those studies carried out in the early years of attachment theory, a large body of research examining the effects of separation and divorce on children has amassed. Some of this literature is discussed in detail in the chapters that follow. They all highlight the detrimental consequences of parental divorce for children's developmental outcomes. Series of meta-analyses by Amato and colleagues have consistently reported supporting evidence (Amato, 2000, 2001; Amato and Keith, 1991a, 1991b; Amato and Gilbeth, 1999). A review by Rogers and Pryor (1998) summed up the findings of over 200 research studies and concluded that separated children have a higher probability of adverse developmental outcomes. Nonetheless, the authors pointed out that long-term negative effects of divorce typically only apply to a small number of children who are about twice as likely to have less favourable outcomes than children living with both parents. These children are more likely to experience poverty, to have behavioural problems, to perform below par at school, to need medical or psychiatric treatment, to leave school or home when young, to be sexually active at an early age, and to suffer from depression.

This chapter explores further the place of socio-genealogical connectedness as a psycho-social developmental theory, as an adjunct to attachment theory. This exploration starts with a reanalysis of the results of Bowlby's (1944) 'Forty-Four Juvenile Thieves: Their Characters and Home-Life'. It is one of his original studies which inspired attachment theory. According to Cassidy (1999) this study, as well as the observations of others (e.g. Goldfarb, 1943; Lorenz, 1935; Spitz, 1945) convinced Bowlby that major disruptions in the parent–child relationship are precursors of later psychopathology. Bowlby's clinical observations led not only to his belief that the relationship with the parent figure is important for later psychological functioning, but also that this relationship is of critical and immediate importance. His initial emphasis on the notion of 'maternal deprivation' as the cause of long-term psychological disturbance stemmed largely from his observations of the frequency with which both delinquency and 'affectionless psychopathy' were associated with multiple separation experiences and institutional care. The results and findings of the study stimulated a variety of investigations by others in the 1950s and 1960s. These investigations also found an association between delinquency and 'broken homes' (e.g. Brown, 1966; Gibson, 1969; Glueck and Glueck, 1950, 1962).

In Chapter 1, we saw that during the 1940s and 1950s secondary drive and psychoanalytic theories provided the dominant explanations for the emotional, intellectual and behavioural problems that separated children are frequently reported to exhibit. Since its inception 60 years ago, attachment theory has supplanted these theories. It has been the dominant approach to understanding the long-term effects of early childhood experiences on their social, emotional and personality development. Thompson (2000) attributes attachment theory's dominance to the fact that theorists and researchers face some of the most compelling, longstanding issues of developmental psychology such as: 'How do early experiences, particularly in primary relationships, affect social and personality development? What are the central features of parenting that have these influences? What internal and external factors mediate continuity and change in socio-personality functioning early in life?' (p. 145). Thompson argues that attachment theory offers developmental psychologists some of their best opportunities to address these questions empirically and to consider new directions based on the answers of current research. The present thesis looks at these issues from a new theoretical and empirical perspective. To start with, unlike other approaches in this field, it does not fully accept attachment theory as a prêt-à-porter explanation for the implications of separation and loss for child development. In addition, unlike attachment theory which was based on clinical observations and insights, the notion of socio-genealogical connectedness is based upon empirical studies involving non-clinical samples.

It is an unquestionable fact that until his death in 1990, at age of 83, John Bowlby was (and continues to be) a highly influential theorist and writer on child development. His legacy still endures. Holmes (1993) has described attachment theory as one of the most important theoretical developments in psychoanalysis since Freud; that the theory has had an enormous impact on child development, social work, psychotherapy, psychology and psychiatry. To this list we must add education and family law, at least in relation to child custody and adoption decisions. Among Bowlby's most important studies was 'The Forty-Four Juvenile Thieves'. This seminal work firmly linked emotional and behavioural problems in childhood with 'broken homes' – maternal (parental) separation – and formed the impetus for attachment theory's development. The study held delinquency and inability to form meaningful relationships to be the consequences of 'broken homes'. Bowlby's later report (1951) to the World Health Organization (WHO) popularized and reinforced this belief:

The evidence is now such that it leaves no room for doubt ... that the prolonged deprivation of a young child of maternal care may have grave and far reaching effects on his character and so on the whole of his future life.

(quoted in Howe, 1995, p. 47)

Together with Bowlby's other claims this became a creed which, bolstered by similar conclusions reached by subsequent studies, has influenced not only research but also family law and professional childcare practice globally.

'THE FORTY-FOUR JUVENILE THIEVES'

In this study Bowlby (1944) compared the behavioural and emotional development of juvenile delinquents (aged between 5.7 years and 16.2 years) with those of a control non-delinquent client group, matched in terms of age and socio-economic status. On the basis of his clinical diagnoses, he classified the children into six character types (see Table 3.1).

The 'affectionless characters' (or 'antisocial psychopaths') were identified as the most incorrigible and troublesome subgroup among the thieves. Their distinguishing features included 'a remarkable lack of affection or warmth or feeling for anyone, solitariness, undemonstrativeness, and unresponsiveness' (Bowlby, 1944, p. 38). They responded neither to kindness nor punishment. Such children truanted and 'wandered', which Bowlby saw as a characteristic sign of indifference to home ties: 'The affectionless character is capable of

Table 3.1 Distribution of thieves and controls by character types

Type	Description	Thieves	Controls	Total
Normal	Children whose characters appear fairly normal and stable	2	3	5
Depressed	Children who have been unstable and are now in a more or less depressed state of mind	9	21	30
Circular	Unstable children who show alternating depression and overactivity	2	1	3
Hyperthymic	Children who tend to constant overactivity	13	10	23
Affectionless	Children characterized by lack of shame or sense of responsibility	14	–	14
Schizoid	Children who show marked schizoid or schizophrenic symptoms	4	9	13
Total		**44**	**44**	**88**

Source: Bowlby (1944: 24, 52).

neither attachment, affection, nor loyalty.' He described them as unique and hard-nosed criminals, compared to the other groups of delinquents, and summarized their character unequivocally thus:

> We can get a Depressive who does not steal as well as one who does, we can find a law-abiding Hyperthymic as well as his antisocial brother. I am doubtful, however, whether the law-abiding Affectionless Character exists. He does not figure among my controls and I have not met him elsewhere, though I have met many other Affectionless thieves besides the fourteen described here.
>
> (p. 39)

Bowlby identified a strong connection between these children's emotional and behavioural problems and their prolonged early separation from their birth parents. He based his conviction mainly on the fact that such separations occurred in 7 (50 per cent) of the 14 affectionless characters, but only in 3 (10 per cent) of the other 30 delinquents.

However, Rutter (1981) has suggested that the affectionless character is associated with multiple changes of parent figure or home in infancy or early childhood rather than separation from a mother figure. This reinterpretation implies that factors other than parental physical separation alone were involved in the affectionless characters' difficulties. As Rutter has argued, deprivation involves a most diverse range of adversities which operate through a number of distinct psychological mechanisms. The present thesis argues that the absence of socio-genealogical knowledge, or adverse socio-genealogical knowledge is one possible mechanism (Owusu-Bempah, 1993, 1995, 2006; Owusu-Bempah and Howitt, 1997, 2000a). A further careful re-examination of Bowlby's case histories supports this contention. The following section examines Bowlby's seminal research and compares it with modern case studies reflecting similar characteristics in which the role of socio-genealogical linkage is apparent.

Bowlby's 44 thieves and socio-genealogical knowledge

The case histories of Bowlby's 44 thieves were reassessed in terms of the amount and quality of information the 'thieves' would have been expected to have possessed about their biological parents at the time of the study. As in previous investigations (Owusu-Bempah, 1993, 1995), these delinquents were categorized in terms of their (hypothetical) possession of:

1   'Full information' about both parents (e.g. those who were living with both biological parents).
2   'Partial information' about both or one of the parents.
3   'Minimal information' (those whose knowledge of both or one of the parents could have been expected to consist of only basic facts, for

instance, name(s), possible whereabouts, but no genealogical information about them).

4   'No information' (those who could not have been expected to know even the names of both or one of the parents).

5   'Negative information' (those who had information about the parents or one of them, but such information could have been expected to be unfavourable or damaging).

Because of Bowlby's relatively small sample and his occasional failure to provide sufficient details, categories (3), (4) and (5) were combined. We will see in this section and later chapters that studies based on the idea of socio-genealogical connectedness and involving community (non-clinical) samples of children of lone-parent families found many of the problems associated with lone-parent upbringing to be much more prevalent among those who had no, inadequate, or unfavourable information about the absent parent. Significantly, these problems often paralleled those associated with Bowlby's 'affectionless characters', such as burglary and attempted suicide.

As Table 3.2 shows, 8 (18 per cent) of the 44 juvenile delinquents, according to the present reanalysis, had no, or only partial knowledge or negative information about one or both of their biological parents. Of these, six (75 per cent) were described by Bowlby as affectionless characters, while only one of the 'normal' and one of the schizoid thieves had no, or partial or negative parental information. The six affectionless characters who fell into this category were the children whom Bowlby listed as Cases 27, 32, 33, 36, 37 and 38. In other words, 43 per cent of the affectionless delinquents possessed no or inadequate or damaging parental information, but this applied to only 2 (7 per cent) of the other 30 delinquents. This is consistent with Bowlby's own findings: 7 (50 per cent) of the affectionless characters had experienced prolonged 'maternal deprivation' compared with only 3 (10 per cent) (including 1 'normal') of the other 30 thieves. The lack of adequate and/or positive parental or

Table 3.2 The 44 thieves and parental information by character type

Type	Full information	No/partial/negative information	Total
Normal	1(50)	1(50)	2(4.5)
Depressed	9(100)	–	9(20)
Circular	2(100)	–	2(4.5)
Hyperthymic	13(100)	–	13(30)
Affectionless	8(57)	6(43)	14(32)
Schizoid	3(75)	1(25)	4(9)
Total	**36(82)**	**8(18)**	**44(100)**

Note: Percentages are in brackets.

Source: Bowlby (1944: 24, 52).

genealogical information seems, therefore, to have been one of the distinguishing features of the affectionless characters. Comparison between Tables 3.1 and 3.2 thus indicates that problems of socio-genealogical linkages might explain aspects of Bowlby's seminal data. By inference, this factor may also have been a missing dimension in many subsequent studies and reviews (e.g. Bowlby, 1973, 1980; Glueck and Glueck, 1950, 1962) of delinquency and childhood and adolescent problems. As such, it may have hindered our pursuit of a fuller understanding of separated children who exhibit such problems.

This is also likely to have been the case with regard to adoption and other instances of separation where the risk of severance of socio-genealogical linkage is obvious. A sense of socio-genealogical connectedness is essential to the general well-being of adopted children (see Brodzinsky and Schechter, 1990, for a review and discussion). Brodzinsky (1987) and Pannor *et al.* (1974) attribute the repeatedly reported intellectual, emotional and behavioural difficulties experienced by many adopted children to the loss of genealogical continuity. Following Shants (1964), many writers have laid stress on the state of confusion and uncertainty found in children lacking knowledge of their biological parents, or possessing only uncertain knowledge of them. This is believed to undermine the child's emotional security and self-concept, leading to a confused sense of identity not only in adolescence but also in adulthood. This has long been recognised.

William James (1890) drew special attention to the serious, adverse implications brought about by the loss of (genealogical) continuity for personal identity. In other words, there seems to exist a deeply rooted psychological need to experience human connectedness. A number of investigators have emphasized the strength of the need for continuity. They compare it with hunger which 'grows with time, experienced subjectively by some adopted persons as equivalent to starvation' (Schechter and Bertocci, 1990, p. 85). Adopted children share with other children, for example, the offspring of donor insemination, some of the problems of maintaining socio-genealogical connectedness.

Also, as we will soon see, many children in some lone-parent families equally lack socio-genealogical information about the absent parent, or possess inadequate or damaging information about them. This appears to be as applicable to some 43 per cent of Bowlby's affectionless characters; in fact, Bowlby unknowingly recognised this:

> ... These children have suffered the complete emotional loss of their mothers or foster-mothers during infancy and early childhood. Such a loss in later life not uncommonly precipitates a Melancholia. It is possible that some such reaction takes place in the mind of the two-year-old, and because of the special circumstances, complete recovery is impossible.
>
> (Bowlby, 1944, p. 39)

The concept of socio-genealogical connectedness does not refer merely to facts or the knowledge component of parent–child relationship. Knowledge about one's parents is not affectively neutral, but may have positive and negative emotional connotations. For this reason, it is important to distinguish between affective links between parent and child and socio-genealogical information links which may entrain emotive issues. For example, the affective parent–child communication or relationship may be essentially innocuous or even negative, but available socio-genealogical knowledge is somewhat positive and beneficial. Knowledge of a socio-genealogical link in itself may contribute to a person's psychological well-being without there ever having been face-to-face contact. So, for example, knowing the biological as well as the cultural and social background of a parent or even a great-grandparent dead long before a child's birth may contribute positively to that child's psychological well-being.

This does not mean that socio-genealogical knowledge, irrespective of its particular content, is always a positive influence on a child's life. Nonetheless, in the absence of experience of one's parent(s), knowledge which is solely bad is unlikely to contribute positively to a child's psychological well-being. Furthermore, the notion of socio-genealogical connectedness acknowledges the possibility that a child may actively shun socio-genealogical knowledge in circumstances where their parents are not valued. Fantasies of being adopted may be an instance of this. This is important in relation to Bowlby's work. Given that his central thesis is that failure to form bonds or disruptions in bonding in early childhood leads to psychological maladjustment, there is a risk of confusing this with the concept of socio-genealogical knowledge. After all, the death of a parent can be construed as both a severance forever in the bonding process and a loss of socio-genealogical knowledge through contact. The difference is that Bowlby saw this as resulting directly in psychological dysfunction, but the notion of socio-genealogical connectedness would argue that the provision of socio-genealogical knowledge could go a long way towards stabilizing or at least mitigating the situation. Of course, depending on the age of the child, there may be a grieving process and a long-term sense of loss, but this need not be harmful in the sense of attachment theory.

It was argued in the preceding chapter that socio-genealogical knowledge is fundamental to our sense of who we are, where we come from and where we belong in the order of things. In the absence of information about one's origins and genealogy it is difficult, if not impossible, to comprehend oneself or one's abilities, potential, or even characteristics, desirable or undesirable. Triseliotis and colleagues (1997) point out that the influence of one's forebears, one's sense of security and belonging, among other things, depend on socio-genealogical identification. The argument being advanced here is that many of Bowlby's affectionless characters are understandable today in terms of severance of socio-genealogical links rather than in terms of physical or spatial separation from their parents per se. In examining this, one is at a slight disadvantage in that Bowlby naturally examined the validity of his thesis rather than the present thesis, so sometimes relevant details are missing. Still, Bowlby's research paper contains many case studies which, as he acknowledged, fail to firmly support his theory. His argument is that most of these are not serious thieves and fail to demonstrate the affectionless personality which is conducive to serious thieving, and which results from childhood separation from parents. Yet, the cases which he rejected in this way are actually the overwhelming majority of his thieves who were referred to his clinic because of their behavioural problems. Consequently, it is reasonable to ask whether these 'excluded' cases demonstrated potential problems in socio-genealogical connectedness any more than they did problems of childhood separation from parents.

Bowlby emphasized the affectionless characters, the 'entrenched thieves', and isolated them as the particularly problematic children. Moreover, the case studies seem to be more thorough for the affectionless thieves than for the other children. This makes it difficult to examine the other case studies with confidence. However, for reasons of illustration, we can take Bowlby's Group B which he described as 'depressed characters' (Table 3.1). Although there is no evidence that they generally suffered the maternal separation which Bowlby described as characteristic of the thieves, they are described in terms seemingly implicating parental information and socio-genealogical connectedness in their difficulties. In other words, for six of the nine children in the depressed category, there seems to have been at least tentative evidence that there might have been problems of parental information or socio-genealogical connectedness (Cases 3, 4, 5, 7, 9, 10). Similar comments could be made of many of the other children discussed in Bowlby's seminal paper. These cases might have included those children who, according to him, never recovered from the loss of their parents.

Failure to form bonds or disruption of bonds? Rutter (1981) asked this question in his review of Bowlby's notion of 'maternal deprivation'. The question which the present thesis seeks to examine relates to whether it is a failure to establish a sense of socio-genealogical connectedness which somehow accounts for separated children's developmental difficulties. In his study of 'The Forty-Four Thieves', Bowlby linked inability to form relationships with separation experiences in early childhood. However, an examination of his case histories suggests that, as Rutter (1981) has pointed out, an 'affectionless' character is associated not so much with a prolonged separation as with multiple changes of parent figure or home in infancy or early childhood. This had occurred in 7 out of 14 affectionless characters, but only 3 of the other 30 thieves. It could well be that frequent changes of parent figures during the period when a sense of connectedness normally is established, in early formative years of development, could have disrupted or impaired the children's development of a healthy sense of connectedness. From a socio-genealogical connectedness perspective, it could well be argued that such circumstances provide no opportunity for establishing genealogical linkage. In fact, failure to develop a sense of socio-genealogical connectedness is likely to erode or corrode a child's sense of socio-genealogical connectedness where this is in a process of formation or consolidation.

Rutter (1981) would endorse this proposition. He has noted that two of the other affectionless characters had spent nine months in hospital unvisited during their second year of life, when attachments would normally be consolidated. Thus, he hypothesized that a failure to form bonds in early childhood is particularly associated with the later development of an 'affectionless character'. He asked: 'Can the disruption of bonds have the same effect?' (p. 105). To this question, his examination of the empirical evidence suggested that the outcome is only rarely a consequence of bond disruption. Thus, he argued that follow-up studies of children admitted to institutions after the age when attachments develop confirm that affectionless psychopathy is not characteristic of children who have developed bonds and then had them broken or stressed by a prolonged separation. Although highly plausible, this conclusion does not take into account the socio-genealogical dimension of personality development. It was suggested in the preceding chapter that a distinction be made between bonds and socio-genealogical connectedness, on the grounds that it will enable us to better understand the developmental difficulties of not only Bowlby's 44 delinquents, but also many of the children in the studies that subsequent research and reviews have examined. The following section considers this question in relation to children in lone-parent families.

SOCIO-GENEALOGICAL CONNECTEDNESS AND CHILDREN OF LONE-PARENT FAMILIES: CASE STUDIES

The following case studies (all names changed) reinforce the above view. In other words, consideration of the notion of socio-genealogical knowledge is likely to enhance our understanding of the developmental needs of today's children, especially separated children of all categories. The cases were qualitative data gathered as part of a quantitative study of the relationship between parental information and the adjustment of children of lone-parent families (Owusu-Bempah, 1993, 1995). Statistical analyses of the results of the studies and their findings are discussed in subsequent chapters. Through in-depth interviews, the study investigated whether the amount and quality of information possessed by the children about the absent parent affected their behaviour, emotional adjustment and academic achievement.

Case study 1: Colin

Colin was 8 years old at the time of the study. He lived with his divorced mother and 6-year-old brother. His mother had been a lone parent for

5.5 years. During that time neither of the children had had contact with their father (not even a birthday card or telephone call from him). According to the mother, the children knew very little about him and his background or even his whereabouts. They occasionally asked her questions about him and expressed a wish to see him. She did not know much about him herself and was unable to provide information to them 'as he turned out not to be the person she thought he was'. Colin was described by his mother as a 'disturbed child':

> Colin is a 'problem child'. He has problems: bedwetting and soiling. He sees a psychiatrist, school psychologist mainly, for his behaviour and the way he talks to people and the way he is with me, but more than anything the way he is with me. He also has behaviour problems at school: fighting, etc., and has been banned from school dinners several times; and he is not doing well academically. He tried to strangle himself about two years ago when he was about 6 years old. He stood on a chair, put his head through a loop (of a washing line) in the garden, and jumped off the chair. Other attempts include climbing and jumping off the garden shed, climbing through upstairs windows.

Colin's school reports confirmed his mother's account of his behaviour at school. Asked what she thought might be the cause(s) of her son's problems, she replied:

> I think that Colin might have less problems if he had contact with his dad. I think that children who have contact with their dad tend to get more love, more affection because they have got the two people still there.

Recognizing the importance of parental contact and, implicitly, favourable parental or socio-genealogical knowledge to children following divorce, she had made several attempts (mainly through correspondence) to make contact with her estranged husband.

Case study 2: Donald

Donald (19 years old at the time of the study) was the oldest of three children (all males) in his family. The mother was a twice-divorced, 38-year-old woman. Donald was the older of two children from her first marriage which lasted two years. She had been divorced from her second spouse, after six years of marriage, for some 11 years. Donald exhibited many of the classic problems associated with lone-parent upbringing (and 'affectionless characters'). This is the mother's account of his problems:

> I have had every kind of trouble with Donald. He started smoking at 13, bunking school, not attending at all by age 16; made to leave school at 16

to avoid me being taken to court; bad behaviour at school – constant detentions. He has been in trouble with the police and courts six times for various offences; sent to G [local prison for young offenders]; spraying paint, petty burglary, shoplifting, motor car theft, nuisance to neighbours. He didn't want to work after leaving school; resorted to burglary since age 13 or 14; drug taking. He started involvement with the police at 14 years; started custodial career from age 16 – has been in G and other places in the country; released from prison less than a year ago. He has been in solitary confinement in G and other places; sentenced to 18 months for burglaries at 18 years.

An epitome of Bowlby's affectionless character? Asked what she would attribute her son's problems mainly to, she replied:

Donald's problems arise from his denial of his father. I think he needs to sit down with a therapist; he needs to go right through his past; he needs to acknowledge the fact that, OK, he doesn't have to see his real father, but I think he needs to sit down, he needs to talk about it, and he needs to sort himself out, sort his head out. I think he's got a chip on his shoulder, Donald has got such a terrible chip on his shoulder. I feel that really he needs to work his problems out. I put it all down to the fact that he has never met his father, and he is unwilling to meet him or even to know who he is.

Donald detested bearing his biological father's name such that at the age of 13 he changed his name to that of his stepfather (with whom he did not particularly get on). At 16, while shopping with his mother, Donald and his father bumped into each other in a local supermarket as total strangers to each other – only the mother knew that it was a 'father–son encounter'.

Why Donald detested his biological father so much that he changed his name into his stepfather's name (a person with whom he reportedly did not get along) may be explained in terms of 'parental alienation syndrome'. This syndrome will be discussed in Chapter 7. In the meantime, his story may be described as a classic case of denial of one's socio-genealogical background, with all its adverse psychological ramifications.

Case study 3: Martin

Martin, a 15-year-old boy, lived with his mother and 17-year-old sister. Martin was 5 years old when his parents divorced. He and his sister had had no contact with their father since then, for some ten years. The father lived abroad and the mother disallowed them to maintain even telephone contact with him. Their mother was so hostile and antipathetic towards their father that, during the interview, she found it emotionally difficult to even mention his name. Asked what their father's name was, she replied without hesitation: 'I just call him "ex-". I don't give him any name . . . I refer to him to the children as "your ex-father".'

Martin was reported by his mother to be acting out more severe emotional problems than his sister. She described him as a very angry youth who vented his anger specifically on her:

> Martin expresses his anger only at home; and he does so in violent ways – foot through the bedroom door, breaking windows and furniture and throwing things about by the week. At other times, he is sullen and withdrawn – locks himself up in his room.

Martin's mother seemed to be in no doubt about why he was angry:

> I suspect that Martin's anger towards me may have something to do with cutting them off from their father . . . They have nothing to remind them of their father . . . there are no mementos of their father in the house . . . not even a photograph.

Like many parents involved in the study, Martin's mother was aware that her son's anger and behaviour were reactions to her disconfirmation of his father, her denial of him and suppression of information about him. She acknowledged that Martin could have benefited from help but said: 'I'm reluctant to seek professional help for him, lest I be labelled an inadequate parent; for fear of having them [the children] taken away from me. I couldn't cope with that.'

It appears that in this case Martin repudiated his mother's apparent disconfirmation or negative account of his father. That his sister was not reported to have been exhibiting any such problems may be explained by the mother's admission that she was aware that her daughter was in secret communication with her father.

Case study 4: Jack

Jack, 19 years old, was the oldest of six children in his family. His parents were not married and he was conceived during a very brief liaison. The mother (40 years old at the time of the study) had been twice divorced. She married another man when Jack was about one year old and had three children with him. Following a divorce, she remarried and had a further two children. Thus, Jack had had two stepfathers but had never met his biological father, about whom he knew virtually nothing. All of the children were reported to be experiencing (or to have experienced) difficulties, but Jack exhibited the severest problems. The following is his mother's description of his problems:

Jack's problems started at an early age. He was taken into care at about fourteen and a half years. The reason he was in care was 'cos he used to run away – he was volatile at home and at school; he used to stay away from home – sleeping out; he never came back without the police escorting him home. Eventually he was taken into voluntary care by social services. As he got older he was constantly in trouble with the police for various offences including car theft, driving. He was eventually expelled from school. He was also involved with the police for violence and sent to G [local prison for young offenders]. He spent his 18th birthday in prison.

The mother summed up the possible causes of Jack's (and her other son Malcolm's) difficulties thus:

I think a lot of the problems the children have had has something to do with not knowing their natural fathers; perhaps not just not knowing but not being able to have a pride in that part of themselves . . . I think that is very important. I think children need to be able to relate to their own family.

Asked what prevented the children from knowing their natural fathers, she replied:

Perhaps the children, especially Jack and Malcolm, would've done better if they hadn't had a stepfather, if I had stayed on my own; the stepfather didn't like them to talk about their father; they weren't allowed to talk about their father when the stepfather was about.

This illustrates not just a case of denial or total absence but of suppression of or an embargo on essential material that Jack and Malcolm needed in order to establish a sense of identity and emotional and behavioural stability.

Case study 5: Andrew

Andrew's circumstances contrasted markedly with the above cases. Andrew was 13 years old at the time of the study. His parents divorced when he was 3 years old and he had lived with his 40-year-old mother since then. However, unlike the above cases, he had regular and continuous contact with his remarried father. Indeed, because his mother's job (nursing) entailed unsocial hours, his father had been babysitting Andrew since the divorce, including picking him up from school and taking him to the mother's residence and looking after him until she returned home from work. Andrew knew no less about his father and his extended kin than he would have done if his parents had stayed married. Both he and his mother stated that he identified a bit more with his father's side (Welsh) than his mother's (English). He was asked the question: 'What sort of things make you happy, besides your birthday and Christmas?' He replied: 'Staying with my grandparents in Wales during school holidays, and going on holidays abroad with my dad.'

In terms of adjustment, his school reports confirmed his mother's description of him as a well-adjusted child, happy and cheerful and doing very well at school, both academically and behaviourally, and being popular with his teachers and other children. Music was his main hobby and he treated the interviewer to a tune or two on his trumpet.

CONCLUSION

To conclude this chapter, several investigators, writers and practitioners have reported an intimate association between family disruptions and emotional and behavioural disturbance in children, particularly of an antisocial nature. Rutter (1981), for instance, has pointed out that it is not the children in institutional or public care but rather those separated from a parent through divorce who have much increased risk of delinquency. As we will see in Chapter 7, parental divorce or separation provides a potentially fertile condition for denial, disconfirmation or negative distortion of socio-genealogical information. This is exemplified by Cases 3 and 4 above. The question of whether it is bond disruption, disruption of relationships (as Rutter, 1981, has suggested), or a lack or distortion of parental knowledge that is responsible for these children's developmental difficulties certainly warrants further consideration. In the meantime, the case studies presented provide support for a culturally acknowledged belief in the importance of knowledge about one's biological parents (and the quality of such information) to a child's overall well-being. This factor was not considered in Bowlby's (1944) study or Rutter's (1981) perceptive and incisive review of Bowlby's idea of 'maternal deprivation' and attachment theory generally. Unsurprisingly, however, many of the parents involved in socio-genealogical connectedness studies spontaneously acknowledged its indubitable importance. It must be pointed out, though, that the above cases are selected cases and so do not necessarily signify how widespread the parents' belief is.

Although consideration of socio-genealogical information or connectedness as a factor in child development is likely to lead to a fuller understanding of separated children's and adolescents' emotional, intellectual and behavioural problems, attachment theory as a whole and studies derived from it have failed to clearly take this factor into account. Also, current notions regarding separation through divorce – parental absence or contact, spousal conflict and economic hardship – on which much research has concentrated fail to consider it.

With respect to spousal conflict and parental absence, this is somewhat surprising in view of the fact that both factors are closely linked, such that they interact to affect contact and communication between the child and the non-residential parent. There seems to be a consensus that contact with parents has long-term benefits (e.g. Cantos *et al.*, 1997; Cleaver, 2000; Guidubaldi *et al.*, 1987; Hetherington, 1989; McWey, 2000; Mitchell, 1983; Peterson and Zill, 1986; Rutter, 1981; Southworth and Schwarz, 1987; Pringle and Clifford, 1962; Wallerstein and Kelly, 1980). Why this should be beneficial requires clarification. Socio-genealogical connectedness theory would hypothesize that the reported long-term benefits of contact may not be due to (physical) parental contact per se, but rather to the parental information acquired by the child during contact. The conflict perspective fails to account for why some children whose mothers never married or cohabited exhibit the problems commonly associated with lone-parent status. Previous investigations found strong correspondence between parental contact and the amount and quality of information possessed by the children about the absent parent (Owusu-Bempah, 1993, 1995). These factors were in turn found to be closely related to the children's overall well-being. Consideration of such relationships and parental contact and their resultant quantity and/or quality of information gathered by the child about the parent(s) was clearly missing in Bowlby's 'Forty-Four Juvenile Thieves'.

A number of studies have suggested that hostility between the parents is likely to result in a decrease in post-divorce contact between children and their non-resident parent (Amato, 1987; Amato, 2001; Amato and Keith, 1991a, 1991b; Amato *et al.*, 1995; Hess and Camara, 1979; Wallerstein and Kelly, 1980, 2000; White *et al.*, 1985; Peterson and Zill, 1986) and, by inference, in the quantity and quality of information possessed by the child about the parent (Owusu-Bempah, 1993, 1995, 2000a). They also highlight the detrimental effects of this state of affairs not only on the children but also on the adults involved. A 38-year-old (and three times divorced) mother of four appreciated this:

> As for the children, if you can remain on a friendly level with your ex-partner it works better for the children, and I've proved that from my own experience. I know that, I need no expert to tell me . . . sometimes that is impossible to achieve, but if you can make friends after, the kids benefit, definitely! That is a decisive piece of information for you there, I've proved that.

We will see in Chapter 7 that in acrimonious situations the information about the absent parent is more likely to be unfavourable, suppressed or unwelcome. This is clearly illustrated by Case studies 3 and 4 indicating that overt conflict between biological parents alone is not a sufficient condition. Rather it is the suppression, distortion or denial of information about the non-resident parent which renders the children vulnerable.

That socio-genealogical knowledge is an essential factor in children's overall adjustment seems undeniable and has been acknowledged historically by various investigators, albeit indirectly (e.g. Bach, 1946; Bharat, 1988; Shants, 1964; Simmons *et al.*, 1973). It is not just the amount of information that children who lack parental information need, but rather that such information should be positive or at least undamaging. For example, Erikson (1950) and Epstein (1976) claimed that the disconfirmation or denigration of a parent diminishes the child's sense of trust in the world. This is clearly illustrated by the serious emotional and behavioural problems exhibited by Donald, Martin and Jack (Case studies 2, 3 and 4).

The importance of the biological parent's value to the child's emotional welfare is even more dramatically demonstrated in child abuse cases:

> All [child protection workers] who have been involved when children are removed from a home have witnessed how youngsters cling even to abusing parents . . . [and] seen children run away from adequate foster homes to inadequate parental homes.
>
> (Cole, 1984, quoted in Palmer, 1990, p. 228)

With regard to socio-genealogical connectedness, the explanation for such seemingly bizarre behaviour is that these children possess the cognitive ability to differentiate the two parts of the parent, to separate the parent as a person who is a part of the child from the parent's abusive behaviour (Owusu-Bempah, 2006). Derdeyn (1977), in similar vein, also warned that even abusing parents have a great value to a child and so ought not to be devalued; that the disconfirmation of the parent results in the denial of the child's self and subsequent splitting off of that self part. That is, the cost to children of seeing their parent as 'bad' or 'undesirable' is too high – children's self-worth is so closely tied to their parent's self-worth. This was acknowledged by many of the parents interviewed and as one of them aptly put it:

> I feel that it is important that children know their fathers, that they know where they come from and that they have a relationship with their father, no matter how bad the father is, unless it is that bad it is a danger to the child. I think that it is something the child has to decide for himself, not what we put in their minds. They need to know their father, and when they are old enough they can make their own judgements. I don't think we can run their lives, much as we would like to. I feel that if a child never met his dad, he would always wonder, and they would feel that the father didn't care about them . . . I think that there would be some sense of a loss.

The evidence contained in this chapter and those that follow indicates that a lack of socio-genealogical connectedness has undesirable consequences for the development and overall functioning of separated children. This has long been implied by a number of investigators and writers (e.g. Freud and Burlingham, 1944; Tessman, 1978; Triseliotis, 1973; Triseliotis *et al.*, 1997;

Wallerstein and Kelly, 1980). The therapeutic value of positive parental information has long been documented, for example, by Auer (1983). Auer claimed that favourable information about one's parents can be a positive influence on a child's sense of trust, self-concept and overall adjustment.

The implications of parental knowledge for theory, policy and professional practice concerning modern families are quite apparent. (Chapter 7 discusses these in detail.) In custody decisions and professional childcare practice, for instance, it is clear that this factor has long been neglected. While few would deny that in custody situations, for instance, unhindered (positive) contact with non-custodial parents ought to be facilitated, this can prove very difficult. Where such contact is already severed or restricted, it will be in the child's best interest for the professionals involved to emphasize to both the resident and non-resident parent the developmental benefits of contact, and to encourage the parties concerned to facilitate the availability of positive or undamaging socio-genealogical knowledge. Contact, where possible, must be extended to include the absent parent's relatives. In the words of a mother who participated in one of the present author's studies: 'Ideally, they [children] need not only two parents, but an extended family as well to get the balance of both sides right.'

Miller (1999), concurring with Bowlby (1944), has stated:

> Scientists hold certain assumptions that lead them to see certain facts more easily than others; in fact, it is difficult to see what we are not looking for . . .
>
> (pp. 15–16)

Theorists and researchers have overlooked the idea of socio-genealogical connectedness and its importance for developmental outcomes. The present thesis identifies and acknowledges it as an important factor in psycho-social development. The chapters that follow describe studies and analyses stressing further its implications for separated children's global adjustment.

4 Socio-genealogical connectedness and the well-being of children of divorce

The large amount of research, reviews and reports accumulated over the last 60 years since Bowlby's (1944) publication of 'The Forty-Four Juvenile Thieves' suggests that, as in the case of other groups of children, those of parental divorce or separation are at particular risk of myriad developmental problems, compared with those living with both biological parents. These difficulties include the frequently reported psychiatric, educational, employment and relationship problems that are closely linked with separation and loss: aggression, violence, burglary, lying, temper tantrums, disobedience, rebelliousness, absconding, truancy, alcohol and illicit drug misuse, promiscuity, and so forth (e.g. Amato, 1993, 1996, 2000; Amato and Keith, 1991a, 1991b; Austin, 1978; Bowlby, 1944, 1973, 1980; Burns and Dunlop, 2002; Chase-Landsdale et al., 1995; Dennis and Erdos, 1992; Elliot and Richards, 1991; Emery, 1988; Glueck and Glueck, 1950, 1962; Hetherington, 1973; Hetherington and Arasteth, 1988; Raphael et al., 1990; Tennant, 1988; Wadsworth, 1976; Wallerstein and Kelly, 1980). In short, there is more than ample research as well as anecdotal evidence that parental divorce or separation often have detrimental effects on children's psychological functioning and overall well-being.

Stewart-Clarke and Hayward (1996), in a study which involved a sample of 187 children aged between 5 and 15, reported that these effects are not large in absolute terms. On measures of psychological well-being, they found that children from divorced families scored, on average, only about one-seventh of a standard deviation below children from non-divorced families. They caution, however, that these averages obscure the fact that although some children in divorced families are doing as well as those in non-divorced families, others are doing considerably worse. Using the rate of recovery from poliomyelitis as an analogy, Bowlby (1973) had previously argued that the fact that only a small proportion of children are severely affected should not preclude us from nor does it provide us with an excuse for not making efforts to find ways to help those children who are adversely affected by separation, including divorce:

> Of all those who contract poliomyelitis less than 1 per cent develop paralysis, and only a fraction of 1 per cent remain crippled. To argue

that, because 99 per cent recover, polio is a harmless infection would be obviously absurd. Similarly, in the field under consideration, to argue that because most individuals recover from the effect of a separation or loss these experiences are of no account would be equally absurd.

(p. 23)

Stewart-Clarke and Hayward (1996) have categorized current research efforts to understand and address the lasting undesirable consequences of divorce for developmental outcomes according to their underlying assumptions into the following:

1   Studies guided by the assumption that continuity of contact or relationship between children and their non-resident parent facilitates their adjustment to divorce; the hypothesis being that children who have contact with both parents are able to maintain their attachment to both parents.
2   Research which tests the hypothesis that children adjust better to divorce in financially favourable circumstances; that is, in the custody of the parent who maintains a reasonable standard of living.
3   Studies guided by the assumption that same-gender custody mitigates the effects of divorce on children.

Seemingly missing from this list of guiding principles is the role of socio-genealogical knowledge. Socio-genealogical connectedness studies and analyses conducted over the past ten years intrinsically tested these assumptions (Owusu-Bempah, 1993, 1995, 2006; Owusu-Bempah and Howitt, 1997, 2000a). The need to empirically examine this factor cannot be overstated, given the accelerating rate of divorce throughout the western world since World War II, and consequently the vast number of children affected by it. Together with Chapter 5 this chapter describes the research and analyses which examined the role of socio-genealogical knowledge in children's post-divorce adjustment. These involved children of lone-parent families.

LONE-PARENT UPBRINGING

In the early 1990s Goode (1992) noted that 'within the Western world, the social conditions of our time have created the highest divorce rates in its history' (p. 11). For example, a survey by Bradshaw and Millar (1991) reported that the UK had over one million lone-parent families – that is, one in seven families was headed by a lone parent. These investigators predicted that as many as a third of all children would experience life in a lone-parent family. In the same period, Haskey (1990, 1997) and Kiernan and Wicks (1992) expressed similar concerns. They also predicted that by the year 2000 only half of all children would have spent the whole of their childhood in a conventional two-parent family. In western Europe as a whole Roll (1992) reported that lone-parent families with children under 18 ranged from 5 to 6 per cent in Greece, Italy and Spain, to over 17 per cent in Britain. As we saw in Chapter 1, more recent large-scale surveys tend to confirm these predictions: that is, these predictions were well founded. Figure 4.1 shows the divorce trend in the UK as a whole in the last 45 years, from 1961 to 2004, while Table 4.1 shows the number of divorce and under 16-year-old children involved during the period 2001–2004 in England and Wales alone.

Thousands

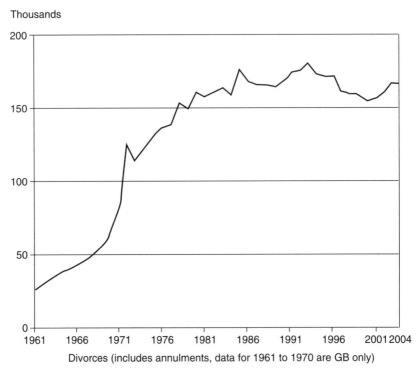

Divorces (includes annulments, data for 1961 to 1970 are GB only)

Figure 4.1 Divorces in the UK, 1961–2004.

Source: Office for National Statistics (2005a).

Table 4.1 Children of couples divorced in England and Wales, 2001–2004

Year	No. of divorced couples	No. of children under 16
2001	145,713	146,914
2002	147,735	149,335
2003	153,490	153,527
2004	153,442	149,275
Total	**598,442**	**599,015**

Source: Office for National Statistics (2005a). *Population Trends 121*, London: Office for National Statistics.

Amato and Keith, for example, have argued that it is now apparent that parental divorce is associated with negative psycho-social effects on offspring both during childhood and as they progress into adulthood (Amato, 1999, 2000; Amato and Keith, 1991a, 1991b). If lone parenthood is a major cause of psychological maladjustment, poor school performance and delinquency, as research suggests, then the current accelerating divorce rates throughout all strata of society must be of grave concern for researchers, policymakers, childcare professionals and society at large. In most cases, parental divorce or separation automatically leaves children living with only one birth parent; no less than 90 per cent of them with the mother. Public concern about lone-parent families typically highlights the so-called burden that they place upon the nation's economic welfare and moral health. This concern is often expressed in moral or disapproving tones: 'Are women neglecting their family duties? Is a breakdown in morals imminent?' 'Absent fathers are neglecting their parental responsibilities and obligations.' 'Should decent citizens have to pay for the welfare support of people who violate traditional family norms [for the results of other people's carnal pleasure]?' (Goode, 1992, p. 11).' Hence much contemporary research has concentrated on the economic or policy implications of lone-parent families for society at large (Brown, 1989) while comparatively less attention has been paid to other factors which may mediate the developmental outcomes for the children involved.

Empirical evidence abounds to support the traditional view that lone-parent families are a detrimental environment to the healthy development of children. That is, children of lone-parent families are frequently presented as being at greater risk for psychological, academic and behavioural difficulties than other children. Granted this to be the case, and coupled with the current accelerating rise in the number of lone-parent families, particularly in the western world (especially in the USA and UK), it is important to understand why lone-parent upbringing adversely affects child development and how it may be mitigated.

It was suggested earlier that contemporary explanations have concentrated on three main notions: parental absence, economic hardship and spousal conflict. Examination of the literature in this area, however, suggests that there may be other mechanisms responsible for these children's vulnerability. Psycho-social research, as opposed to policy research, has for a long time emphasized children's social, emotional and intellectual well-being. Such research suggests that children of divorced or separated parents do worse throughout the life cycle: as adults they have lower educational attainment (Burns and Dunlop, 2002; Dennis and Erdos, 1992; McLanahan, 1985; Spencer, 2005; Sergrin *et al.*, 2005); earn less income and are more likely to be dependent on welfare (state benefit) (McLanahan, 1985; Ross and Mirowsky, 1999). They are also likely to bear a child out of wedlock (Amato, 1996, 2000; Amato and Keith, 1991b; McLanahan and Bumpass, 1988); get divorced (Amato, 1996; Glenn and Kramer, 1987; Sergrin *et al.*, 2005); and to be the head of a lone-parent family (McLanahan and Bumpass, 1988). It has been suggested that these problems of adult children of divorce, in turn, may be associated with lower psychological well-being (Burns and Dunlop, 2002; Glenn and Kramer, 1985; Ringbäck *et al.*, 2003; Ross and Mirowsky, 1999; Tennant, 1988). A series of meta-analyses and other investigations by Amato and colleagues support these and other findings (Amato, 1999, 2000; Amato and Booth, 1991; Amato and Keith, 1991a, 1991b). In line with attachment theory, Anthony (1974) speculated that loss of a parent through separation, divorce or desertion leaves the child vulnerable to acute psychiatric disturbance, and as adults to avoidance of marriage, to divorce, and to various psychiatric disorders.

Past and current research conducted in different nations provides evidence supporting these views. For example, a British study of the cohort of children born in one week (5–11 April, 1970) found that 5-year-old children of single mothers were more neurotic and antisocial, and had lower scores on vocabulary and visuo-motor co-ordination tests (Wadsworth *et al.*, 1985). In Australia, single mothers reported higher rates of both emotional and physical disorder (validated by medical records) in their children (Underwood and Kamien, 1984). Offord (1982) compared Canadian children on probation from juvenile court with controls matched for age, sex, school, school performance, and social class. Offord's study reported that delinquent children were more likely to be from lone-parent homes than other children. American surveys reported increased deviance (contact with the law, school discipline, truancy, absconding and smoking) among children from lone-parent homes (Dornbusch *et al.*, 1985), and adverse effects of divorce on behaviour, psychological well-being and academic performance (Allison and Furstenberg, 1989). More recently, a Swedish population-based study of almost one million children (Ringbäck *et al.*, 2003) reported twofold increased risk associated with living in a lone-parent family of psychiatric illness, suicide, attempted suicide, alcohol and drug-related problems amongst boys and girls. Ringbäck reported a close association between all of these and mortality in boys compared with those in two-parent families.

If we cannot deny that lone parents' children are at increased risk, and so accept that this is to be prevented, then a crucial issue to be addressed is the basis of their vulnerability. Since not all children of lone-parent families and other separated children are damaged and many succeed extremely well (Bowlby, 1973; Rogers, 2004; Rogers and Pryor, 1998; Rutter, 1999; Stewart-Clarke and Hayward, 1996), it is important to identify the characteristics of high-risk children. Over the years, a number of explanations, besides attachment theory, have been proposed to account for why lone parenthood adversely affects children's lives. It was pointed out earlier that currently three notions dominate: (a) parental absence – the view that lone-parent families constitute a less congenial environment for socializing children properly; (b) economic disadvantage – the view which emphasizes financial factors rather than the absence of a parent; (c) family conflict – the perspective which attributes the problems to animosity heralding or accompanying divorce or separation (Amato and Keith, 1991a; Buchanan *et al.*, 1996; Stewart-Clarke and Hayward, 1996; Dunn, 1996; Rutter, 1981/1991). However, a meta-analysis of 92 studies involving 13,000 children (Amato and Keith, 1991a) found only modest support for marital conflict in accounting for the range of emotional, academic, social and general behaviour problems commonly associated with children of lone-parent families. It is therefore a plausible assumption to make that there are other mechanisms that at least interact with other factors which may account for the problems associated with lone-parent families, and which the children involved may continue to experience in adulthood.

The notion of socio-genealogical connectedness proposes that the quality and quantity of information that children possess about the non-resident parent play a key role, in that parental knowledge leads to children's general well-being. Evidence for this can be gleaned from the research on adopted children (and adults). Chapter 6 discusses some of the evidence and reviews which clearly indicate that many adopted children, for example, demonstrate the kinds of problem held to be the consequences of lone-parent upbringing. Shants (1964), Brodzinsky (1987) and Pannor *et al.* (1974) attributed these problems directly to loss of genealogical continuity, and hence loss of 'self'. Such evidence stresses a state of confusion and uncertainty in children who have either no knowledge of their biological parents or only uncertain knowledge of them. Furthermore, it suggests that this state of uncertainty could fundamentally undermine the child's security and result in the development of insecure self-image and confused sense of identity in adolescence. Giddens' (1991) recent suggestion, for instance, that gaps in one's biography result in a sense of fractured or fragmented self further reinforces this view.

From a cognitive-developmental perspective, Schechter and Bertocci (1990) suggest that the need for understanding of causal relationships is an inherent human attribute, so that inadequacies and inconsistencies or discrepancies in birth information or biography result in an array of fantasies and in cognitive dissonance or mental unrest that demands appeasement. These authors emphasize that the intrapsychic valence (or drive) to search for or experience genealogical connectedness is innate. In other words, there exists a driven need to experience human connectedness. Indeed, they equate the strength of this need with starvation.

Likewise, Brodzinsky (1987) has suggested that what has been termed pathogenic in the adopted child's behaviour is nothing more than the unrecognized manifestation of an adoptive grieving process. These may be likened to the experiences of children of lone-parent families as well as other groups of separated children. Namely, extant research evidence seems to imply that the emotional experiences associated with adoption may be applicable to those of children of lone-parent families who have no genealogical information about the birth parent, or where such information is inadequate or negative. This suggestion is made more plausible by Bharat's (1988) study of children in a slum area of Bombay. Bharat reported that although the prevalence of juvenile delinquency, drug addiction and other delinquent behaviours was found to be low (contrary to the findings of western studies), children in lone-parent families involved in the study felt a sense of loss regarding the absent father. The study to be described in this and the following chapter adds to extant evidence.

Most of the studies on lone-parent families have involved large-scale surveys which may not always be conducive to detecting the intricacies and subtleties of family dynamics. There are substantial variations in the ways in which lone parents relate to their former spouses or partners and portray them to their children. Some children will know nothing of their other biological parent while others will have contact with and a warm view of them. Some will have them portrayed as selfish, unpleasant and lying cheats while others will be taught not even to ask questions about the absent parent. None of these scenarios are predictable from lone-parent status alone although, as we see in Chapter 7, they might be expected to be more commonly negative among divorced or separated families.

The research available indicates that knowledge of the non-resident parent has an impact on children's adjustment. Current British social policy (Adoption and Children Act 2002 and the Human Fertilisation and Embryology Act 1990), for example, accepts this (explicitly or implicitly) in connection with adopted children and children resulting from donor insemination respectively. Such socio-genealogical knowledge is easily available within a two-parent family. However, things are clearly more haphazard when it comes to lone-parent families which will vary in the amount of information and emotional tone. Thus, reviews of the literature examining the impact of separation through parental divorce, for example, indicate that the negative consequences of family disruption for children vary. In short, we must acknowledge the complexity of the psycho-social mechanisms involved in adjustment to separation and loss.

In comparison to adoption, studies on children separated through parental divorce or separation and those born outside marriage or stable relationships are a new phenomenon. Reported studies regarding the psychological well-being of children resulting from donor insemination remain even more scant. Nonetheless, in these areas research reports similar findings. Given that the western world holds a continuous parent–child relationship as the ideal situation for children's development, research findings and the conclusions drawn from them are hardly surprising. Thus, children's problems following separation or discontinuity of parent–child relationships, such as delinquency and educational difficulties, are readily attributed to physical separation.

EMPIRICAL EVIDENCE

This section and the next chapter report research and analyses which empirically tested the main assumptions of the theory of socio-genealogical connectedness. The studies examined the role of parental information in children's adjustment to parental divorce or separation. The independent variables were the amount and quality of information possessed by the children about their non-resident parent and the dependent variables were: (1) emotional well-being; (2) behaviour (i.e. social functioning); (3) academic achievement.

The sample

This study was carried out in the East Midlands of England. Participants were recruited through advertisements placed in the local media (radio) and press and leaflets placed in community centres and general practitioners' surgeries. Of the 74 families who initially responded to the advertisements, 36 families were included in the final sample. Families were excluded either because of the children's ages (under 5 years old), because the children had learning difficulties not associated with family status, or there was a history of physical and/or sexual abuse (actual or suspected).

All of the parents were female and white, except for one male and one female of Indo-Chinese origin. The parents' ages ranged from 20 to 47 years and the mean age at which they had their first child was 25 years – the range was from 13 years to 40 years. They had been single parents from 1.5–19 years (mean = 6 years). Two of them had had three partners (at different times), eight had had two partners, and the remaining 22 had been involved in one relationship each. In terms of marital status, 20 (56 per cent) of the parents were divorced; 4 (11 per cent) widowed; 10 (28 per cent) separated from their co-habitees; and 2 (5 per cent) had always been single. The length of their relationships with their last partner ranged from 6 months to 15.5 years (mean = 6.5 years). A large proportion (75 per cent) of them described their relationship with their children as 'very good', and 25 per cent of them as 'good'. None of them described their relationship with their children as 'bad' or particularly difficult. With regard to employment, 31 per cent were in full-time employment, 25 per cent in part-time regular employment, and 44 per cent were not in paid employment. Occupationally, 44 per cent belonged to the semi-professional class (nurses, teachers and social workers); 17 per cent belonged to the clerical/secretarial category; 39 per cent were in the semi-skilled/unskilled category. Regarding housing, 61 per cent owned their homes; 33 per cent were local council tenants; and 6 per cent were housing association tenants. Geographically, 28 per cent of the 36 families lived in an inner-city area; the rest (72 per cent) were either suburban or rural residents. .

The children

The final sample consisted of 50 children – 31 males and 19 females. Forty (80 per cent) were white and ten (20 per cent) were described by their parents, or described themselves, as of 'mixed parentage'. The resident parents of 36

(72 per cent) of these children were divorced, 10 (20 per cent) were widowed, 2 (4 per cent) were separated (from co-habitees), and another 2 (4 per cent) had always been single. Of the children 34 per cent attended inner-city schools and 66 per cent attended either suburban or rural schools. The majority of the children (84 per cent) attended predominantly white schools. Only 8 per cent of them attended schools where the other children were predominantly black; a further 8 per cent attended racially 'fairly mixed' schools. Ten (20 per cent) had lost their other parent (fathers) through death. Of the remaining 40, 38 per cent had frequent and regular contact with the non-resident parent (at least once a month on average); 17 per cent had infrequent and irregular contact (less than once a year); and 45 per cent had no contact at all (not even birthday cards from the non-resident parent).

The interviews

Semi-structured interviews were used. Separate questionnaires were designed to gather information from (a) the resident parent and (b) the child. The questionnaires related to the following: personal details; parental information; academic achievement; emotional well-being; and behaviour. In-depth, tape-recorded interviews were then conducted with each of the custodial parents and some of the children. Interviews took place at the participant's home; and where there was more than one child involved they were interviewed individually. School reports were also obtained from the parent for further corroboration of the information regarding the children's behaviour, emotional well-being and school performance.

On average, each interview lasted about one and a half hours. Participants were encouraged to talk as freely and generally as possible, but prompts were given occasionally by raising topics and issues. The recorded interviews were later transcribed and the information used to complete a schedule for each participant. Information from the child was to corroborate that provided by the custodial parent. Other sources of information, such as the child's contact with the non-resident parent and/or the parent's relatives and the relationship between the custodial parent and the non-resident parent, were also examined for further corroboration of the information supplied by either the parent or the child (or both).

Results

Analysis of the results, using χ^2 test (2-tail), concentrated on the influence of parental information (i.e. the amount and quality of information about the non-resident parent) on: (1) academic achievement (school performance); (2) behaviour (misbehaviour, aggression or delinquency) (3) emotional well-being (depression, anxiety, anger, loneliness or cheerfulness). With regard to the amount of information, the children were categorized and compared according to: (a) those who possessed full information about the non-resident parent (i.e. as much information as they would have if they were living with the parent); (b) those with partial information about the parent (not so much information as they would have had the parent been present); (c) those with minimal information (children whose knowledge of the parent consisted of basic facts, e.g. name, 'race'/ethnicity, possible whereabouts, but no genealogical information about the parent; this group included two children who did not even know the name of the other parent).

Amount of information and behaviour

As Table 4.2 shows, the analyses revealed a significant difference between the groups in terms of behaviour ($p = < 0.05$). Namely, of the 23 children who were described as very well-behaved, 65 per cent had full information, 9 per cent had partial information and 26 per cent had minimal information. On the other hand, none of those with full information were described as badly behaved, while 43 per cent and 57 per cent of those with partial and those with minimal information respectively were described as badly behaved. However, a greater difference was observed between those with full information and the other two groups combined ($p = 0.01$) (Table 4.3). The groups were also compared in terms of behaviour or delinquency which led to professional contact or involvement with social services, the police and the

Table 4.2 Amount of information and behaviour ($n = 50$)

	Behaviour			
Information	Very Good	Good	Bad	P
Full	15 (65)	9 (45)	0 (0)	
Partial	2 (9)	5 (25)	3 (43)	< 0.05
Minimal	6 (26)	6 (30)	4 (57)	

Source: Reprinted by permission of Sage Publications Ltd from Owusu-Bempah, J. (1995). Information about the absent parent as an important factor in the well-being of children of single-parent families. *International Social Work*, 38 (3), 253–275.

Table 4.3 Amount of information and behaviour: full vs partial and minimal ($n = 50$)

	Behaviour			
Information	Very Good	Good	Bad	P
Full	15 (65)	9 (45)	0 (-)	< 0.01
Partial and Minimal	8 (34)	11 (55)	7 (100)	

Source: Reprinted by permission of Sage Publications Ltd from Owusu-Bempah, J. (1995). Information about the absent parent as an important factor in the well-being of children of single-parent families. *International Social Work*, 38 (3), 253–275.

courts, the probation service, or psychologists/psychiatrists, such as violence, assault, illicit drug use, burglary, shoplifting, truancy and car theft (Table 4.4). Six of the children had had such contact and the analyses revealed that only those with partial information and those with minimal information (33 per cent and 67 per cent respectively) had had professional contact. None of those with full information about the non-resident parent had engaged in behaviour which led to the involvement of any of the above professionals ($p = < 0.05$).

Amount of information and emotional well-being

As Table 4.5 indicates, there were significant differences emotionally between the three groups. Only 9 (18 per cent) of the children were described as having or experiencing emotional problems (ranging in seriousness from nocturnal enuresis, withdrawal, aggression, anger and fire-setting to suicide attempts). Of these, only 1 (11 per cent) had full information, 3 (33 per cent) had partial information, while 5 (56 per cent) had minimal information ($p = < 0.05$). The most significant difference was, however, found between those with full information and the other two groups combined ($p = 0.01$) (Table 4.6).

Table 4.4 Amount of information and professional contact ($n = 50$)

Information	Professional contact		
	Yes	No	P
Full	0 (-)	24 (55)	
Partial	2 (33)	8 (18)	< 0.05
Minimal	4 (67)	12 (27)	

Source: Reprinted by permission of Sage Publications Ltd from Owusu-Bempah, J. (1995). Information about the absent parent as an important factor in the well-being of children of single-parent families. *International Social Work*, 38 (3), 253–275.

Table 4.5 Amount of information and emotional well-being ($n = 50$)

Information	Emotional well-being		
	Yes	No	P
Full	1 (11)	23 (56)	
Partial	3 (33)	7 (17)	< 0.05
Minimal	5 (56)	11 (27)	

Source: Reprinted by permission of Sage Publications Ltd from Owusu-Bempah, J. (1995). Information about the absent parent as an important factor in the well-being of children of single-parent families. *International Social Work*, 38 (3), 253–275.

Table 4.6 Amount of information and emotional well-being: full vs partial and minimal

Information	Emotional well-being		
	Yes	*No*	*P*
Full	1 (11)	23 (56)	< 0.01
Partial and minimal	8 (88)	18 (44)	

Source: Reprinted by permission of Sage Publications Ltd from Owusu-Bempah, J. (1995). Information about the absent parent as an important factor in the well-being of children of single-parent families. *International Social Work*, 38 (3), 253–275.

Amount of information and academic achievement

The influence of parental information on the children's academic performance was also examined. The children were therefore categorized into those who were described by their custodial parents (validated by school reports) as: above average; average; and below average. Analyses comparing all three primary groups yielded an overall statistically significant difference between them (p = < 0.05) (Table 4.7). However, further analyses revealed that the difference was between those with full and those with partial information (combined) and those with minimal information. Namely, there was no significant difference between those who possessed full information and those who possessed partial information about the non-resident parent.

Quality of information

The effects of the quality of information on the dependent variables were also examined. The children were therefore categorized in terms of the type of information they possessed about the non-resident parent: (1) favourable information; (2) unfavourable information; (3) neutral information (including two with no information). The analyses revealed significant differences

Table 4.7 The effect of amount of information on academic achievement ($n = 50$)

Information	Academic achievement			
	Above average	*Average*	*Below average*	*P*
Full	10 (56)	11 (52)	3 (27)	
Partial	6 (33)	2 (10)	2 (18)	< 0.05
Minimal	2 (11)	8 (38)	6 (55)	

Source: Reprinted by permission of Sage Publications Ltd from Owusu-Bempah, J. (1995). Information about the absent parent as an important factor in the well-being of children of single-parent families. *International Social Work*, 38 (3), 253–275.

between the groups with regard to behaviour and emotional well-being (Tables 4.8 and 4.9). In other words, those children who had positive or favourable information about the non-resident parent were better behaved than those who possessed unfavourable or neutral information about the non-resident parent ($p = < 0.05$).

As Table 4.8 shows, 45 children were included in the analyses. Of these 51 per cent were described as very well-behaved; and among this subgroup 17 (74 per cent) had positive information and the other 6 (26 per cent) had neutral information; none of those with negative information were described as very well-behaved.

As indicated by Table 4.9, of those who were described as experiencing emotional difficulties, only 2 out of 31 (6.5 per cent) of those possessing positive information, and 3 out of 6 (50 per cent) of those who had negative information, while only 1 out of 7 (14 per cent) who had neutral information had such problems ($p = < 0.05$). In this respect, negative information appeared to have been more detrimental to the children's emotional well-being.

Other findings

Sex, age, and race differences were also examined regardless of information (see Tables 4.10–4.12). As far as age and race/ethnicity were concerned, no

Table 4.8 Quality of information and behaviour ($n = 45$)

Quality of information	Behaviour			
	Very good	*Good*	*Bad*	*P*
Favourable	17 (74)	12 (71)	2 (40)	
Unfavourable	0 (–)	4 (23)	2 (40)	< 0.05
Neutral	6 (26)	1 (26)	1 (20)	

Source: Reprinted by permission of Sage Publications Ltd from Owusu-Bempah, J. (1995). Information about the absent parent as an important factor in the well-being of children of single-parent families. *International Social Work*, 38 (3), 253–275.

Table 4.9 Quality of information and emotional well-being ($n = 45$)

Quality of information	Emotional well-being		
	Yes	*No*	*P*
Favourable	2 (6.5)	29 (93.5)	
Unfavourable	3 (50)	3 (50)	< 0.05
Neutral	1 (14)	7 (86)	

Source: Reprinted by permission of Sage Publications Ltd from Owusu-Bempah, J. (1995). Information about the absent parent as an important factor in the well-being of children of single-parent families. *International Social Work*, 38 (3), 253–275.

Table 4.10 Sex and emotional well-being (*n* = 45)

Sex	Emotional well-being		
	Yes	*No*	*P*
Males	8 (89)	23 (56)	< 0.05
Females	1 (11)	18 (44)	

Source: Reprinted by permission of Sage Publications Ltd from Owusu-Bempah, J. (1995). Information about the absent parent as an important factor in the well-being of children of single-parent families. *International Social Work*, 38 (3), 253–275.

Table 4.11 Sex and professional contact (*n* = 50)

Sex	Professional contact		
	Yes	*No*	*P*
Males	6 (100)	25 (57)	< 0.05
Females	0 (0)	19 (43)	

Source: Reprinted by permission of Sage Publications Ltd from Owusu-Bempah, J. (1995). Information about the absent parent as an important factor in the well-being of children of single-parent families. *International Social Work*, 38 (3), 253–275.

Table 4.12 Sex and academic achievement (*n* = 50)

Sex	Academic achievement			
	Above average	*Average*	*Below average*	*P*
Males	11 (61)	10 (48)	10 (90)	< 0.05
Females	7 (39)	11 (52)	1 (10)	

Source: Reprinted by permission of Sage Publications Ltd from Owusu-Bempah, J. (1995). Information about the absent parent as an important factor in the well-being of children of single-parent families. *International Social Work*, 38 (3), 253–275.

significant differences were observed with regard to any of the variables under consideration. However, with regard to sex, as Tables 4.10–4.12 indicate, significant differences were observed on the following measures: emotional well-being, behaviour (contact with professionals) and academic perform- ance. Nine of the children were reported to be experiencing emotional dif- ficulties at the time of the study. Of these, 8 (89 per cent) were males and only one (11 per cent) was female ($p = 0.05$). Similarly, all of the 6 (100 per cent) children who had had contact with professionals – the police, psychologists, psychiatrists, social workers or the probation service – were males ($p = 0.05$). Academically, an overall statistically significant difference was also found between the sexes ($p = 0.05$): the school performance of the males was better than that of the females. Of the 18 children who were described as academically above average, 61 per cent were males, while 39 per cent were females. Of those described as average 48 per cent and 52 per cent were males and females respectively. However, amongst the below-average students, 90 per cent were males while only 10 per cent were females. These results are consistent with those of previous studies (e.g. Amato, 1987; Amato and Keith, 1991a; Amato and Ochiltree, 1987; Brady *et al.*, 1986; Emery, 1982; White *et al.*, 1985).

The data were also analyzed to determine whether there were any differences between the children in terms of their area of residence and school location. They were therefore categorized into: (1) inner-city children; (2) suburban; (3) country children. The analyses revealed no significant differences between the groups with respect to their emotional well-being, academic achievement and general behaviour. Analyses using Pearson's product-moment co-efficient of correlation revealed a high correspondence between the amount of information the children possessed about the non-resident parent and the quality of that information ($r = 0.775$; $p = 0.001$). Thus, further computation was performed on the data to determine the degree of correspondence between the amount and quality of information and the following variables: parental contact (contact with the parent); behaviour; professional contact; emotional well-being; and academic achievement.

Table 4.13 shows a high correspondence between parental contact and the amount and quality of information possessed by the children about the non-resident parent ($p = < 0.001$); that is children who had more contact with the non-resident parent possessed quantitatively more and qualitatively more favourable information about the parent. Likewise, the amount of information was found to be related to the children's behaviour, professional contact (or delinquency), emotional well-being ($p = < 0.01$) and academic achievement ($p = 0.05$).

However, while the correspondence between amount of information and behaviour was in the positive direction, that between amount of information and professional contact and emotional adjustment was in the negative direction. That is, the less contact there was between the child and the parent,

Table 4.13 Pearson's product-moment co-efficient of correlation

Variable	Amount of information	Quality of information
Parental contact	0.831***	0.775***
Behaviour	0.352**	0.034
Professional contact	−0.414**	−0.176
Emotional difficulties	−0.356**	−0.174
Academic achievement	0.3163*	0.231

Source: Reprinted by permission of Sage Publications Ltd from Owusu-Bempah, J. (1995). Information about the absent parent as an important factor in the well-being of children of single-parent families. *International Social Work*, 38 (3), 253–275.
*** = <0.001; ** = <0.01; * = 0.05.

the more likely it was for the child to be delinquent. Similarly, the less the child knew about the non-resident parent the more likely it was for the child to experience emotional difficulties. These results are consistent with previous and recent findings (e.g. Amato, 1996, 2000, 2001; Amato and Keith, 1991a, 1991b; Buchanan *et al.*, 1996; Furstenberg *et al.*, 1983; Wallerstein and Kelly, 1980).

Discussion of results

Sixty years of research, stimulated by attachment theory, has yet to provide conclusive evidence as to why children reared by one parent are at particular risk of negative psycho-social developmental outcomes. This failure is often attributed mainly to poor research design – methodological inadequacies (e.g. Blechman, 1982; Spencer, 2005). The present results seem to support a plausible, if partial, explanation for those problems. In this study, it was found that, irrespective of the reasons for parental loss, children who possessed adequate and favourable information about the non-resident parent fared better on measures of behaviour, academic achievement and emotional well-being than those who either had no information or inadequate information about him, or where such information was unfavourable. Conversely, many of the problems associated with lone-parent status were found to be prevalent amongst the latter group of children. Contrary to the hardship hypothesis, this appeared to have been the case regardless of the material circumstances in which the children lived. That is, in this study, parental or socio-genealogical knowledge was found to be a major influence on the children's behaviour, emotional well-being and academic achievement.

On the basis of these findings, it is plausible to suggest that the psychological vulnerability of children of lone-parent families may lie more in parental information than in many of the superficially striking features of the family. The essential factor, nonetheless, appears to be the quality of the information: it needs to be positive or at least undamaging in order to have favourable developmental outcomes.

It was pointed out earlier that the conventional notions on which research in this area has concentrated suggest a number of hypotheses, including parental absence, economic circumstances and spousal conflict (Amato and Keith, 1991a; Ross and Mirowsky, 1999; Rutter, 1981; Simons *et al.*, 1999; Stewart-Clarke and Hayward, 1996). However, the parental absence perspective and the conflict perspective are most germane to the present study. Two related hypotheses are possible: (1) that the adverse effects of growing up in a lone-parent household are partly mitigated if non-resident parents maintain close relationships with their children; (2) that the frequency and quality of contact with the non-resident parent is positively related to children's well-being. Both of these hypotheses were indirectly supported by the present findings. However, the present findings indicate that the long-term positive effects of contact may be due not necessarily to physical parental contact per se, but rather to the parental information acquired by the child during contact. Wallerstein and Kelly (1980) alluded to this when they suggested that having contact with the non-resident parent was more important to a child than what happened during contact.

For a long time, research has consistently supported the conflict hypothesis. However, it has inherent weaknesses. One of the main limitations of the conflict perspective is that it fails to account for why children whose mothers never married or co-habited should experience those problems commonly associated with divorce or separation. Still, this perspective was indirectly supported by the present findings: a strong correlation was found between parental contact and the amount and quality of information that the children possessed about the non-resident parent ($r = 0.775$; $p = < 0.001$). These factors were in turn found to be related to the children's global well-being. It is commonsense that the better the relationship between the divorced or separated parents, the more contact there is likely to be between the child and the non-resident parent (and/or the parent's relatives), and consequently the more and better information the child is likely to possess about the parent. As many investigators have reported, this leads to better outcomes for the child (e.g. Amato, 2001; Bianchi and Setzer, 1986; Stewart-Clarke and Hayward, 1996; Dunn, 1996; Hetherington, 1989; Imbimbo, 1995; Lowenstein and Koopman, 1978; MacKinnon, 1989; Mitchell, 1983; Smith and Gollop, 2001; Wallerstein and Kelly, 1980). Conversely, continued acrimony between the divorced or separated biological parents is likely to lead to a decrease in contact between children and their non-resident parent (Amato, 1987, 2000; Amato and Keith, 1991a; Bradshaw and Millar, 1991; Furstenberg *et al.*, 1983; Hess and Camara, 1979; Smith and Gollop, 2001; Wallerstein and Kelly, 1980; White *et al.*, 1985), and hence in the quantity and quality of information that the child possesses about the parent. We will see in Chapter 7 that in such relationships information about the non-resident parent is more likely to be unfavourable, suppressed or unwelcome. This was the case in a conflict-ridden relationship between the divorced parents of one of the families involved in the present study whose mother disconfirmed the father (Chapter 3, Case 3).

Several other studies carried out in the last 60 years provide indirect support for the notion of parental information as an essential factor in children's development and overall well-being. For example, Bach (1946) compared latency-aged boys who had no father present in the home with boys who did. He found that boys without a father living with them had idealistic, fantasy pictures of their fathers. Simmons *et al.* (1973) also found that post-divorce children who had strong self-concepts had stronger ties to both birth parents than those who did not. The authors suggested that the normal process of continuity and integration (self-concept) are often interrupted when a child loses contact with one of the parents. Other writers have also drawn particular attention to the importance of positive information about the non-resident parent. For example, Erikson (1950) and Epstein (1976) claimed that when the biological parent is devalued or disconfirmed over time, the child's sense of trust in the world diminishes. This was clearly evident in two of the families who participated in the present study (Cases 3 and 4) described in the preceding chapter. Derdeyn (1977) took the issue further in suggesting that even abusing parents have a great value to a child and so ought not to be devalued. As far back as the early 1950s Bowlby noted:

> The attachment of children to parents who by all ordinary standards are very bad is a never-ceasing source of wonder to those who seek to help them
>
> (Quoted in Rutter, 1981, p. 112)

The assumption is that children derive a sense of security from socio-genealogical knowledge. Thus, the denial or denigration of the parent results in the negation of the child's self and subsequent splitting off of that self part. The cost to children of seeing their parent as 'bad' is too high: children's self-worth is so closely tied to their parent's self-worth. Many of the parents involved in the present study acknowledged this.

The plausibility of parental information as an important and influential factor affecting the development and overall functioning of children of lone-parent families has been implied by other investigators and writers, albeit indirectly. For example, Tessman (1978) suggested that even children who had never seen their absent biological parent had a mental picture (idealized) of that parent. From socio-genealogical connectedness perspective, this cognitive or internal representation of the non-resident parent is very likely to consist not only of the parent's physical characteristics, but also their genealogical and social background. As far back as 1944, Freud and Burlingham argued that even children with no parents tend to invent their own mother and father figures to satisfy their need for the lost object. More recently, Wallerstein and Kelly (1980) emphasized the continuing psychological importance of two parents, and the fact that the non-resident parent does not fade in psychological significance. That is, abandonment or rejection does not dim children's awareness of the parent or the children's longings for them. These longings are likely to contribute to what Wallerstein and Kelly (1980) have described as developmental interference in children of lone-parent status; for example, low self-esteem, depression and continued anger.

In the light of the present findings and the preceding discussion, therefore, deliberate denial or negative distortion of parental information to a child may be equated with deliberate infliction of emotional abuse on that child (Melzak, 1992), which is as psychologically damaging as sexual abuse and may be as physically detrimental as starvation. Owusu-Bempah (1995) concurs with this view.

Therapeutically, Auer (1983) highlighted the importance of a child's continued contact with the non-resident biological parent after separation or divorce. Auer firmly believed that such contact can be a positive influence on the child's sense of trust, self-concept and overall adjustment. A large body of research involving various groups of separated children, including those resulting from donor insemination and other methods of assisted reproduction, supports Auer's belief (e.g. Lifton, 1994; Triseliotis, 1973; Turner and Coyle, 2000). Nevertheless, as suggested earlier, this positive effect seems to derive more from the quantity and/or quality of socio-genealogical information which the child gains from such contact than from contact itself.

The implications of the present results for theory, policy and professional practice are patent. To know why and to what extent lone-parent status affects children is of importance not only to researchers but also to parents and professionals who seek to help families and children. For instance, in custody decisions consideration needs to be given to the need of the child to have unhindered contact with the non-resident biological parent or, where possible, their immediate relatives, especially grandparents. Where such contact is already severed or restricted, it will be in the child's interest for social workers or therapists to inform the custodial parent of the benefits of contact, and to encourage the parties concerned to facilitate contact. Indeed, some writers and practitioners advocate this in respect of looked after children (i.e. those in the public care system). They argue for the importance that professionals should attach to enabling the children to make such connections (Cleaver, 2000). Those who set policies which affect the functioning of families also need to give this factor due importance. Apparently, no previous empirical study has directly considered parental information as a factor affecting the social and intellectual development and psychological functioning of children growing up in lone-parent families. However, in this study, correspondence was found between contact and the quantity and quality of information possessed by a child about the non-resident parent, and the child's psychological and social adjustment, academic achievement and general behaviour.

THEORETICAL LINKAGES

In Chapter 3 it was shown that, as applied to child development, classic psychoanalytic theory, learning theory and psychodynamic theory all concerned personality development. Nevertheless, the research reviewed in this book so far indicates that Bowlby's notion of attachment has been the dominant theoretical framework for studying and understanding psycho-social developmental outcomes. This is largely because of the theory's proposition that a failure to experience positive attachment relationships has undesirable consequences for personality development. There is consensus amongst theorists, investigators and childcare professionals that this failure renders a person particularly susceptible to emotional problems, as well as relationship difficulties. This susceptibility is claimed to be fostered by negative attachment experiences, such as inconsistency or disruptions in the parent–child relationship, parent–child separation, and threats of abandonment (actual or perceived). The literature overwhelmingly suggests that children experiencing insecure attachment for any of these reasons are likely to develop shaky internal working models of themselves and others, especially significant others: in other words to lose their secure base (Bowlby, 1988).

Given that for the past 60 years, childcare professionals have regularly incorporated ideas derived from attachment theory into their work with children and families, one may wonder what the implications of socio-genealogical connectedness may be. The preceding discussion and case studies presented in Chapter 3 indicate clearly the importance of socio-genealogical connectedness in the development and overall functioning of children; and hence the need to seriously consider its place in developmental psychology, childcare policy and practice. This by no means implies that socio-genealogical connectedness is an alternative to attachment theory. In fact, they overlap and complement each other. For example, successful and undisrupted attachment, as propounded by Bowlby, would be seen as evidence of a satisfactory sense of socio-genealogical connectedness. Nevertheless, the latter theory is in certain subtle ways distinct from the former. To start with, it extends our theoretical understanding of the concept of self-identity, its genesis and development. Another distinguishing feature of socio-genealogical connectedness is that it does not construe contact or physical presence as such as the essence of the matter. Thus, it may be argued that its assumptions better reflect the broad diversity of modern families. It also allows the practitioner to extend the range of professional interventions from those based upon attachment theory, insofar as it has a wider focus on the child–parent/carer relationship than Bowlby's etho-psychoanalytic attachment theory.

Bowlby (1951) averred that mother love in infancy and childhood was as important for mental health as vitamins and minerals are for physical health. The present discussion suggests that adequate and favourable parental or socio-genealogical information is important to emotional, mental and intellectual well-being. It suggests the idea of socio-genealogical connectedness to be a useful and viable framework for studying and understanding the psycho-social developmental needs of separated children.

5 Further research evidence: the gender question

It is now well established that separation does not necessarily nor always result in developmental difficulties. There is, therefore, a need for a proper understanding of those factors which mitigate the adverse influences of separation. This need is reiterated here in spite of the acknowledgement concerning the complexity and interlocking nature of the factors, including their duration and intensity, which impact on children. It is also recognized that the difficulty in trying to disentangle or unravel these factors is further compounded by the fact that children's resilience to the harmful consequences of separation and other psychological stressors is affected by their endogenous as well as exogenous characteristics. These characteristics include gender, age, temperament, intellectual ability, family environment, economic status, parenting skills, social networks and so forth.

The preceding chapter examined some of these characteristics and identified a sense of socio-genealogical connectedness or lack of it as another important factor which may positively or negatively affect the children's resiliency. The evidence presented in Chapters 3 and 4 implies that, as a mitigating factor, its efficacy may be enhanced through warm, regular and sustained contact or relationship with the biological parent(s). This chapter explores further the central tenets of the theory in relation to the characteristics of lone-parent families and the overall welfare of children in these families.

It was pointed out in Chapter 1 that prolonged or permanent separations do occur for a variety of reasons, so that to understand their various effects better we must differentiate those effects according to their causes. Research and reviews concerning the impact of parental separation and loss, for instance, indicate that the negative consequences of parental divorce for children do vary (e.g. Amato, 1993; Amato and Keith, 1991a, 1991b; Evans and Bloom, 1996; Hetherington, 1989; Wallerstein, 1991; Zaslow, 1989). In other words, children do not react automatically or uniformly to parental separation or loss. This means that we must take cognizance of individual variations in our examination of the extent to which such effects are experienced in not only childhood and adolescence but also are carried into adulthood, the degree to which they influence later life. That is to say, the quest for detailed investigations into and evaluation of the multiple dependent variables that mitigate or compound that impact must continue. We must constantly bear in mind Bowlby's (1973) plea not to diminish the seriousness of this impact, even though it may have lasting effects on only a proportionately small number of children.

Various investigators have identified some of the factors believed to differentially affect children's post-separation adjustment. Besides those mentioned previously, they include: (a) their life situations; (b) the type and quality of the relationship existing between the child and the birth parent(s) (e.g. Emery, 1982; Felner *et al.*, 1975; Lengua *et al.*, 1995; Ross and Mirowsky, 1999; Rutter, 1981, 1994; Wallerstein and Kelly, 1980). Obviously, a child's response to parental separation is dependent not only on the presence or absence of these factors, but also on their combination or permutation.

Today, the three most favourite assumptions which guide research in this area have been outlined already. The first is that if children continue to have relationships with their non-resident parent(s), they will not suffer the pain of losing an attachment object that divorce often causes. The second is that children fare better if the resident parent offers the child a favourable environment in which to adjust and develop; it emphasizes the resident parent's standard of living as well as their emotional ability and/or preparedness to provide adequate care. The third assumption emphasizes same-gender parenting as a key factor in children's adjustment to parental divorce, on the grounds that they need a same-gender parent model in order to develop appropriate identity and gender attitudes and behaviour.

The results and findings reported in the preceding chapter provided further support for only the first hypothesis. Thus, the following analyses focused on the third hypothesis and also examined the role of those innate attributes associated with resiliency in childhood and adolescence following parental divorce. They are reanalyses of the quantitative data presented and discussed in the preceding chapter. Specifically, they examined the role of sociogenealogical connectedness and same-gender parenting as mediating factors in children's adjustment to parental divorce. These type of analyses are necessary in view of the contested evidence suggesting that children in the custody of their father are more likely to maintain contact with their mother and so do better than children in the custody of their mother (e.g. Bianchi and Setzer, 1986; Grief, 1997; Stewart, 1999; Stewart-Clarke and Hayward, 1996). What is uncontroversial, though, is the evidence that children fare better post-divorce if they have continuity of relationship with both parents (see Owusu-Bempah and Howitt, 2000a, for detailed analyses).

THE ANALYSES

The main aim of the present analyses was to examine the role of sociogenealogical connectedness relative to other identified mediating factors, such as parent–child relationship, gender, age and academic ability in the long-term adjustment of children of lone-parent families. The expectation was that doing so would provide a greater insight into the relationships of socio-genealogical connectedness to other aspects of life experience. Factor analysis and multiple-regression procedures were used to enhance understanding of the structure of the relationships.

RESULTS

The main research focused on psychological (emotional), social (behavioural) and academic measures. Thus, as in previous studies (Owusu-Bempah, 1993, 1995), a number of developmental measures were coded in the analyses. These were as follows:

1 *Behavioural adjustment* – this was rated on a three-point scale from very good, through good to bad.
2 *Contact with professional child care agencies* (such as social services, psychologists/psychiatrists, police) – coded in a binary form.
3 *Emotional problems* – this was coded as being present or absent.
4 *Sociability* – the children were rated on a three-point scale: popular, not so popular, unpopular.

In addition, the following measures regarding general attitude towards school were analyzed:

5 *General school orientation* – this was evaluated on a three-point scale: good, fair, bad.
6 *Attitude to school* – evaluated as either generally positive or negative.
7 *School attendance* – this was coded on a three-point scale from very good, through good to bad.

Psychological and social problems measures

Pearson correlation co-efficients were computed between each of these indicators of adjustment. On examination, it was found that all of the correlation co-efficients were positive and statistically significant. The smallest correlation was between behaviour and attitude to school ($r = 0.35$, $p < 0.05$, 2-tailed test), and the largest was between emotional adjustment and contact with professionals such as social workers or psychiatrists ($r = 0.74$, $p < 0.01$, 2-tailed test). The pattern of moderate to strong correlations between the variables suggested that these seven varied indicators of psychological and social problems reflect a constellation of interrelated adjustment difficulties. This interpretation was confirmed by a principal components factor analysis of the correlation matrix which indicates that all of these variables cluster together.

As Table 5.1 shows, only one significant factor emerged on which all of the

Table 5.1 Principal components factor analysis of psychological and social problems indicators

Problem indicator	Factor loading
Behaviour	0.78
Emotional	0.87
Social	0.67
Professional contact	0.85
School attendance	0.85
School attitude	0.73
School general	0.82

Source: Reprinted by permission of Blackwell Publishing Co. from Owusu-Bempah, K. and Howitt, D. (2000). Socio-genealogical connectedness: on the role of gender and same-gender parenting in mitigating the effects of parental divorce. *Child and Family Social Work*, 5(2), 107–116.

psychological and social problems variables loaded highly. This indicates that there is a syndrome of closely intertwined problems involving the child's school, social, behavioural and emotional adjustment. In other words, the different variables are measuring much the same thing. Thus, the seven different indicators of adjustment problems were combined to form a total problem score by computing the factor score of each child on the single factor which had emerged in the factor analysis (Howitt and Cramer, 1997). The total problems score was used throughout the rest of the analysis as the key indicator of the extent of a child's problems. Not only is this statistically the most satisfactory solution, but conceptually it is in keeping with the view that children's psychological and social adjustment difficulties do not occur independently of each other; that is, a child with behavioural problems at home is likely to have problems in relation to school, or vice versa. In other words, these problems coexist and manifest themselves in a variety of situations.

Socio-genealogical information

A number of socio-genealogical variables were assessed from the interviews. These reflected both qualitative and quantitative aspects of socio-genealogical information ranging from the quality of information about the non-resident parent to amount of regular contact with that parent:

1 *Information:* this was assessed on a four-point scale from full information, through partial information and minimal information, to no information.
2 *Nature of information:* this was rated on a three-point scale from positive, through neutral to negative.
3 *Contact with the non-resident parent:* this was rated on a three-point scale from frequent, through infrequent to none.

Table 5.2 shows that these three variables correlated significantly with one another. However, since the purpose of these analyses was to examine which aspects of socio-genealogical connectedness were the most important in ensuring a socio-psychologically satisfactory childhood, each of these aspects of socio-genealogical information was retained as a separate variable in the analyses.

Other measures

A wide range of other variables was assessed from the interviews and examined, including academic achievement, and demographic variables such as race/ethnicity, sex, age and relationships with and between the parents. The ethnic composition and urban/rural location of the school attended were also included.

Academic achievement

For both boys and girls, psychological and social problems were much more frequent in the lower academic ability strata ($r = 0.61$ for boys, 0.66 for girls,

Table 5.2 Pearson correlation coefficients between socio-genealogical and other variables

	Contact	*Information*	*Nature of information*	*Total problems*
Boys and girls combined				
Contact	1.00			
Information	0.60**	1.00		
Nature of information	0.76**	0.36*	1.00	
Total problems	−0.41**	−0.44**	−0.35*	1.00
Boys only				
Contact	1.00			
Information	0.63**	1.00		
Nature of information	0.80**	0.45*	1.00	
Total problems	−0.52**	−0.61**	−0.45*	1.00
Girls only				
Contact	1.00			
Information	0.56*	1.00		
Nature of information	0.68*	0.22	1.00	
Total problems	−0.09	0.01	−0.02	1.00

Source: Reprinted by permission of Blackwell Publishing Co. from Owusu-Bempah, K. and Howitt, D. (2000). Socio-genealogical connectedness: on the role of gender and same-gender parenting in mitigating the effects of parental divorce. *Child and Family Social Work*, 5(2), 107–116.

** significant at 0.01 (2-tailed test). * significant at 0.05 (2-tailed test).

both significant at 0.01 with a 2-tailed test). That is to say, psychological and behavioural problems appeared to be associated with those least intellectually able to deal with them, or reappraise their circumstances. This renders some support for the assumption that cognitive ability plays an important mediating role in children's adaptation to parental divorce and separation and loss.

Gender

One of the major assumptions underlying the present study is that knowledge, and the affective tone of knowledge, about the non-resident parent as well as contact (in terms of amount and/or quality) are important prerequisites for the psychological and social well-being of children of divorce. It suggests that many of the psychological and social problems in children from lone-parent families are the result of a lack of a sense or experience of continuity with the non-resident parent. Hence, Pearson correlation co-efficient was calculated between these measures of socio-genealogical connectedness and the total psychological and social problems measure.

The analysis revealed that for boys and girls combined there were modest correlations between the socio-genealogical measures and relative freedom from psychological and social problems. That is, the following variables: contact ($r = 0.44$), information ($r = 0.37$) and the nature of information ($r = 0.39$) all correlated significantly with a lack of problems at better than the 1 per cent level of significance with a two-tailed test. (The results of this analysis are to be found in Table 5.2.) In other words, problems in a child's sense of socio-genealogical connectedness were associated with greater levels of psychological and social problems. Thus, the major hypothesis underlying the theory of socio-genealogical connectedness was supported.

However, like most lone-parent families, the non-resident parents in the families studied were the fathers (with the exception of one mother) while the resident parents were the mothers. This raises the question of whether or not the basic socio-genealogical hypothesis is too general or encompassing, and thus masks crucial differences in the ways in which personal identity develops in girls and boys. It has been repeatedly suggested that self-identity in boys develops differently, with the same-sex parent being in many ways more essential to satisfactory identity formation than with the opposite-sex parent (e.g. Stewart-Clarke and Hayward, 1996; Imbimbo, 1995; Studer, 1993; Zaslow, 1988). With regard to the association between parental death and delinquency or antisocial behaviour, for example, studies and reviews suggest that parental death is associated with only a very slight (and usually statistically nonsignificant) rise in delinquency rate. In other words, 'which parent dies seems to be of possible importance, in that studies have found ill-effects to be most marked following the death of same-sex parent' (Rutter, 1981, p. 66). This does not, of course, mean that the opposite-sex parent has no role in the development of their children's identity, but that their individual role may be different.

Since the overwhelming majority of lone-parent families are female headed (Burns and Scott, 1994; Hoyt *et al.*, 1990), there is therefore a possibility that relationship with the non-resident father is more important to boys than it is to girls in these families. Hence, the data were reanalyzed for the boys and girls separately. As shown in Table 5.2, it is obvious that, for the boys, there were strong relationships between the socio-genealogical connectedness variables, particularly the information variables, and psychological and social problems. Again, the expectations of the socio-genealogical connectedness hypothesis were supported. It is, therefore, important to note that Table 5.2 fails to show any support for the hypothesis when applied to the girls – none of the socio-genealogical connectedness variables correlated with the total psychological and social problems variable for the girls considered separately.

The variable which seemed to have the most bearing on the psychological and social problems exhibited by the girls was their relationship with their mothers ($r = 0.65$, $p < 0.01$, 2-tailed test). The relationship with their fathers (the non-resident parent) seemed to have no significant relationship to their psychological and social adjustment. The pattern was a little different for the boys. For them the quality of their relationships with both parents correlated with their freedom from psychological and social adjustment problems. Difficulties in the relationship with the mother correlated 0.51 with psychological and social problems; and difficulties with the father correlated 0.48 (both: $p < 0.01$, 2-tailed tests). Again, this seems to suggest that the relative adverse impact of the absence of the father was rather less on the girls than it was on the boys. Nevertheless, their relationship with their mother was more or less equally important for the psychological and social well-being of both sexes.

Age

Perhaps it is worthy of note, in this context, that the girls' psychological and behavioural difficulties actually declined with age ($r = -0.37$), whereas the boys' increased with age ($r = 0.28$). There was a statistically significant difference between these trends at the 0.01 level (Edwards, 1966). While this is somewhat inconsistent with extant literature (e.g. Hetherington *et al.*, 1985; Parosaari and Laippala, 1996; Wallerstein, 1991), it is precisely what one would expect if identity crises of development were responsible for the psychological and social problems. Controlling for age in the boys' data produced a change in the pattern of the relationship between socio-genealogical information and psychological and social problems. On the other hand, both contact and the nature of information remained strong (inverse) predictors of problems – the amount of information itself correlated less significantly with problems. This may suggest that amount of information beyond the optimum may be of less significance to a child's sense of connectedness than its content, be it favourable or unfavourable. This interpretation is consistent with other reports (e.g. Triseliotis, 1973; Triseliotis *et al.*, 1997).

Multiple regression analysis

Because of the complex interacting patterns among the variables in this study, it was decided to subject the boys' and the girls' data to multiple regression in order to ascertain the simplest combination of factors which would predict psychological and behavioural adjustment problems. Table 5.3 indicates that, for the girls, low academic ability was associated with psychological and behavioural problems – no other predictor variable, including age, ethnicity, school location, relationship between the parents, relationship with the non-resident parent or resident parent (any of the contact variables) was necessary, statistically, to account for psychological and social problems. As we have seen, this is because there were few correlates of problems in girls and these, in turn, correlated with the girls' academic performance.

Things were different for the boys. As Table 5.3 shows, higher academic achievement was associated with fewer psychological and behavioural problems, just as it was for the girls. However, the information variable was independently predictive. That is, for the boys only, the presence of optimum information about the father was negatively associated with psychological and social problems, just as the socio-genealogical hypothesis would predict.

Table 5.3 Stepwise multiple regression analysis to predict psychological and social problems

Girls

Variable	B	SEB	Beta	T	Sig T
Academic	0.45	0.18	0.66	2.50	0.04
(constant)	−1.08	0.31		−3.51	0.01
Multiple R	0.66				
R square	0.44				

Variables eliminated from equation: age, contact, information, nature of information, race, relationship with absent parent, relationship between custodial and absent parent, school location, school racial mixture and relationship with custodial parent.

Boys

Variable	B	SEB	Beta	T	Sig T
Academic	0.77	0.22	0.54	3.44	0.01
information	−0.58	0.17	−0.54	−3.43	0.01
(constant)	0.48	0.74		0.65	0.53
Multiple R	0.81				
R square	0.66				

Variables eliminated from equation: age, contact, information, race, relationship with absent parent, relationship between custodial and absent parent, school location, school racial mixture and relationship with custodial parent.

Source: Reprinted by permission of Blackwell Publishing Co. from Owusu-Bempah, K. and Howitt, D. (2000). Socio-genealogical connectedness: on the role of gender and same-gender parenting in mitigating the effects of parental divorce. *Child and Family Social Work*, 5(2), 107–116.

To stress the point, this means that information and academic ability were sufficient to predict psychological and social problems exhibited by boys. It does not mean, however, that other variables do not correlate with problems; it merely implies that they co-vary with the successful predictors. This seems to suggest that the socio-genealogical hypothesis has some validity for boys, but not for girls in lone-parent families. Apart from academic ability, socio-genealogical connectedness seems to be the best predictor of psychological and social adjustment problems in boys growing up in lone-parent families.

DISCUSSION OF RESULTS

The results and findings of these analyses demonstrate the complexity and interrelatedness of the factors associated with children's adjustment to separation. The findings also clearly reinforce the role of parental information or a sense of socio-genealogical connectedness in the psychological, emotional, behavioural and intellectual functioning of children of divorced or disrupted families. Socio-genealogical connectedness would hypothesize this to be equally applicable to other children in similar circumstances – the offspring of donor insemination, adopted children and those in the public care system. On adopted children and those separated through kidnapping or trafficking, for example, who have no contact or information (or only inadequate information) about either one or both of their biological parents, the effects may be more pronounced and felt equally by boys and girls.

The finding suggesting that socio-genealogical connectedness may be less important to the personality or identity development of girls than to that of boys growing up in lone-parent families is of particular interest. The explanation may be one of gender, but it may equally be the result of an interactive effect of the gender of both the child and the resident parent. Besides those factors already discussed, the literature points clearly to gender as a factor which buffers girls against the adverse impact of parental divorce. Currently, our insight into its mechanisms, in this respect, is limited. One hypothesis is that the female gender is an endogenous protective factor which independently mitigates the effects of psychological or emotional adversity, including separation and loss in childhood and adolescence (e.g. Rutter, 1994; Zaslow, 1989). Rutter (1994), for example, has likened the greater male psychological susceptibility, relative to females, to their susceptibility to biological stress. That is, psychological stress appears to have more deleterious effects on boys than it does on girls.

As a psychological stressor, Rutter's claim is consistent with various empirical studies and secondary analyses examining the impact of parental divorce on boys and girls. These studies and reviews indicate that male children show more adverse reaction; the most consistent finding being higher levels of externalizing problems, such as substance misuse, aggression and antisocial behaviour in response to parental divorce than in daughters, both immediately and over time. This is claimed to be especially the case for boys living with an unmarried mother (Grych and Fincham, 1992; Stewart-Clarke and Hayward, 1996; Zaslow, 1989). Such findings may at least partly account for the sex differences observed in the present analyses regarding the role of socio-genealogical connectedness in the children's overall adjustment. Further support for this finding derives from studies (Amato, 2001; Amato and Keith, 1991a, 1991b; Amato and Gilbreth, 1999; Fincham and Osborne, 1993; Stewart-Clarke and Hayward, 1996; Zaslow, 1989) which indicate that sex differences in children's responses to parental divorce are not confined to clinical samples of individuals involved in divorce.

Others, on the other hand, argue that its mediating quality derives from its interaction with relevant exogenous factors, such as the parenting skills of the resident parent, the extent of the non-resident parent's involvement in the children's upbringing and lives as a whole (Amato, 2000; Eme and Kavannaugh, 1995; Samuelson, 1997; Simons *et al.*, 1999; Zaslow, 1989). Studies which have considered what factors might boost children's resiliency to the risk of divorce or separation and help determine ways of supporting their well-being generally agree that family dynamics are clearly an important factor in how well children adjust to their parents' divorce or separation. For example, Amato (2000) and Samuelson (1997) have suggested that children are protected from the effects of divorce by active coping skills and support from the extended family and friends. Other investigators believe that an amicable relationship between the ex-spouses or ex-partners and the frequency and nature of children's contact with non-resident parents is an important protective factor. A series of meta-analyses and reviews by Amato and colleagues (e.g. Amato, 2000, 2001; Amato and Gilbert, 1999; Amato and Keith, 1991a, 1991b), for example, suggests that warm, authoritative fathering and positive, supportive, co-operative co-parenting behaviours are part of a pattern associated with children's resiliency after divorce, whereas negative, hostile behaviours (toward the child or the former partner) are associated with risk for children.

A number of others studies in this field have found sex differences in many areas of child development (e.g. Amato and Keith, 1991a; Emery, 1982; Hetherington, 1989; Hetherington *et al.*, 1998; Imbimbo, 1995; Kelly, 2000; Lengua *et al.*, 1995; Wallerstein and Kelly, 1980). In a study which examined sex differences in identity formation in college students aged 17–25 years of divorced families, Imbimbo (1995) found evidence suggesting that the absence of the father and the altered traditional role of the mother had a differential impact on male and female children in mother-headed families. Imbimbo found male children tended to be more adversely affected. Ten years previously, Hetherington and colleagues (1985) had concluded from their extensive research and reviews that growing up with a lone mother impacts differently on the development of boys and girls, with boys experiencing more cognitive and social deficits than girls. They also suggested that it may be a precursor to developmental difficulties, including identity problems in boys. In short, gender is believed to be one of the mediating variables in children's adjustment to separation. From this perspective, it is not surprising that Bowlby's (1944) 44 juvenile thieves were all males. It is likely, therefore, that the importance of socio-genealogical knowledge to the well-being of children in divorced families is at least partly mediated by gender, as the present analysis suggests.

Yet another factor claimed to be associated with resiliency in children of divorce is social support networks. Again, girls appear to be at an advantage here. Research indicates that girls use social support networks more than boys. For example, a Swedish study by Samuelson (1997) which involved children (9 to 16-year-olds) found that girls with lone parents knew more adults outside the family circle than their male counterparts. The study also found that during adolescence girls in the sample tended to have more intimate or meaningful friendships than boys and more adult friends; it was girls and not boys who found emotional closeness outside the family. Samuelson concluded that lack of adult contacts may be one of the factors contributing to the greater emotional and behavioural vulnerability of boys, relative to girls, of lone-parent families. This in some way reinforces Diehl *et al.*'s (1996) claim that girls use different and more socially acceptable strategies for coping with divorce-related stresses, including a shaky sense of socio-genealogical connectedness, for instance, by internalizing their difficulties. The social acceptableness of this strategy makes these difficulties appear normal.

From the perspective of the present thesis and in the context of the present analyses, an alternative but perhaps less plausible explanation for the unpredicted finding is that problems only arise as a consequence of a failure to achieve a solid and healthy sense of connectedness with the same-sex non-resident parent. This would produce a gender difference simply because of the lack of male-headed lone-parent families in the sample, due to their underrepresentation in the community at large. Overall, however, the results of the analyses are consistent with extant evidence which shows that children in the custody of the same-sex parent following divorce make better adjustments than those in the custody of the opposite-sex parent (Imbimbo, 1995; Peterson and Zill, 1986; Warshak, 1986, 1992, 2000; Zimiles and Lee, 1991). For example, Imbimbo (1995), concurring with Hetherington and colleagues (1985), has suggested that the absence of a father contributes to male children's developmental deficits. Young girls, on the other hand, have been reported to adjust better to divorce or father absence than young boys (Hetherington *et al.*, 1985; Rutter, 1991, 1994). Other researchers, of course, refute the claimed benefits of same-sex residence or custody (e.g. Downey *et al.*, 1998; Downey and Powell, 1993)

The apparent preponderance of research suggesting that in divorced families girls fare better than their brothers must not be construed as suggesting that the girls are not affected by parental divorce; it does not always nor necessarily mean that girls are unaffected in any way. This is evinced by studies comparing adolescent girls of divorced families to those in non-divorced families. Such studies have also reported girls of divorced families to be more likely to exhibit divorced-related difficulties, such as anti-social behaviour, depression and withdrawal, in addition to difficulties in sexual behaviour (promiscuity in adolescence) and relationships with boys (e.g. Amato, 1993; Johnson *et al.*, 1995; Simons *et al.*, 1999; Studer, 1993).

For example, a study by Simons and co-researchers (1999) examined the extent to which differences in adolescent adjustment problems between divorced and two-parent families (biological) can be explained by the follow-ing factors: loss of family income, parental conflict, the psychological adjustment and parenting practices of the resident parent, and the level of involvement of the non-resident parent. The sample comprised 328 non-divorced and 206 divorced families. Hierarchical regression analysis was employed to assess the importance of these variables. The results indicated that the quality of the mother's parenting and the father's involvement in parenting explain the association between divorce and boys' externalizing problems, whereas the quality of mother's parenting and post-divorce con-flict explain the relationship between divorce and girls' internalizing prob-lems. These researchers concluded that divorce elevates a girl's risk for depression because it increases the chances that her mother will become depressed, which in turn reduces the quality of her parenting. This conclu-sion suggests clearly that factors other than divorce per se are implicated in children's post-divorce adjustment problems, an obvious one being their rela-tionships with the parents. As found in the present analyses, the mother–child relationship was important for both sexes.

PARENT–CHILD RELATIONS AND CONTACT

Researchers have found differential parenting of boys and girls in divorced families (e.g. Buchanan *et al.*, 1996; Eme and Kavannaugh, 1995; Emery and Coiro, 1995; Zaslow, 1989). A longitudinal study of parent–child relation-ships by Emery and Coiro (1995), for example, reported that boys receive more negative and punitive parenting from their divorced mothers than girls. Such studies suggest also that mother–son problems tend to protract, com-pared to those with daughters, particularly if the mother remains unmarried. Facing difficult situations like this is likely to intensify their longing for the father (presumably to be an arbiter or problem solver). In other words, the quality of children's relationships with one or other parent after divorce has been consistently found to be a significant factor in children's adjustment.

Further studies reveal that adolescents with the same-gender custodial par-ent are less likely to be delinquents, less prone to antisocial behaviour and depression and less likely to drop out of school (MacKinnon, 1989; Peterson and Zill, 1986; Stewart-Clarke and Hayward, 1996; Zimiles and Lee, 1991). It may seem trite to suggest that warm, accepting relationships with both par-ents facilitate post-divorce adjustment in both male and female children and adolescents. Indeed, evidence accumulated over the years indicates that it is a commonplace but important mitigating factor (Bauserman, 2002; Buchanan *et al.*, 1996; Hetherington, 1973; Hetherington *et al.*, 1982; Lamb, 1976; Peterson and Zill, 1986). Evidence concerning the positive effects of a good relationship with either or both biological parents is, nonetheless, not so clear-cut. While some research indicates that a good relationship with either parent is associated with better outcomes than poor relationships with both parents, other data suggest that a good relationship is beneficial only if it is with the custodial parent (e.g. Bauserman, 2002; Johnston, *et al.*, 1989). If this is so, then the question is whether or not the gender of the custodial parent makes any difference.

The straightforwardness of this question in fact disguises its complexity. Because of the gender bias in children's residence arrangements following parental divorce or separation, such sex differences may thus reflect several facts, a major one being the observation that in 90 per cent of divorce settlements involving young children the mother becomes the custodial parent (Hoyt *et al.*, 1990; Poussin and MartinLebrun, 2002; Smith and Gollop, 2001). This tendency persists owing to the traditional belief that the child's interest is best served by the mother rather than the father. In terms of personal identity development, this situation provides a clear identity figure for young girls, a suggestion strongly backed by research evidence (Hetherington *et al.*, 1998; Lye, 1999; Peretti and Divitorrio, 1992; Rutter, 1981; Stewart-Clarke and Hayward, 1996). Research addressing the above question has predominantly involved children in mother custody. Unsurprisingly, many of these suggest that boys fare worse than girls in maternal custody. Zaslow (1988, 1989) examined 27 studies of school-age children in maternal custody and reported that in 16 of the studies boys did worse; in five girls did worse; and in the remaining six there was no difference.

Other studies also indicate that younger children do better with their mother than their father, or that the sex of the resident parent makes no difference for boys (Maccoby and Mnookin, 1992). Yet others claim that boys with fathers and girls with mothers experience fewer behaviour problems, are less aggressive, have higher self-esteem and are more acceptable to same-gender playmates (Camara and Resnick, 1988). Based on such evidence there has been a call for same-gender custody after divorce. The research which has been most frequently used to support the same-gender hypothesis is by Warshak and Stantrock (1983). Warshak (1992, 2000) strongly suggests that there is an advantage to having a resident parent of the same gender or of having a good relationship with the non-resident parent. The notion of socio-genealogical connectedness would regard the non-resident parent–child relationship as the crucial factor, as the gravamen of the gender question.

On balance, there seems to be no clear dispute concerning the benefit to children of maintaining post-divorce good relationships with both parents. To have a healthy relationship with the non-resident parent of the same or opposite sex, of course, necessitates contact with them in the first instance. It appears that whether or not a child has or maintains contact with the non-resident parent is influenced very much by the resident parent. Thus, Stewart-Clarke and Hayward (1996) tested the same-gender hypothesis by evaluating children's psychological well-being and relating it to the gender of the resident parent. The participants comprised a total of 187 school-age children: 72 in paternal custody (39 boys and 33 girls) and 115 in maternal custody (56 boys and 59 girls). Compared to similar studies, this study contained an unusually high proportion (39 per cent) of custodial fathers. The investigators also tested two other hypotheses in order to determine if children's psychological well-being (self-esteem, anxiety, depression and behaviour problems) is related to: (a) the extent and nature of the child's contact with the non-resident parent; (b) the psychological and economic status of the custodial parent. The results revealed, inter alia, that it was not the frequency of contact or financial standing so much as the type of contact that was related to children's well-being. Namely, the children's relationship with the non-resident parent was strongly and consistently related to their contact with the parent: the relationship with the non-resident parent was more positive if parent and child had more frequent and longer visits, lived closer to each other, participated in a wider variety of activities and spent holidays together.

On all of the measures that Stewart-Clarke and Hayward's study tested, boys did significantly better in the custody of their father. Furthermore, children in the custody of their father, irrespective of their sex, maintained a more positive relationship with their mother. Yet another advantage of father custody was that children living with their father were more likely to continue to think of their mother as part of the family and less likely to think of them in negative terms than children in maternal custody. Statistically controlling for the custodial parent's psychological status and financial circumstances did not eliminate the observed differences. In summary, the results showed that the advantage of father custody was especially marked for boys, but there was no indication that girls did better in a same-gender custodial arrangement. Their analyses of the children's relationships with their parents showed no significant interaction effects, and only two main effects for gender of parent. Nevertheless, they found children in paternal custody to be less negative toward the non-resident mother than children in mother custody were to the non-resident father. Stewart-Clarke and Hayward concluded:

> If there is one major finding in this study, it is the demonstration of the importance of fathers for the psychological health of children after divorce. The significance of fathers' contribution to children's well-being has been suggested by researchers previously . . . but it has never been so clearly and unequivocally demonstrated for children of school-age. For girls in this study, positive contact with the non-resident parent was the *only* significant predictor of psychological well-being from among all the family variables.
>
> (p. 260, emphasis added)

These findings clearly reinforce the stress of socio-genealogical connectedness on the importance of continuity of children's post-divorce relationship with the non-resident parent. It needs reiterating that this applies to other groups of separated children. They also need continuity with their socio-genealogical background. Evidently, as already pointed out, socio-genealogical connectedness makes a distinction between the amount and nature of contact. Stewart-Clarke and Hayward's findings and conclusion are indeed just what the theory of socio-genealogical connectedness would expect. That is, it is not just the frequency that is important but rather the quality of contact, especially one which provides the child with an opportunity to gather socio-genealogical information that will enhance post-divorce adjustment and general psychological well-being and integrity, including mental health.

What the foregoing discussion shows is that it is not just the relationship with the mother that matters. It is a matter of course that in most cases the mother generally has more contact with very young children and so exercises greater and in most cases enduring influence on them. On the other hand, as Lamb (1976) emphasized many years ago, the father–child relationship is just as important and may in certain circumstances be the most influential and enduring. Briefly, both parents influence their children's development, although which parent is more important varies with the child's age, sex, temperament and the ecology in which the child is raised (Bronfenbrenner, 1979, 1992; Whiting and Edwards, 1988). Accordingly, it is not always meaningful or helpful to regard the influence of each parent as separate and independent. In *Maternal Deprivation Reassessed*, Rutter (1981) clearly recognized this and so advised: 'A less exclusive focus on the mother is required. Children also have fathers' (p. 127).

A closer exploration of the literature in the area of divorce and its detrimental impact on psycho-social developmental outcomes for children shows that, although difficult resident parent–child relations may contribute to or aggravate children's emotional, academic and behaviour problems, a good relationship with at least one parent can boost a child's resilience to deal with divorce-related stresses. That is to say, where difficulties exist in the mother–child relationship, the role of a good relationship with the father in the child's adjustment to the divorce becomes particularly important, as socio-genealogical connectedness theory would predict. Given that one of the most important characteristics of resilient children is a good relationship with at least one adult, either within or outside the family, and given that boys are less inclined to seek adult contact outside the family or utilize social support networks than girls (Samuelson, 1997), it is not surprising that the non-resident parent–child relationship seemed more important to the boys than it did to the girls in the present analyses.

Sadly, there exists a substantial body of evidence which shows that many non-custodial fathers lose contact with their children following divorce, thereby depriving the children of an essential source of psychological sustenance and emotional support (Barn, 1993; Bianchi and Setzer, 1986;

Stewart-Clarke and Hayward, 1996, Stewart, 1999). Here too, that is in terms of contact, a prerequisite for parent–child relationship, examination of the literature reveals a stark gender asymmetry. Namely, there exists evidence demonstrating that a higher proportion of children in paternal custody sustain contact with their mother. Conversely, a lower proportion of children in maternal custody maintain frequent and regular contact with their biological father (see Table 5.4). From a socio-genealogical connectedness perspective, the implications of such findings for the children warrant further investigation, especially in view of their ramifications for family law – child custody decisions – and professional childcare practice.

In one of their analyses of a US national survey involving 1500 children, Bianchi and Setzer (1986) outlined the variables commonly reported to influence children's contact with the non-resident parent. They found three of the most influential variables to be: (1) the length of time that has elapsed since divorce; (2) gender; (3) the post-divorce marital status of either or both parents. Regarding time, they identified the length of time a child's parents have been divorced or separated as a significant factor. That is, children who, due to divorce, have been living apart from a biological parent for one year or more are much less likely to see that parent on a frequent and regular basis than children who have been separated from a parent for shorter periods of time. The frequency of a child's contact with a non-resident parent as well as the quality of their relationship is proportional to the length of time the parent has been absent in the child's life. However, Bianchi and Setzer's data show that children in paternal custody are more likely to have regular contact with their mother than vice versa. From the point of view of socio-genealogical connectedness and other studies, the implications of this for boys' developmental outcomes are obvious.

Hetherington *et al.* (1985) and (Rutter, 1981), for example, have highlighted the difficulty that boys have in identifying with a father whom they very rarely or never see. Like Eme and Kavannaugh (1995) and other investigators, they emphasize the importance of the biological father as a role model. It may be hypothesized, therefore, that this factor contributes to the particular vulnerability of boys noted in many studies, to the extent that it is fathers who are most often absent. Additional to length of time and gender, Bianchi and Setzer found the marital status of either parent to be an influential factor. Their data show that children of a remarried non-resident parent are much less likely to maintain regular contact with that parent than children living with an unmarried parent, more so in the case of a remarried mother. Table 5.4 summarizes the results of their analyses relating to this variable.

As Table 5.4 shows, among children living in a lone-parent household headed by their biological father, 29 per cent saw their mother at least once a week; only 14 per cent never saw their mother. Among those living with a remarried biological father, 16 per cent saw their mother at least once a week, while 24 per cent never saw her. For children living with only one biological parent, their frequency of contact with the non-resident parent depended

Table 5.4 Non-resident parents' contact with their children by marital status

Head of household	Contact with other parent	
	% per week	Never
Lone father	29	14
Remarried father	16	24
Lone mother	24	31
Remarried mother	8	46

Source: Summarising some data reported by Bianchi and Setzer (1986).

largely on whether the non-resident parent had remarried. Of those living in a lone-parent household headed by their biological mother, 24 per cent saw their father at least once a week; 31 per cent never saw their father. In comparison, among children living with a remarried biological mother, only 8 per cent saw their father at least once a week, while 46 per cent (nearly half) never saw their father.

Subsequent studies have reported similar findings. These studies predominantly tend to stress, in the absence of inter-parental conflict, the benefits of parental contact to the children's general well-being (Amato, 2000, 2001; Amato and Keith, 1991b; Allison and Furstenberg, 1989; Cherlin *et al.*, 1991). Many of these studies also suggest the desirability of contact or a relationship with the non-resident parent to the children. More recently, in New Zealand, Smith and Gollop (2001) conducted a study which focused on children's perspectives regarding parental contact. The study involved a total of 107 children of divorced or separated parents (male = 52; female = 55, in 73 families). The children were aged between 7.41 and 18.65 years. The researchers concluded that, on the whole, children enjoy access with non-custodial parents and that many children would like more contact, though they are only rarely consulted about access arrangements.

Bianchi and Setzer (1986) examined other factors which distinguish children who have some contact with the non-resident parent from those who never see the parent. In addition to the length of time since divorce or separation and the presence of a step-parent, they found several other characteristics which influence whether a child has any contact with the non-resident parent, including, among other things, the following:

- Children born outside of marriage or long-term relationship (including those whose mother self-inseminated) are less likely ever to see their father than those whose parents were married or in a long-term stable heterosexual relationship.
- Children are more likely to have contact with their non-resident biological mother than their non-resident biological father.
- Children adopted by relatives such as their grandparents are more likely to have frequent and regular contact with their biological parents.

The findings of socio-genealogical studies are consistent with these findings. The third finding is particularly pertinent to the notion of socio-genealogical connectedness.

CONCLUSION

Bianchi and Setzer (1986) rightly counsel caution. Before concluding that all children should be placed in father custody after divorce, we should take other things into consideration:

- We must be mindful of the tried but true cliché that correlations do not prove causation.
- We must not generalize beyond the sample.
- Although children in father custody as a group are often reported to be doing better than those in mother custody, in many studies they were not doing better than the children in maternal custody who had high levels of contact with dad. In terms of psychological well-being, close contact with dad (for children in mother custody) fully compensated for the advantages of living with dad (for children in father custody).
- Children's psychological well-being is a function of many factors and those identified in any given study are only but a few.
- Bianchi and Setzer stress that the significance of their results and findings for practitioners is not that it provides a blunt instrument for obtaining more custody for fathers; the positive associations obtained in the study demonstrate the benefits for children of paternal custody and of continued contact with both parents but do not necessarily imply that custody and contact are the whole story.

To inform and help childcare professionals in particular, Eme and Kavannaugh (1995) take the story a step further. From their scrutiny of the literature, they provide the following summary of the exogenous factors commonly adduced for the greater male relative to female vulnerability to parental divorce:

- Father absence has a greater adverse effect on boys [than on girls] because of the absence of a male role model.
- Boys are more likely than girls to respond to parental divorce with externalizing, antisocial behaviours requiring firm, consistent and decisive discipline or control in parenting them; following divorce, however, the discipline of custodial mothers tends to be erratic, inconsistent and harsh.
- Parents entrapped in marital conflict often come to resent an opposite-sex child who is perceived as a constant reminder of the ex-spouse or partner; since the mother is usually the primary caretaker of the children, this sort of resentment may be experienced more frequently by boys than girls.

- In times of stress, boys are less able than girls to disclose their feelings and to solicit and obtain support from parents, other adults and peers.

Regarding the first explanation, socio-genealogical connectedness would specify the biological father or his close relative, especially the paternal grandfather, as the crucial male model rather than any male. The third explanation may be seen as a sign of parental 'alienation syndrome'. This is discussed in Chapter 7.

Together, the evidence reviewed so far may account for an unexpected finding of the present analyses concerning the differential impact of paternal information on boys and girls in the families studied. In other words, the relative impact of the relationship with the non-resident father appeared to be less on the girls in the socio-genealogical studies than it was on the boys. Even though the pertinent literature remains inconclusive, this finding contradicts the prediction of socio-genealogical connectedness. Although unpredicted, the finding is by no means surprising. It may be explicable in terms of a number of factors including those already mentioned, such as the children's relationships with their mother, social support networks and coping strategies.

The world of children of divorce is a complex one. Further research on all aspects of the social, psychological and emotional development of children brought up in male-headed lone-parent families is clearly needed. Otherwise, it is impossible to explain effectively the lack of support for the socio-genealogical theory when applied to girls in this study. It could be that there is a genuine gender difference which makes girls less susceptible than boys to acting out (externalizing) problems of socio-genealogical connectedness.

6 Socio-genealogical knowledge and identity

> A genealogically bewildered child is one who has either no knowledge of his natural parents or only uncertain knowledge about them. The resulting state of confusion and uncertainty fundamentally undermines his security and thus affects his mental health.
>
> (Shants, 1964, p. 133)

Can any description of the feeling of rootlessness be more vivid than Shants' portrait of it, except perhaps, Stonequist's (1937) portrayal of 'the marginal man'? It epitomizes the significance of genealogical knowledge to one's psychological integrity and mental health. It also makes clear that while Bowlby saw 'mother love' as essential for mental health, Shants regarded ancestral knowledge as a prerequisite. Shants employed the term genealogical bewilderment to describe the presenting problems of a large number of adopted children he saw in a child guidance clinic in north Wales. His clinical observations of the adjustment difficulties which the children were experiencing led him to suggest that, in addition to the general causal factors of their adjustment problems, adopted children have the burden of what he called adoption stress; that is, the stress to which adopted children are subjected as a result of their adoptive status. Those observations revealed genealogical bewilderment to be a major factor in adoption stress.

Shants recognized that it is not only adopted children who may lack knowledge of their birth parents; that genealogically bewildered children may be found in any family where one or both of the genetic parents are missing (or denigrated). Thus, stepchildren and foster children may also show this symptom. So may those reared by one biological parent, most notably children of unmarried mothers by choice, the offspring of donor insemination, as well as children in divorced families.

What genealogically deprived children share in common is at least one unknown parent or one of whom the child's knowledge is inadequate or doubtful. Shants also recognized that although children of parents whose origins are unknown or maligned may not always show overt concern about their lack at every stage of their development, at some time, usually in early adolescence, they will begin searching for clues. Both historical and contemporary investigators and writers agree with Shants that once they have begun their preoccupation with the task can reach disturbing proportions. They will gather directly or indirectly every shred of evidence which they feel will put them on the right trail. Some have described the preoccupation as amounting to an obsession, in that genealogically deprived children seem to believe that solving this problem will lead to solutions to all their troubles (Triseliotis, 1973; Triseliotis and Hill, 1990; Triseliotis *et al.*, 1997; Baran and Pannor, 1993; Walby and Symons, 1990). Uncertainty and confusion resulting from ignorance about one's exact origins appears to stimulate pressure of such magnitude that the desire to know or find out becomes virtually uncontrollable.

According to Shants, the child who has no knowledge of their natural parents or only fuzzy knowledge about them may become genealogically bewildered. The resulting state of confusion and uncertainty may undermine their sense of belonging and identity. Studies suggest that the achievement of a clear sense of identity and a sense of security for separated children growing up in 'substitute' forms of care is linked to several factors, including:

- the quality of caring and relationship experiences in childhood
- the level of knowledge and awareness about their heritage and personal history
- their experience of how other people perceive them and behave towards them, as well as how they see themselves in relation to the rest of society.

In the absence of negative experiences, a positive outcome for the child in these three areas should enable them to satisfactorily perform a wide range of life tasks and roles covering personal and social relationships, occupational, marital and parenting roles. More recently, other researchers (e.g. Roche and Perlesz, 2000; Schechter and Bertocci, 1990) have drawn particular attention to the implications of the loss of genealogical history for not only the development of self-esteem, but also for policy and childcare practice.

SELF-IDENTITY AND THE OEDIPUS COMPLEX

Shants considered the psychological ramifications of a lack of socio-genealogical knowledge in relation to self-identity and the Oedipus complex. Like many psychoanalytic theorists and writers of his time, Shants very much believed in the importance of the self-concept in mental health. For example, he agreed with Hurlock (1955) that 'until the individual establishes a stable concept of self he will be uncertain about his ability, his status in the group, and how he compares with others . . . Those with stable self-concepts have higher levels of self-esteem' (quoted in Shants, 1964, p. 134).

In describing the emergence of the self-concept, Shants also drew on the work of Flugel (1921). He agreed with Flugel that from the first year onwards children's awareness of their social environment gradually extends from their mother or mother figure to other members of the family; that is, it progressively expands from the dyad through to the macro-system. At each stage of development, children seek to establish a stable concept of themselves by fostering a sense of belonging to their extended social environment because feelings of not belonging aggravate their anxieties of parental rejection. To allay such anxieties and establish a secure sense of belonging, the developing child extends their feelings towards their parents to more distant relatives, to the family as a whole and finally to other units so that they are accepted as a full members, the clan, the neighbourhood, school, village or town and nation. Shants quotes Flugel to support this claim:

> In certain persons . . . especially in members of an aristocratic caste or in others who are able to trace their descent through a long line of ancestors some important aspects of the parent-love come to be attached to the idea of the whole family of which they form a part; the tendencies to esteem, obedience, admiration or idealisation originally aroused by the child's immediate parents being transferred to the family or clan regarded as a social group, which has existed in the past, exists now in those of its members who happen to be living and will continue to exist in the descendants.
>
> (Flugel, 1921, quoted in Shants, 1964, p. 134)

Looking back to Chapter 2 reveals the similarity between Flugel's description of the process and role of socialization (or socio-genealogization) in identity development and that described by Wiredu (1998) and Gbadegsin (1998).

In adolescence, when maturing children are normally detaching themselves from their parents or establishing personal identity through extending warm sentiments or feelings to wider groups such as the peer group, the clan or the community, Shants argued that genealogically deprived adolescents are handicapped by their ignorance of the family or clan to which they belong. He described such children as confused or disturbed as a consequence of feeling displaced. He suggested that what needs to be examined is why genealogically deprived children who are denied an extension of their self-concept into their hereditary family feel so emotionally deprived. He presented the story of 'The Ugly Duckling' to illustrate the emotional and psychological plight of the genealogically deprived.

For readers who may not be familiar with this story, it is about a swan deprived of its genealogy by being hatched in a duck's family and later fostered by an old woman who already had two animals, a cat and a hen. The swan is rejected by the cat and hen because it lacks the typical genetic endowment of each member of the family. For example, the old woman can feed and take care of them, the chicken can lay eggs and the cat can curve its back and purr, but the swan can do none of these things. Their rejection and mocking drive the swan into depression and wandering (symptoms found so often in genealogically deprived children). The story ends happily because the swan eventually reunites with its kind; it finds itself among a flock of other swans and is admired as a beautiful swan. Shants used this analogy and his clinical experience to conclude that when a child of unknown parentage is encountered the consequences of his deprivation become revealingly apparent. He pointed out, however, that because very few of us are in this unfortunate position, it is difficult for the majority of us to envision the extent of the consequences, what it really means to the genealogically bewildered.

According to Shants (1964), unlike Bowlby (1973), for example, the child's efforts to extend their self-concept transcend the immediate family and relatives. Ancestors too have an important role in the process of developing a healthy self-concept. Many writers agree that in every culture people identify with their ancestors; indeed, some regard ancestors as mediators between themselves and their 'creator'. For those holding this belief it would be perturbing not to know the identity and possible status of one's mediators (Holdstock, 2000; Horton, 1967; Hountonji and Zegeye, 1989; Mbiti, 1969; Owusu-Bempah and Howitt, 1995, 2000b; Sawyer, 1970; Sogolo, 1998; Wiredu, 1998; Witte, 2001). Shants quotes from a leader article in *The Times* (1961) to demonstrate how universal the phenomenon of ancestor worship is, even in so-called 'scientific' or 'postmodern' societies:

> Few men are completely without interest in their forebears, because at its lowest this is mainly an extension of their interest in themselves . . . For children, for instance, how swiftly and eagerly they respond to tales about their great or greater grandparents . . . Perhaps that is part of the secret of the hold that grandparents so often seem to have upon their grandchildren: they have already, as it were, a foot in the ancestor clan . . . Some few families are equipped with everything that feeds such curiosity, with portraits and letters and priceless heirlooms of varying degrees of beauty. Some try to fill the gap with research.
>
> (quoted in Shants, 1964, p. 137)

The currently growing popularity and interest in genealogy, spurred by the advent of the internet, is testimony to the universality of ancestor worship.

Through the process of identification and repudiation, other people, including ancestors, are incorporated into the self-concept. Anthropological observations, nevertheless, suggest that 'the relation to the body image of others is determined by the factor of spatial nearness and remoteness and by the factor of emotional nearness and remoteness' (Shants, 1964, p. 138). Such observations suggest emotional nearness and remoteness of ancestors. In other words, the dead (the living dead) do not disappear from the community of the living. Rather, they remain in the community of the living for as long as their pictures are revived or stories about them narrated orally or in literature within the family, clan or the wider community (e.g. de Witte, 2001; Holdstock, 2000; Mbiti, 1969; Owusu-Bempah and Howitt, 1995, 2000b). Shants and others cite anthropological evidence which indicates that related ancestors have a special emotional nearness, and it is they who appear normally to be incorporated into our self-concept or psyche – Hinde's (1979) notion of 'penetration'.

From a psychodynamic perspective, Erikson conceived of the self-concept as the integration of integrations. As such, he saw it as the essence of psychological integrity:

> The process of identity formation emerges as an evolving configuration – a configuration which is gradually established by successive . . . syntheses throughout childhood. It is a configuration gradually integrating constitutional givens, idiosyncratic libidinal needs, favored capacities, significant identifications, effective defenses, successful sublimation and consistent roles.
>
> (Erikson, 1968, p. 168)

In *Childhood and Society* (1950), Erikson's description of the process of identity development is not unlike the one presented above. He stressed the developing child's need for recognition and figures with whom to identify. He argued that identity formation involves expanding self-awareness and more conscious exploration of self. He acknowledged the role of not only the parents but also the extended family and wider environment, including culture. He opined that true personal identity depends on the support which the child or young person receives from the collective sense of identity which characterizes the social groups significant to them: their class, nation and culture. Erikson stressed that understanding any person requires knowledge of the cultural, social and historical context in which they live. In other words:

> Human development is always embedded in some social group context. This ranges from the minimal (mother and child) to the maximum case of collective institutions of infinite membership.
>
> (Valsiner, 2000, p. 86)

Erikson reinforced the generally accepted idea that one of the main tasks in life is the quest for identity. He employed the term identity to refer to 'a conscious sense of individual identity . . . an unconscious striving for a continuity of personal character . . . a criterion for the silent doings of ego synthesis . . . a maintenance of an inner solidarity with a groups' ideals and identity' (1950, p. 102). Stated differently, identity involves the awareness, understanding and acceptance of both the self and one's biological, cultural and social roots. Throughout life we ask 'Who am I?' All this implies that, apart from the important contribution of biological parents, identity is a convergence or composite of other family and socio-cultural influences. Evidence from studies based upon the notion of socio-genealogical connectedness suggests that it is the quality or ratio (positive versus negative) of these constituents that determines, to a large extent, the kind of personal identity or personality a child develops (Owusu-Bempah, 1993, 1995, 2006; Owusu-Bempah and Howitt, 1997, 2000b).

In line with historical theorists (e.g. Cooley, 1902; James, 1890; Mead, 1934) and contemporary writers on the concept of identity, Triseliotis and Hill (1990) employ the term to denote the kind of consciousness that we all carry within us about 'who' we are, how secure and worthy we feel in what we are, and hence the kind of self-identity, the type and clarity of the mental map of ourselves, that we convey consciously or unconsciously about ourselves to others. We must bear in mind, though, that one's mental or cognitive map of one's sense of security gives the overall sense of identity, while being simultaneously its product. Contingent upon its quality and clarity, a sense of identity conveys feelings of self-worth or self-esteem, subjective expectancy or self-efficacy – one's confidence in accepting and undertaking a whole range of life roles and tasks in life, such as marriage, parenthood, employment, and so forth. We must be mindful, though, that one's identity is inseparable not only from one's cultural background but also from one's ancestral history. It is simultaneously a conglomerate and amalgamation of other identities: parents, grandparents and ancestors, cultural and social groups.

DONOR INSEMINATION

The rest of this chapter focuses mainly on donor insemination and its psychological implications for the offspring's identity development. Where pertinent, the discussion draws evidence from the adoption field. Golombok and colleagues (2002) claim that the first reported case of donor insemination, arranged by the husband, took place in 1884, a century before Mary Warnock chaired the Committee of Inquiry into Human Fertilisation and Embryology in England and Wales. In this case, even the woman involved was (supposedly) not told by her doctor that she had received another man's sperm. This case shows that donor insemination predates today's other medically assisted reproduction techniques, and has been and continues to be practised in almost every human society. In the western world today, the clientele of assisted conception consist of heterosexual married couples, lesbian couples and single women. Ordinarily, assisted conception takes the following forms:

- donor (artificial) insemination
- in vitro fertilization (IVF)
- surrogacy.

Donor (artificial) insemination

This procedure entails simply introducing sperm (semen) inside a woman's vagina (near the cervix) or uterus by means other than sexual intercourse. A syringe is a convenient tool for this purpose.

In vitro fertilization (IVF)

This technique is used when a woman has no fallopian tubes, has had them removed, or where the tubes are blocked. A ripe egg, extracted from the ovary before it is released naturally, is mixed with sperm in a dish (in vitro), in laboratory conditions, so that fertilization can occur. When the fertilized egg starts to develop it is then inserted into the woman's womb to develop naturally.

Surrogacy

This involves one woman undertaking gestation for another with the intention of handing the child over at birth. It can take a number of forms which may include: the egg of the carrying mother being artificially fertilized by the commissioning father or a donor; the embryo being entirely a product of donation; or the embryo a product of the commissioning parents where the commissioning mother is unable to carry the pregnancy. (See Snowden and Snowden, 1993, for a detailed non-technical description of these procedures.)

Donor insemination is the least expensive assisted conception procedure and is claimed to have the same rate of success as normal sexual intercourse; it is simple to perform. Hence, it is reported to be by far the most common of the above techniques (Baran and Pannor, 1993). However, we will see soon that its simplicity conceals its psychological complexity. For example, Baran and Pannor have rightly pointed out that each case of donor insemination involves more than two individuals. It involves: first, a biological or genetic mother; second, a donor (usually anonymous); third, a child. In a heterosexual couple, this threesome is joined by the woman's husband, who becomes the child's social father. In lesbian couples, this triangle becomes a quadrangle, a second 'mother' serves as a foil to her partner and the family as a whole. Single mothers by choice retain full control of their parenthood. In actual fact, in each of these cases, the resulting child has one genetic mother and one genetic father. Whatever the successful means of assisted conception employed, in most cases the offspring is deliberately left in ignorance with regard to the other half of their biological inheritance, their paternal (or maternal) half. The crucial psychological question relates to the implications of this secrecy for them, the possible accompanying feeling of socio-genealogical bewilderment.

DONOR INSEMINATION, KNOWLEDGE AND IDENTITY

> I ask to be no other man than I am, and I will know who I am . . . I must
> pursue this trail to the end, till I have unravelled the mystery of my birth.
> (King Oedipus, quoted by Shants, 1964, p. 139)

The legendary King Oedipus story evidently raises questions of self-
knowledge or self-identity. Traditionally, adoption has dominated research
and literary works in this area. Using adoption to illustrate the experiences of
childhood separation, research over the years has consistently reported and
stressed the importance of socio-genealogical knowledge to self-identity.
Anecdotal evidence supports this. More recently, Grotevant (1997), for
example, has provided anecdotal reports from adopted adults to reinforce the
importance of identity for adopted persons and other socio-genealogically
disconnected children and adults:

> I seem to have a compelling need to know my own story. It is a story
> that I should not be excluded from since it is at least partly mine, and it
> seems vaguely tragic and . . . unjust that it remains unknown to me. We
> adoptees are missing a crucial piece of ourselves.

> (p. 12)

The feeling of inner unrest and torment expressed by the legendary character,
Oedipus, typifies and encapsulates the world of not only adopted persons
(which Oedipus accidentally discovered he was), but also the inner world of
all groups of socio-genealogically disconnected individuals. The story of
Oedipus describes the social, psychological and emotional worlds of individuals whose ancestral linkages have been severed. It also signifies that the
need for biological and cultural linkage is one of the most basic human needs,
on a par with the need for air, water and food. Furthermore, it illustrates that
recognition of this need – the unyielding need of disconnected individuals to
know their hereditary roots – is ancient. It is not simply a quest for information for medical or other non-psychological reasons, as many point out (e.g.
Human Fertilisation and Embryology Act 1990; Landau, 1998; Lifton, 1994;
Triseliotis *et al.*, 1997; Walby and Symons, 1990). Rather, as the idea of socio-
genealogical connectedness suggests, the potent driving force is the need for
self-knowledge, the compelling need to know who one is: to be able to answer
such fundamental questions as 'Who am I?' 'Where did I come from?' 'Where
do I belong?'.

For the individuals concerned the question 'Who am I?' is not a mere
philosophical or epistemological question, but rather one of psychological
and practical significance. Hence, in the case of the offspring of donor insemination, the story of King Oedipus is very pertinent. A person resulting
from gamete donation, like everyone else, is made up of two sets of genetic
material. Although they know the origin of one set, in most cases this does

not minimize their need to achieve psychological wholeness. Both clinical and anecdotal accounts of their experiences as a result of their donor offspring status support this (Baran and Pannor, 1993; Ehrenshaft, 2005; Landau, 1998; Snowden *et al.*, 1983; Snowden and Snowden, 1993; Turner and Coyle, 2000). Their experiences, as documented by numerous investigators and writers in the adoption field, parallel those of adopted individuals. All these reports indicate that socio-genealogical information is essential for a sense of emotional security and mental health.

The pioneering study on adoption by Triseliotis (1973), *In Search of Origins*, looked at the search behaviour of adopted people in Scotland and provided a number of insights that link identity formation with knowledge about origins and the past. The study came to the conclusion that a vital part in the tapestry of identity formation is knowledge about one's background and forebears, including the history of one's family, culture and ethnic group. Subsequent studies lend support to Triseliotis' findings and conclusion (e.g. Baran and Pannor, 1993; Baran *et al.*, 1975; Brodzinsky, 1987; Brodzinsky *et al.*, 1992; Haimes and Timms, 1985; Lifton, 1994; Schechter and Bertocci, 1990; Owusu-Bempah, 2006; Shants, 1964; Snowden *et al.*, 1983; Triseliotis and Hill, 1990). Compared with adoption, there is a dearth of reported research concerning the implications of donor insemination for the personal identity of children who result from this procedure. This is surprising given that both adoption and donor insemination have an equally long history.

THE OFFSPRING IN ADOLESCENCE

As in adoption, research examining the psychological implications of donor insemination for the offspring indicates that the developmental stage at which curiosity about being 'different' or the need to seek one's origins varies for the individual. For those who are aware of their origins or whose curiosity gets the better of them, the need to know usually peaks in adolescence. This is hardly surprising, given our knowledge of adolescent psychology. Developmental psychologists, from the days of Hall (1904), Freud (1916/1963) and Erikson (1968), to mention a few, through to the present agree that the need to complete one's self, to attain ego strength (or rounded personality), intensifies during adolescence. It is the phase of development which Hall, for example, described as the period of stress and storm, when the individual undergoes a deep emotional turmoil, with the search for identity gyrating, among other things, around one's parents and forebears. Erikson, likewise, described adolescence as the period when establishing a personal identity is paramount, when the individual is confused or uncertain about themselves, their sexual orientation, vocational role and the expectations of society. Erikson also saw adolescence as the age of hero worship, of identification with what is seen as a greater and more complete personality. Regarding hero worship, it seems not to matter whether the figure is dead (ancestor worship) or alive, historical or contemporary. In other words, in his formulation, one of the main developmental tasks of adolescence is to emerge with an independent identity, as a unique individual, although an amalgamation of past and present other independent identities or unique individuals.

Fahlberg (1991) concurs with Erikson that the major psycho-social developmental task facing the adolescent is to seek satisfactory answers to the following questions about themselves: Who am I? Where do I belong? What can I do or be? What do I believe in? Satisfactory answers to these questions do not reside solely within the adolescent. They are provided largely by one's parents, family (including the extended family), social group, ancestors and culture. As such, a true feeling of security means a sense of socio-genealogical continuity. As we saw in Chapter 2, this is more easily achieved in some cultures than others. In some cultures the process is facilitated by the whole community through the easy availability of information about one's birth family, extended family and clan. Metaphorically, the community is a reference library containing every individual member's socio-genealogical fingerprint or details and it is open all hours.

Hartman and Laird (1990) provide an archetypical example from Polynesia. According to these researchers there is no 'adoption' in Polynesian culture because children do not 'belong' to their parents. Rather, they 'belong' to the whole community and so move at various points, for various reasons, to different homes. To provide a further example from the African continent: 'A child is held to be the property of the community, and it is the community who are going to see to it that the individual child becomes a significant member of the community, as an asset to all' (Teffo and Roux, 1998, p. 145). In other words, as the African adage goes: it takes a whole village to raise a child.

If adolescence is a period of stress and storm, a period of emotional and psychological unrest, a period of struggle for identity, then having an incomplete biography is obviously an additional factor with which donor offspring and other socio-genealogically disconnected adolescents have to contend. Having gaps in their history renders them emotionally and psychologically vulnerable in that it impedes their development of a sense of continuity, which William James (1890) saw as sine qua non for identity and mental health. James saw a sense of personal identity as precious to psychological well-being, so that disruptions to it are inimical to mental health. He stressed that personal identity arises mainly by combining the experiences of continuity and 'distinctiveness'. These were, for James, the most essential experiences for a stable and healthy self-identity. He strongly believed that any difficulties emanating from these types of experience have serious consequences for one's sense of self and hence mental health. He presaged: 'The worst alterations of the self are associated with disruption in identity fostered by a loss of continuity and distinctiveness' (James, 1890, p. 207). A sense of continuity is what most donor offspring lack.

In Erikson's conceptualization, one aspect of identity involves coming to terms with the 'givens' in one's life, with one's biography. Triseliotis (1973) and Giddens (1991), for example, concur with Erikson and argue that the self-identity of all of us is largely founded upon our history, on what our parents and ancestors have been, spanning many generations. Triseliotis argues further that adopted individuals, like the rest of us, wish to anchor themselves not only in their adoptive parents but also in what their birth parents are and forebears have been, going back many generations. Although Triseliotis' observation is in relation to adoption, it is applicable to donor insemination offspring and other separated individuals. Based on his pioneering and extensive research on adoption, he agrees with many of his respondents and reiterates their collective view that no person should be cut off from their origins; that separated individuals need full and undamaging or honest information about their origins and genealogy. It stands to reason, therefore, that the availability of such material would make it unnecessary for many of them to have a burning need to 'unravel the mystery of their birth', to shift every grain of sand in pursuit of their origins, in order to achieve a sense of continuity or connectedness.

Whilst one cannot gainsay the validity of these theorists' and investigators' insights, it must be stressed that later provision of the missing link, of the information necessary to establish a sense of continuity, does not automatically or necessarily lead to immediate relief or establishment of consonance. Turner and Coyle's (2000) insight into the experiences of their donor-offspring respondents reinforces this view:

> The account given by . . . seemed to reflect her confusion of emotions following the shock of disclosure. The safety of her 'familiar' world had been lost and she was faced with trying to reappraise her identity. The shock and reappraisal of her identity was perhaps indicative of a feeling of *genetic discontinuity*, i.e. a disruption of her identity as a biological product of both of her parents, which was common amongst many participants.
>
> (pp. 2044–2045, emphasis added)

That the provision of honest information, or unfavourable information tempered with discretion, about one's origins is essential for a healthy sense of identity is reinforced by Grotevant (1997). In agreement with Erikson (1968), she argues that an examination of identity development and an analysis of its constituents bring to light those aspects over which adolescents and young adults have greater personal control; control over which available elements of their origins to integrate or to repudiate. She claims that such an exercise unearths what components are lacking in the identity mural. For example, as we have already seen, many adopted persons feel that they are missing a crucial piece of their personal history because of a lack of knowledge about their birth parents, and so find the process of identity development not only more complex than it is for others, but also emotionally arduous.

Accepting, for example, the proposition by Erikson and others (e.g. Giddens, 1991; Triseliotis, 1973; James, 1890) that an important aspect of identity is continuity across the past, the present and the future leads to the suggestion that the provision of full genealogical information to the adopted person or the offspring of donor insemination is likely to minimize the complexity and accompanying emotions of the process of identity development. They require socio-genealogical information principally to complete this process of development. One of the participants in Triseliotis' pioneering study stated: 'Not because you want to go and live with your natural parents, but without this information you cannot be a whole person' (1973, p. 143). Various investigators have reported similar anecdotal evidence:

> When I found my natural mother, I felt deep inside me that I had finally found myself. I could fill so many empty pockets: who I looked like; where my mother came from; where I got my interests, talents and even allergies.
>
> (A respondent, quoted in Baran *et al.*, 1975, p. 38)

Socio-genealogically disconnected individuals' labours to establish psychological wholeness must be seen as a manifestation of their legitimate need to make sense of and ground themselves in reality by achieving a sense of belonging. As the evidence reviewed so far indicates, a lack of socio-genealogical continuity, a feeling of incompleteness and low self-esteem, is an important contributory factor in affected children's and adolescents' mental health and other psychiatric problems.

A common theme that emerges from the literature on adoption and donor insemination is that searching emanates from the sense of socio-genealogical severance, with all its psychological and mental health ramifications. It is a clear sign of one's need to anchor the self in one's origins; of an unmistakable need to connect with one's socio-genealogical roots. Thus, in the same vein as Erikson described the problems of unformed identity, the problems associated with a lack of a sense of socio-genealogical connectedness do not disappear on emerging from adolescence, on reaching adulthood or old age. In many cases, they continue throughout one's life and manifest especially in times of crisis, such as marital or relationship breakdown and bereavement (Baran and Pannor, 1993; Baran *et al.*, 1975; Erikson, 1968; Fahlberg, 1991; Humphrey and Humphrey, 1989; Lifton, 1994; Sachdev, 1992; Shants, 1964; Triseliotis, 1973; Turner and Coyle, 2000).

Much of the research examined so far indicates that the emotional needs of adults who lack a sense of connectedness tend to present the associated problems through generalized depression and low self-esteem, employment difficulties and relationship and marital problems.

SECRECY AND ANONYMITY: IN WHOSE INTEREST?

> For the child's sake particularly I prefer that absolutely nobody but the parents themselves and myself should know of the insemination therapy.

My last advice to the parents is that under no circumstances should they, or need they, ever tell the child the method of conception – in fact they should forget about it themselves.

(Bloom, 1957, p. 207)

Traditionally, secrecy and anonymity have symbolized donor insemination and other forms of assisted conception. The advice to those contemplating donor-assisted conception has been to maintain secrecy, especially as far the resultant children are concerned. Consequently, parents of children born following any method of conception other than through copulation are reluctant to inform children of their genetic origins, even though they may have confided in trusted friends and/or other family members (Golombok *et al.*, 1996). Research evidence from various nations confirms the entrenched secrecy around donor insemination. It indicates that parents who have used donor conception are unlikely to tell their children about it (e.g. Baran and Pannor, 1993; Blyth and Farrand, 2004; Brewaeys *et al.*, 1995; Golombok *et al.*, 1995, 2002b; Giwa-Osagie, 2002; Hunter *et al.*, 2000; Lycett *et al.*, 2005; McWhinnie, 2000; Savage, 1995; Snowden *et al.*, 1983). It shows that the tradition of keeping the fact of donor insemination and donor identity concealed from the child is widespread and continues.

Snowden and colleagues (1983) and Baran and Pannor (1993) provide two of the pioneering studies. Snowden and associates' study involved 899 couples in Devon, England who underwent donor insemination treatment between 1940 and 1980. They reported similar findings to those of studies on adoption. Of the 57 couples who had given birth to a child about five years prior to the study, only 3 (5 per cent) had decided to tell the child in the future; 6 (11 per cent) were undecided; the vast majority, 48 (84 per cent), had firmly decided not to tell the child. (See also Snowden and Snowden's *The Gift of a Child*, 1993.)

The other pioneering study in California, USA by Baran and Pannor (1993) involved 171 individuals directly connected with donor insemination from February 1980 through December 1982. The participants included 19 donor offspring between the ages of 16 and 68. None of the offspring had been told of the facts of their conception by their parents. Rather, they had learnt of their origins by accident because of a breakdown in the family's attempt to keep the secret. Subsequent research by various investigators supports the findings of Snowden and colleagues and Baran and Pannor (e.g. Brewaeys *et al.*, 1995; Cook *et al.*, 1995; Giwa-Osagie, 2002; Golombok, *et al.*, 1995, 1999; McWhinnie, 1996; Vercollone *et al.*, 1997).

More recent studies have reported that the majority of people seeking donor insemination do not intend to tell a future child (e.g. Golombok *et al.*, 1995, 1999; Gottlieb *et al.*, 2000; Inhorn, 2006; Li and Lu, 2005; Lycett *et al.*, 2005; McWhinnie, 2000). Golombok *et al.* (1999) interviewed 45 families with a child conceived by donor insemination. None of the parents had told or planned to tell their child about their method of conception. McWhinnie

(2000) interviewed the parents of 23 families who had undergone donor-insemination treatment between 0 and 12 years previously. She found that none of the parents had told the child about their origins.

Golombok *et al.* (1995) investigated the openness of two sets of parents: those with children conceived through sperm donation and those with children conceived via egg donation. None of the parents with a child conceived by sperm insemination, and only one set of egg-donation parents, had told the child about their method of conception. A statistically significant difference was found between the groups with respect to the parents' attitude toward telling the child. The sperm-insemination parents were most against telling, with 82 per cent having decided never to tell, compared with 38 per cent of the egg-donation parents.

In another study, Golombok and colleagues (1995, 1999) examined the developmental outcomes of three types of families: donor-insemination families ($n = 37$); adoptive families ($n = 49$); families with children conceived through copulation ($n = 91$). Of the 37 donor-insemination families, only 2 (5 per cent) had told the children about their genetic origins. In contrast, all of the adoptive families had told the children about their adoption. In spite of the donor-insemination parents' decision not to tell, the investigators reported that the children, at ages 4–8 years, were functioning well and did not seem to be experiencing negative consequences arising from the absence of a genetic link with their father, or from the secrecy surrounding the circumstances of their birth. Golombok and colleagues' findings and conclusion invite two obvious comments. Regarding adoption, knowledge of one's adoptive status does not equate knowledge about one's genetic or socio-genealogical origins. As we have already seen, it does not automatically fulfil the adopted person's need for socio-genealogical linkage. The second comment relates to the age of the children involved in Golombok and associates' study. Given the young age of the children, any conclusion from that finding may be regarded as hasty, especially in view of the previous discussion concerning identity formation. Besides, children of that age are unlikely to demonstrate any symptoms associated with being donor offspring, especially if they believe both parents to be their genetic parents, something which the secrecy, if maintained, specifically ensures.

Research from outside western world nations indicates that the practice of secrecy and anonymity in assisted conception is a universal phenomenon (e.g. Giwa-Osagie, 2002; Hunter *et al.*, 2000; Inhorn, 2006; Li and Lu, 2005; Savage, 1995). For example, Giwa-Osagie (2002) reports the findings of a series of surveys he conducted in Lagos, Nigeria. Of 150 heterosexual couples, all of them (100 per cent) chose not to tell anybody about their treatment if it was donor insemination; 70 per cent would tell nobody of it, irrespective of whether the semen used was from husband or a donor; 30 per cent of the women would have preferred even their husband not to be told they were receiving donor semen; while 80 per cent of men whose wives required donor insemination would have preferred this not to be revealed to their wives. Of 30 couples who rejected donor insemination as therapy, 17 accepted insemination with mixed (donor/husband) semen. Bloom's (1957) advice about secrecy would have struck a sweet chord with these parents. In each of these cases the women's main concerns were about the appearance of the baby (presumably they were hoping for some family resemblance), the mental health of the baby and the absence of antisocial behaviour such as stealing and drunkenness. In only 3 (1 per cent) of 267 consecutive pregnancies by donor insemination did the parents reveal this fact to anybody. Giwa-Osagie (2002) reports further that among the first 15 in-vitro fertilization babies in Lagos, only 6 parents were happy to reveal this fact to other persons once the babies were born.

PSYCHOLOGICAL IMPLICATIONS

In the UK, many years after publication of the pioneering study by Snowden and colleagues (1983), the question as to whether there are any adverse effects of anonymity and secrecy on the welfare of the child in donor insemination is still unresolved (Blyth and Farrand, 2004; Shenfield and Steele, 1997). More recently, from a psychological point of view, Turner and Coyle (2000) asked:

> So what does it mean for those donor offspring who do know of their donor-insemination conception? What (if any) psychological implications have the secrecy surrounding the practice of DI had for their identity development and how might this information shape therapeutic practice with this group?
>
> (p. 2041)

These investigators recognize that it is not the practice per se, but rather the circumstances surrounding it – the effects of the accompanying secrecy and anonymity – that need to be studied. This task is not simple either; the question of the psychological effects of donor insemination on the offspring is a perennially contentious one.

Since the seminal studies by Snowden and colleagues (1983) and Baran and Pannor (1993), various researches have highlighted the genetic, medical, psychological and ethical implications of the secrecy in which donor insemination is shrouded, not only for the offspring but also for all concerned. These investigators stress the complex nature of donor insemination, that it is far from easy. For example, Baran and Pannor (1993) highlighted the following psychological implications not only for the child, but also for all those involved. For the husband of a heterosexual couple, donor insemination means that the baby will inherit his wife's genes but not his and that his wife will, in fact, be carrying another man's child. It means the loss of family blood line, genetic continuity and sense of immortality for him. From their survey, they suggested that in some cases the husband feels inferior to the genetic father and the child on the assumption that they are more endowed than he is, especially intellectually, since donors tend to be mainly medical or university students. The husband may also feel at a disadvantage vis-à-vis the biological mother in matters regarding the child's upbringing, feeling that he must yield to her views as a 'real' mother. In lesbian and single parent families, there is no secrecy about the child being a donor offspring. There is, nevertheless, secrecy about the identity of the donor.

These views support Snowden and associates' (1983) suggestion that many infertile husbands who have become parents through donor insemination tend to feel that they are only 'minders' of 'their' children; that the donor is the 'real' father. Discussing the ethical dilemmas that donor insemination entails, Bloom (1957) gave consideration to such questions as: whether the father would be left in the cold with regard to family interactions and relationships; the likelihood that he may become jealous or hostile of the child, given that the child will not be his own genetically. He conceded that one might expect a feeling of inadequacy in the husband for these and other reasons. In relation to lesbian couples and single women, the lack of fuller documentation of donor-assisted conception unfortunately makes it impossible to know clearly how these women are affected by not knowing anything of the identity of the father of their child. Nonetheless, Golombok *et al.* (1999) reported that a number of participant lesbian mothers claimed not have been affected.

Landau (1998) sees the donor offspring as the shoulder upon which rests, ultimately, the weight of the psychological implications of donor insemination; that is to say, they are the persons most affected by the anonymity and deception inherent in donor insemination. The evidence reviewed previously suggests that the majority are ignorant of their real paternal lineage. If their parents are a heterosexual couple, they will grow up in an atmosphere of secrecy and taboo regarding their true origins. Their environment will also be saturated with all sorts of unexplained phenomena, for example, different anatomical features, talents, interests, mannerisms, and so forth from other members of the extended family, especially on the father's side. The ultimate question must therefore, be: What does it mean to be a donor offspring? Only the offspring themselves can provide a satisfactory answer to this important question. Anything short of this is bound to be refuted by many. Blyth (2002) recognizes the difficulty in finding the answer to this question. He argues that in any discussion of what is known about the views of donor offspring themselves, it is necessary to note that the secrecy that has accompanied the practice of donor-assisted conception has limited the information which might be accepted by sceptics as constituting irrefutable empirical evidence.

Turner and Coyle (2000) have likewise noted that detractors of available evidence indicating the psychologically adverse effects of the secrecy and anonymity surrounding donor insemination on the offspring often reject or play down the significance of such evidence on the grounds that it derives from anecdotal accounts or self-report, small-scale surveys, comparisons with adoption or sheer speculation. Knowledge of what donor-conceived people, or at least some of them, actually think is derived first from a number of personal accounts (see e.g. Hamilton, 2002; Turner, 1993). A second source of information comes from a few small-scale studies that have sought the views of donor-conceived people (e.g. Baran and Pannor, 1993; Snowden and Snowden, 1993; Turner and Coyle, 2000). Any research questions designed to seriously address this perennial question effectively must include items related to socio-genealogical connectedness.

OPENNESS: TO TELL OR NOT TO TELL?

In spite of the ongoing controversy, few people today would question the idea that knowledge about one's socio-genealogical background is essential for mental health. Empirical and anecdotal evidence supporting this view is generally accepted by childcare professionals, yet many separated children lack this knowledge. Even where it is available, access to it is very often hindered or denied to them, to the detriment of their emotional, social and behavioural development. We saw earlier that Shants (1964) warned against the suppression or distortion of socio-genealogical information to adopted children and other separated children, whatever the circumstances surrounding their separation. In contrast to Bloom's (1957) counsel, Shants argued that however tragic the circumstances, the child may be happier with his own judgement based on the facts rather than being subjected to attitudes based on attempting to behave as if the event had never occurred. To press home this point, he referred to a principle in psychotherapy that conscious acceptance of the known facts, intolerable though they may appear to be, tends to improve rather than worsen relationships between adopted children and their adoptive family. The following sections consider the pros and cons of openness in donor insemination.

Not to tell

Shenfield and Steele (1997) see the main criticism of secrecy and anonymity in donor insemination as stemming from experience in the field of adoption. On the basis of this, they claim that the crucial question to be answered is if there exists evidence to support whether anonymity is beneficial or harmful to the prospective child. They extend this question to the secrecy which the majority of prospective parents across the world who choose donor insemination as the means of conception maintain. Walker and Broderick (1999) refute the importance of this question. They claim that the practice is psychologically innocuous. They suggest that there is evidence from genetic testing for paternity indicating that as many as 20 per cent of the entire population of Australia are not the children of the men they think are their fathers. Extrapolated to the UK today, for example, this would amount to some 13 million people of dubious paternity. In a somewhat sarcastic tone, they dismiss Shants' (1964) notion of genealogical bewilderment: 'Given these "false paternity" rates, one fifth of the community ought to be bewildered' (p. 40). The authors deny that there is any analogy between donor insemination and adoption and conclude:

> The . . . basis for the therapeutic injunction in donor-insemination relies on presumed parallels with the area of adoption. It is claimed donors of sperms, eggs, and embryos, and their families, will maintain a bond with the unknown children they cannot nurture . . . that children born through the use of donated material will be driven to search for, and seek reconciliation with, their biological ancestors; and that identity development in children who do not know their biological ancestors will be impaired . . . There is little evidence for these processes in the adoption area.
>
> (Walker and Broderick, 1999, p. 40)

By extension, this conclusion also denies these processes in donor insemination.

A number of investigators support Walker and Broderick's (1999) view. For example, in studies with donor offspring aged 4 to 8 years, Golombok *et al.* (1995, 1996) reported no statistically significant differences in the emotional welfare of donor offspring, compared to adopted children, children conceived through copulation and children conceived through in vitro fertilization. However, it was pointed out earlier that the age group into which the children fell precludes generalization of the findings to older children, adolescents and adults, particularly in the light of the importance of the adolescent years for identity formation (Erikson, 1968; Kroger, 1989).

In another study, Golombok *et al.* (1999) examined the relationship between family functioning and the socio-emotional functioning of children conceived through donor insemination (by sperm or egg donation). One of the findings was that a 'strong desire for parenthood overrides the importance of genetic relatedness for fostering positive family relationships, and that conception by sperm donation did not appear to have an adverse effect on the socio-emotional development of the child' (p. 520). Again, caveat emptor! This seems to assume that the parents' strong desire for a child is more important than the child's (later) psychological need for genetic linkage. Evidence from adoption studies, as we saw earlier, suggests rather positive correlation between possession of socio-genealogical information and family relationships.

The belief in the value of secrecy is not confined to the western world. For example, reporting from Africa, Savage (1995) argues vehemently and cogently in support of its maintenance and perpetuation. She champions it on the grounds that while openness with regard to donor insemination is now strongly advocated and publicly accepted in the western world, it is inimical to other cultural contexts. Like Giwa-Osagie and many others, Savage acknowledges the tradition and widespread practice of donor insemination in Africa. Nonetheless, she expresses grave concern about the current trend of openness on the continent. Indeed, she is emphatic in her opinion that it is inappropriate in the African context:

> Does the apparent need for secrecy in AID (artificial insemination by donor) need to be re-examined, particularly within the African context, where social parenthood is a well-known and acceptable practice? Is the present trend for secrecy simply an automatic transfer and/or a blind adoption of Western models within a different social and cultural context? The possibility of advocating a policy of openness in AID remains questionable in Cameroon. Human reproduction, assisted or not, still remains a very private affair.
>
> (Savage, 1995, p. 88)

Fonseca (2002) has advanced a very similar argument in defence of child circulation (i.e. informal adoption) amongst the Brazilian working class. Fonseca advocates passionately against the replacement of open adoption in Brazil with sealed adoption: first, it is counter to traditional social and economic practices among some working classes; second, like Savage, Fonseca regards it as a shameful adoption of western archaic models by Third World nations, as auto-colonialism. Other writers have advanced similar arguments in relation to psychology and psychological practice in Africa and other Third World countries (Akin-Ogundeji, 1991; Holdstock, 2000; Howitt and Owusu-Bempah, 1994; Owusu-Bempah and Howitt, 1995, 1997, 2000b).

Savage asserts that donor insemination is generally perceived by potential clients (both fertile and infertile) in Cameroon as a 'fine' and 'acceptable' technique to assist infertile persons. Nonetheless, she points out that its acceptance is contingent upon its being carried out in secrecy. Once done, the secrecy is maintained afterwards and the resultant offspring are raised as 'normal' children, as children conceived through the physical/genetic contributions of both parents. Thus, she argues that the possibility of providing donor-insemination offspring with non-identifying, let alone identifying, information about the donor or of establishing future contact is presently unthinkable in Cameroon. She reports that Cameroonian women seeking assisted conception are particularly insistent on these conditions because they feel the need to protect, maintain and continue to project the virility of their spouses to themselves and society at large.

Similarly, in Nigeria, Giwa-Osagie reported that 30 per cent of the women in his study preferred even their male spouses not to be told that they were receiving donor semen; while 80 per cent of men whose wives required donor insemination preferred their female partners to be kept ignorant of the fact. In these instances, the apparent conspiracy of secrecy and anonymity is basically to save the men's faces, to protect their 'virility'. Thus, Savage asks whether the policy of openness in artificial insemination by donor (AID), which the notion of socio-genealogical connectedness would obviously endorse, is feasible in Cameroon. Her answer to this question is that in traditional societies infertile husbands have been known to give their wives tacit permission to bear children by other men in order to avoid the stigma of infertility. Often, other males within the male partner's family, for example, brothers or uncles were chosen as donors – presumably to ensure that the baby comes with some family resemblance. In such situations, the donor and the 'social' father would be from the same family or lineage. In these circumstances, Savage claims that when a child or adult finally becomes aware (by accident or design) of his biological parentage, they experience no emotional or psychological trauma. Likewise, there is no social stigma or embarrassment attached to the revelation.

Baran and Pannor (1993) have argued that there is a close connection in the emotional effects expressed by all of the parties involved in donor insemination, adoption and high-tech babymaking because human need for genealogical and historical connections is universal, the same for people everywhere, no matter how they were conceived or gestated, whether through semen donation, in vitro fertilization, embryo transfer or surrogate mother-hood. They believe that being open and honest and sharing the facts with the offspring are universally necessary. So, how do the offspring of donor insemination and other methods of assisted conception in such societies as Cameroon thrive emotionally and psychologically, in spite of the guided secrecy surrounding their coming into being? How do they meet their human need for genealogical and historical connections? Although speculative, these questions might be explicable by reference to cultural differences, cultural variations in values and attitudes to children.

In Chapter 2 we saw how children are socialized in traditional societies with regard to their lineage. In these societies, not only the extended family but also the community at large play an active role in their upbringing, in inculcating into them a sense of belonging and identity. In these societies, a child is part of a large social group rather than belonging exclusively to one couple; the child is valued as the embodiment of the family genes into the future. In matrilineal societies, where descent is traced through the mother rather than through the father, the child is valued as the embodiment and carrier of the maternal genes into the future. The apparent rationale under-lying this practice is that, in most cases, a child can be sure of who their real (biological) mother is, but cannot be so sure who their real father is. In this case, the genes of the father seem to be of less significance as far as the child's lineage is concerned. On the other hand, in bilateral societies which western cultures commonly typify, descent is traced through both the father and the mother, so that one's knowledge of and, consequently, connection to both biological sides becomes essential for one's identity and mental health.

To tell

Landau (1998) has examined the question from genetic, psycho-social and ethical perspectives. She argues that the lack of knowledge of one's genetic origins that is implicit in donor anonymity has psycho-social implications, on the basis that our genetic heritage is part of our identity. Like Baran and Pannor (1993), she argues further that such secrecy and anonymity are detrimental for all concerned, both medically and psycho-socially and, moreover, that it is ethically unjustifiable. As Baran and Pannor have pointed out, the issue becomes even more perplexing and less justifiable when the true facts of origins are more difficult for the child to understand and accept; for instance, when an individual comes into being as a result of a mixture of egg and sperm donors, in vitro fertilization, embryo implantation or surrogate motherhood, their lineage is obviously confusing (Baran and Pannor, 1993).

Turner and Coyle's (2000) study, accepting that secrecy is the norm amongst donor-insemination families concerning identifying information about the donor, sought to address the following issues: (a) what it means for those donor offspring who do know of their donor-insemination conception; (b) what psychological implications does the secrecy surrounding the practice of donor insemination have for identity development; (c) how this information might shape therapeutic practice with this group. By posing these questions, they sought to deal with the criticism of their detractors (e.g. Golombok *et al.*, 1995, 1999, 2000a, 2000b; Shenfield and Steele, 1997; Walker and Broderick, 1999).

In the absence of evidence from research with adult donor offspring, the study aimed to address these issues by asking individuals about their experiences as donor offspring. The participants comprised 16 adults (13 male, 3 female; age range 26–55), and were recruited internationally through donor-insemination support networks in the UK, USA, Canada and Australia. They completed semi-structured questionnaires sent by email and post. The researchers examined the data qualitatively by means of 'interpretative phenomenological analyses'. They further employed an 'identity framework' to interpret the participants' accounts. Among other things, they found that the participants consistently reported mistrust within the family, negative distinctiveness, lack of genetic continuity, frustration in being thwarted in the search for their biological fathers and a need to talk to a significant other (i.e. someone who would understand). With regard to searching, all the participants had made some initial inquiries about searching for their donor fathers. One participant is reported to have stated: 'How could doctors think . . . that we wouldn't need or want some honest answers about our heritage? Without all this information, I will never feel complete' (Turner and Coyle, 2000, p. 2047). The investigators summarize the participants' searching experiences thus:

> Unable to complete their searches, participants reported a sense of loss and grief about never being able to know their biological origins. They expressed a need and a right to know who their donor fathers are. These experiences could be postulated as being indicative of a struggle to assimilate, accommodate and evaluate information about their new

identities as donor offspring. It seems, therefore, obvious that for these donor offspring, 'non-identifying' information might not be sufficient to meet their identity needs.

(p. 2050)

The authors point out that this is in contrast to the claims by Shenfield and Steele (1997) and Walker and Broderick (1999) that donor offspring do not share the same identity problems as adopted persons in relation to genealogical bewilderment.

We have already seen that these feelings are commonly expressed by adopted persons and donor offspring who have been thwarted in their efforts to seek information about their origins; information which would enable them to establish their true identity. Turner and Coyle therefore counsel psychotherapists and counsellors about the need to be aware of these identity issues if they are to meet the needs of donor offspring with therapeutic practice. They reported further that their participants expressed feeling devalued socially by those who failed to understand their need for socio-genealogical information; that they perceived a sense of abandonment of responsibility by their donor fathers and the medical profession. This echoes the experiences expressed by participants involved in several studies, including those reviewed in previous chapters and in this chapter.

In summary, as Blyth (2000) has pointed out, the principle of right to information about genetic origins is well established as inalienable in adoption practice. He argues further that it is illogical as well as ironical that, in the case of children resulting from gamete donation and human fertilization procedures, governments, decision makers and practitioners believe that the right of a child to information is to be proscribed. The protection of the donor's anonymity and the possibility of donors being deterred by the prospect of more information being made available appear to be empirically unfounded (Blyth, 2000; Daniels and Taylor, 1993; Rumball and Adair, 1999). The 'protection' of the prospective parents is questionable from a number of standpoints, including that of the interests of the parents themselves. Shants (1964) bewailed the fact that the psychology of heredity has been neglected with the consequent neglect of genealogical deprivation. Given our current knowledge of the psychology of donor insemination, the psychological implications of its inherent secrecy and anonymity for all concerned, it would be unethical as well as irresponsible to dismiss outright any evidence, especially from the offspring themselves, suggesting the psychological benefits of openness to them or the ill-effects of secrecy on them.

From a moral and ethical perspective, many investigators, writers and observers (e.g. Baran and Pannor, 1993; Blyth and Farrand, 2004; Daniels and Taylor, 1993; Landau, 1998; Rumball and Adair, 1999) have advocated the free provision of background information to donor offspring. They argue that each individual should be entitled to know the truth about his conception and his heritage. Socio-genealogical connectedness would support this argument, although from a psychological perspective; that one's sense of identity is intractably tied up with one's family history or lineage. Many donor-conceived people who are aware of the true facts of their conception consider that only knowledge of the donor's identity will help them make sense of their own identity and that access to information about their identity is their fundamental right, not only in civil terms, but also in human terms.

7 Divorce and parental alienation syndrome

Socio-genealogical implications

Chapters 3 to 5 discussed studies which involved children of lone-parent families. The studies tested the basic assumptions of the notion of socio-genealogical connectedness. This chapter considers parental alienation syndrome (PAS), a common feature of parental divorce and separation, and its implications for the children's sense of socio-genealogical connectedness. Chapter 3 also highlighted the extent and preponderance of divorce and parental separation in western societies. In the UK, various estimates indicate that one in three or more marriages end in separation or divorce. According to *Population Trends* (Office for National Statistics, 2005a), in a four-year period (2001 to 2004), more than a half of a million (598,442) couples divorced in England and Wales alone. In these, a total of 599,015 children under the age of 16 were involved. This figure obviously excludes the large number of children who resulted from casual relationships or whose parents never co-habited. In about 90 per cent of these cases, the children and young people will be living with the mother, and a large number of them permanently separated from the father through loss of contact.

Even in a small country like the Netherlands, Spruijt *et al.* (2005) estimate that some 20 per cent of children lose contact with their non-resident father after parental divorce or separation. Across the western world, the implications of these statistics for the sense of socio-genealogical connectedness of the massive number of children affected must be incalculable. The following discussion postulates that the concept of parental alienation syndrome, originated by an American psychiatrist, Richard Gardner (1985, 1991, 1992, 1999, 2001, 2003) has serious implications for these children's sense of socio-genealogical connectedness, and thus warrants serious research, practice and policy consideration.

PARENTAL ALIENATION SYNDROME

Orthodox attachment theory proposes that a child's attachment to a parent is innate, a biological given whose principal function is to meet the basic needs of the child, particularly their survival and developmental needs. It also proposes that once established the resultant emotional tie between an infant or child and the parent endures throughout the child's life. This is frequently adduced as a key explanation for why most children and adolescents of divorce naturally want to maintain unbroken relationships with both parents. For example, in a non-clinical sample of 131 children from 60 divorced families, Rand (1997) found that the majority of the children were keen to visit and spend more time with the non-resident father than the usual alternate weekend arrangement. This finding held at follow-up studies 18 months and five years later. Those children whose father did not show much of an interest in them found the apparent rejection hurtful, but their longing for him did not abate; rather it intensified. Rand interpreted these findings in terms of attachment theory, just as many others would do.

Besides Rand's findings, in earlier chapters we came across suggestions that children's yearning for their absent parents defies parental inadequacies. In spite of the general awareness, understanding and acceptance of this fact, research evidence suggests that when one parent enlists a child in a vendetta against the other, the bond between the child and the other parent can be ruthlessly undermined or destroyed. This is strange in view of attachment theorists' insistence that the tie formed between child and parent endures over time. However, when this happens, it is at considerable emotional and psychological cost to the child and eventually to all concerned. This was first identified by Richard Gardner (1985). He used the phrase 'parental alienation syndrome' to represent this phenomenon. Since then, he has continued to define it as:

> The parental alienation syndrome (PAS) is a disorder that arises primarily in the context of child-custody disputes. Its primary manifestation is the child's campaign of denigration against a parent, a campaign that has no justification. It results from the *combination* of a programming (brainwashing) parent's indoctrinations and the child's own contributions to the vilification of the target parent. When true parental abuse and/or neglect is present, the child's animosity may be justified, and so the parental alienation syndrome explanation for the child's hostility is not applicable.
> (Gardner, 2001, p. 61)

Various researchers give various descriptions of the syndrome. Nonetheless, they are closely similar to Gardner's. For example, Ward and Harvey (1993) have described parental alienation syndrome and the alienated child in the following terms:

> the creation of a singular relationship between a child and one parent, to the exclusion of the other parent. The fully alienated child is a child who does not wish to have any contact whatsoever with one parent and who expresses only negative feelings for that parent and only positive feelings for the other parent.
> (p. 1)

Kopetski (1998a) views it as:

> a form of psycho-social pathology. It is most frequently identified in the process of divorce, although it is not a condition limited to divorcing families. It is not caused by the divorce ... it is exacerbated by legal procedures that coincide with and strengthen the pathological defenses alienating parents use to avoid experiencing the psychological pains of internal conflict, ambivalence, narcissistic injury ... like many forms of psychological pathology, parental alienation syndrome occurs when there is an unfortunate 'fit' between the internal psychological dynamics of an individual and a cultural opportunity for living out pathology in an interpersonal setting.
>
> (p. 65)

King (2002), like Gardner, sees parental alienation syndrome as a 'disorder' that arises predominantly in the context of child-custody disputes. He agrees with Gardner that its primary manifestation is the child's unjustified campaign of disparagement of a parent, that it results from a combination of a programming or brainwashing, a parent's indoctrination and the child's own contributions to the vilification of the target parent.

WHICH PARENT?

There is a consensus that in a majority of instances, the father is the victim, the target of parental alienation syndrome. Dunne and Hedrick (1994) examined 16 cases taken from Gardner's (1985) caseloads. In 14 of the 16 cases, the mother had primary custody and was the alienating parent. In one case the non-resident mother was the alienating parent and in another the non-resident father was the alienating parent. This means that in 94 per cent of the cases the mother was the alienator. Similarly, in a study involving a sample of 40 adults whose parents divorced during their childhood, Baker (2006) reported that in 34 (85 per cent) of the cases, the mother was the alienating parent. The present author conducted an analysis of 99 cases in which Gardner (2001) was professionally involved. In all of the cases, Gardner advised the court to order visitation (in severe cases) or a transfer of primary residential custody to the alienated (the target) parent. In 74 (75 per cent) of these cases the alienator was the mother, while the father was the culprit in the other 25 per cent of cases, in one of which the alienator was the father's female cousin, an unmarried and childless woman. In other words, although every now and again the situation is reversed so that it is the mother who is left out of the family constellation, most often the term refers to mothers. Predominantly, fathers are the victims of this syndrome, principally because the courts and western societies tend to regard mothers as better equipped than fathers to meet their children's needs, so that child-custody decisions are frequently in the mother's favour.

Research and reviews examining parental alienation syndrome tend to paint a judgemental picture of the alienating parent. Generally, they indicate that many alienating parents justify their efforts to expunge the target parent out of the child's 'system' on the grounds that it is in the child's interest, that he is unimportant to the child. Kopetski (1998a, 1998b) goes further and in true parental alienation syndrome cases oppugns the 'best-interest-of-the-child' claim. She goes further and argues that the alienating parent's motive for severing the child's relationship with the other parent is self-serving rather than altruistic. She believes that the parent's motive is sinister; that it is a ploy by the alienating parent to manipulate the social and legal systems. She acknowledges, though, that the alienating parent may or may not be consciously aware of manipulating the child and these systems; that is, to get the courts to sanction her actions and to elicit vindication and support from friends and family.

Other investigators (e.g. Baker, 2006; King, 2002; Vestal 1999) who also regard the syndrome as a disorder are in agreement with Kopetski concerning the conscious and unconscious dynamics of the alienating process. These investigators agree that it is a disturbance in which a child is preoccupied with idealizing one parent and demonizing the other. In this process, as Baker (2006) and King (2002) describe it, conscious and unconscious words and actions of the alienating parent cause the child to align with her in rejecting the father. These parents often believe that the grounds (often accusations) on which they justify the exclusion of the other parent are based on facts; but investigators, including Gardner himself, believe that they have developed those beliefs through a faulty reasoning process.

The literature suggests that the completely alienated child extols the alienating parent (usually the mother) to the skies, but demonizes the alienated parent (the father); that is to say, the child views the alienating parent as all good and the other as all bad. Many see this unusual behaviour as resulting from brainwashing by the alienating parent. Gardner (1999), however, sounds a cautionary note about attributing parental alienation syndrome simply to a process of brainwashing. He regards this perception of the process as constricted. Such accounts ignore the alienated parent's contribution, however small it may be:

> The term 'brainwashing' implies that one parent is systematically and consciously programming the child to denigrate the other parent. The concept of the parental alienation syndrome includes much more than brainwashing. It includes not only conscious but unconscious factors within the preferred parent that contribute to the parent's influencing the child's alienation. Furthermore (and this is extremely important), it includes factors that arise within the child – independent of the parental contribution – that foster the development of the syndrome.
>
> (Gardner, 1999, p. 14)

THE CHILD'S CONTRIBUTIONS TO PARENTAL ALIENATION SYNDROME

An integral feature of Gardner's formulation of the concept of parental alienation syndrome is that the disturbance or disorder results from a combination of parental brainwashing and the child's own contributions. His portrayal of the characteristics of the alienated child includes a 'lack of normal human ambivalence'. A closer examination of the clinical literature suggests, however, that it may be more correct to describe the child as one whose demeanour exudes an aura of a lack of ambivalence. In a large number of cases, the child's attitude masks their inner world of grief and bewilderment. This is not to deny that a few adolescents in this situation may have become alienated or detached sufficiently to be callous and unconcerned about the target parent.

Rand (1997) has examined the traits of the children which prime them to participate in devaluing their parent. The most influential endogenous characteristic appears to be age: children most susceptible to parental alienation syndrome have been found to be those aged between 7 and 15. High-conflict divorce children in this age group are particularly vulnerable to developing parental alienation syndrome. Other factors within the child which have been shown to contribute to the formation of strong alliance with the alienating parent are the child's need: (a) to protect a parent who is depressed, panicky or needy as a result of the divorce; (b) to ward off the wrath of a powerful, dominant parent (often the resident parent on whom the child is dependent); (c) to hold on to the parent the child is most afraid of losing.

Other researchers have pointed to gender as an important factor regarding the parent with whom to align. For instance, Johnston (2003) found that boys who are psychologically more troubled – as indicated by their having more emotional and behavioural problems – are more likely than other children to reject their mothers. Girls who demonstrate more social competence and those who experience more anxieties at separation from their fathers (especially younger ones) are more likely to have negative attitudes towards the mother and to avoid contact with her. Johnston also noted that children's attitudes towards their parents ranged from positive to negative, with relatively few being extremely united or rejected.

In summary, the child's contribution to the parental alienation syndrome has been postulated to be due to one of several factors:

- the child's need to protect and cared for an angered and disturbed alienating parent
- the child's sense of powerlessness in an intractable parental conflict situation – in a high conflict situation the child is likely to capitalize on the conflict between the parents as a means of gaining greater control and power

- adolescents seeking freedom may use the parental alienation situation to gain greater freedom from the stricter parent.

According to researchers (e.g. Johnston, 2003; Rand, 1997; Vassiliou and Cartwright, 2001), this very often fuels the negative view that the more permissive parent holds of the other and weakens the more permissive parent's ability to control the child. The child may then engage in more acting out behaviour and worsen the already volatile situation.

PARENTS' CONTRIBUTIONS

The findings of Johnston and Rand as well as those of other researchers suggest that rejection of a parent has multiple determinants, with both the aligned and rejected parents contributing to the problem, in addition to vulnerabilities within children themselves. Johnston (2003) lists the following determinants or factors:

- the rejected parent's psychological adjustment
- the aligned parent's psychological adjustment
- marital conflict, such as family violence
- divorce, conflict and litigation
- the relationship between the rejected parent and the child
- the relationship between the aligned parent and the child
- age of the child
- the child's response to the parents (which is in turn influenced by all the other factors).

In contrast to parental alienation theory which views the indoctrinating parent as the key player in the child's alienation, Johnston concludes from her findings that the determinants of children's negative behaviour and attitudes towards a parent are manifold. In other words, both the alienating and the alienated parent are implicated in the problem, in addition to the child's own contributions.

Rejected parents, whether fathers or mothers, appear to be more influential architects of their own alienation in that deficits in their parenting capacity are more consistently and most strongly linked to their rejection by the child (Johnston, 2003). Alternatively, they have been rendered powerless, according to Johnston, to parent the child effectively by the alliance against them. On the other hand, these findings support the idea that alienating parents (mothers in particular) contribute substantially to alienating a child's affection from the father. Johnston acknowledges that because of the mother's greater involvement in childcare, she can sabotage the father–child relationship more effectively than can the father undermine the mother–child relationship.

Research in the area of cognitive development indicates that children are highly susceptible to adults' perception of reality, especially parents'. Thus, Kopetski (1998a, 1998b) has proposed that their emotional and cognitive malleability can be easily exploited by adults. The alienating parent is in a unique position to establish an 'independent thinker' relationship with their child. Namely, alienating parents and their children very often share a common delusion that one and only one other human being, the alienating parent, can provide the child with the relationship necessary for their emotional and psychological survival: 'I'm all you have got in this cruel world.' The alienating parent believes and communicates to the child that only she or those given proxy by her can be trusted. This, of course, gives her a great deal of power – much more than is the case if the child knows more than one safe, dependable, trustworthy adult. Kopetski (1998b) argues that a child who does not know that there is a nurturing someone else 'out there', separate from the symbiotic unit with the parent, can only be terrified of leaving the only safe world that, in the child's experience, does exist. The child's participation in alienation is thus easy to achieve by blurring the distinctions between myth and the reality.

FORMS, METHODS AND DYNAMICS

Although parental alienation syndrome is a relatively new concept, it has generated many studies and reviews. There is a consensus amongst researchers and commentators concerning the forms and dynamics of the syndrome (e.g. Baker, 2006; Cartwright, 1993; Dunne and Hedrick, 1994; Gardner, 1987, 1991, 1999, 2001, 2003; Johnston, 2003; Johnson *et al.*, 1985; King, 2002; Kopetski, 1998a, 1998b; Price and Poiske, 1994; Rand, 1997; Roseby and Johnston, 1998; Spruijt *et al.*, 2005; Ward and Harvey, 1993; Waldron and Joanis, 1996; Walsh and Bone, 1997; Warshak, 2000). These investigators agree that the principal characteristic of this disorder is a child's compulsive and unjustified detestation for a parent, induced by the alienating parent:

> Some tale she told me to turn me against my father – so many incidents it's simply impossible to list them all. I became my mother's puppet, her ally against my father. I grew to detest him, with a truly visceral hate. I couldn't stand to be in the same room with him, or even talk to him or have him talk to me.
>
> (Adult interviewee, quoted in Baker, 2006, p. 72)

Contrary to the common claim that the syndrome chiefly occurs in divorced families, the case quoted above took place in a non-divorced family. Regardless of the type of family in which it occurs, typically, as the above quotation shows, the child is obsessed with 'hatred' for a parent. Gardner (1999), however, uses the word *hatred* guardedly because, according to him and others (e.g. Kopetski, 1998b; Rand, 1997; Walsh and Bone, 1997), in most instances, the child still harbours many tender and loving feelings toward the 'despised' parent that they are not allowed to demonstrate, especially in the alienator's presence. Namely, an alienated child may show affection for the 'bad' parent when alone, but will never do so in the presence of the 'good' parent. Walsh and Bone regard this chameleon character of the syndrome as a diagnostic hallmark.

In extreme cases of the syndrome, the repugnance often spills over from the target parent to include that parent's extended family and social network: family friends and even grandparents with whom the child may previously have had warm and loving relationships become loathsome to the child. Presents, seasonal cards and postcards sent to the child by any of these individuals are rejected (unopened) or discarded, generally in the presence of the idealized parent (Gardner, 1999). In many cases, the alienating parent destroys or returns them before the child even sees them (Baker, 2005), to convince them that no one but she cares: 'Otherwise why can't your "daddy" even be bothered to write. That is not too much to ask, is it?'

The present author has witnessed this extreme form of parental alienation syndrome in an alienating family. In this particular instance, the then 13-year-old boy's hatred spilled over from his mother and her extended family and family friends to his own 9-year-old sister with whom the mother moved out of the family home. At 18 now, he still refuses to have contact with any of these individuals, including his mother and sister. Indeed, the author saw it from its embryonic stage through full-term gestation some four years before the boy's parents separated and eventually divorced, by which time the father had virtually completed his job of alienating his son – he only had to consolidate it further. This seems not to tally with Gardner's (1985, 1992, 1999, 2001) claim that the syndrome arises almost exclusively in the context of child-custody disputes. It is obviously also inconsistent with attachment theory's emphatic claim that the child–parent bond is for ever. As we will soon see, the idea of socio-genealogical connectedness offers at least a partial explanation for this apparent paradox. The consequences of parental alienation syndrome for the child's sense of socio-genealogical connectedness will be discussed in a later section. In the meantime, it must be highlighted that they warrant further research, especially given the claim that the problem is growing in western societies to the extent that it now affects 80 per cent to 90 per cent of all children in custody litigation (Gardner, 1992).

Gardner (1999) has expressed misgivings about the claim that brainwashing is a key feature of the process; that 'brainwashing and programming' are used by parents seeking to alienate their children from another parent. Seemingly in response to his concern, other investigators have identified a range of methods usually used by the alienating parent to induce alienation against the target parent, including intimidation, threat and guilt induction. They include subtle techniques: 'Oh! I was left on my own and nobody really thinks of me' (to the child on return from visitation to the father); 'buy-off', playing the victim, promises to change themselves and/or conditions, over-indulgence and permissiveness; telling the child the 'truth' about past events; and suggesting that the child or parent will experience loneliness and fear – 'I didn't bring my friends home. I felt like I was supposed to be there all the time. I felt like if I associated with anyone other than her I was betraying her' (Interviewee, quoted in Baker, 2006, p. 69).

Although the phenomenon of one parent turning the child against the other is ancient and commonplace, it has historically been not so easy to identify its mechanisms. Gardner (1991) initially identified the following eight broad signs of the syndrome.

First, the child engages in a campaign of continuing expression of antipathy towards the target parent. Gardner has observed that this is easily precipitated or triggered by professionals involved such as social workers and court officials, and is often most strong in the presence of the 'hated' parent. In interviews, the child begins to withdraw from the parent, speaks indirectly, for example: 'You tell Daddy to go away, I don't want to see him.' The child refuses presents from Daddy for fear of incurring the displeasure or even wrath of the alienating parent.

Second, there is a weak, frivolous or absurd rationalization given by the child for deprecating the lost parent. In parental alienation syndrome, the hostility of the alienating parent just never seems to be reasonably linked to the seriousness of the incidents alleged. The alienating parent often relies blithely on the child's professed refusal to see the other parent as evidence of the inadequacy of the other parent:

> A derogatory statement was made by . . . that Billy is going to be 'just like his father.' The nurse inquired as to Mr . . . 's well-being. Mrs M. related details of the recent divorce and custody litigation, and added that she would do all she could to ensure that Mr M. never gained custody of Billy. The nurse asked Billy about his relationship with his father. Billy, in adult language, stated, 'Daddy is an alcoholic and a womaniser and doesn't deserve to have children. I hate him, and never want to see him again.'
>
> (Price and Poiske, 1994, p. 9)

Third, the alienating parent persistently impresses upon the child how much better off both of them are without the target parent, such that in the end there is no question of both being of two minds regarding the target parent's 'defective' character. As far as both the alienating parent and the child are concerned, that parent is an 'alcoholic', 'drug-addict', 'rogue', in short, a completely worthless person:

> She never said anything good about him. She said he was worthless. He was an alcoholic . . . she said all these terrible things about him my whole life.
>
> (Interviewee, quoted in Baker, 2006, p. 68)

Fourth, there is contention that the decision to reject the parent is the child's own. This is referred to by Gardner (1992) as the 'independent thinker' phenomenon and is often invoked by alienating parents in court-room testimony. 'I want him to see his father but *he* doesn't want to, I will fight to the end to ensure *his* decision is respected.' However, Gardner has rightly argued that since children are not born with a genetic disposition to reject a father, such hatred is environmentally induced and the most likely person to have brought about the alienation is the mother.

Fifth, there is an almost automatic, reflexive support by the child for the loved parent. This support may flow from a belief that the loved parent is an ideal person who can do no wrong or from the child's perception of the loved parent as the weaker of the two parents who needs defending. 'She impressed upon me that my real ties were with her' (Baker, 2006, p. 69). While Gardner describes the child's support for the alienating parent as spontaneous, Baker, on the other hand, regards it as a process of identification with the aggressor. Baker's perception of the alienator is consistent with Johnston's (1994) defin-ition of post-divorce conflict. Johnston defines post-divorce conflict as verbal and physical aggression, overt hostility and distrust. According to her, conflict or 'entrenched conflict' does not necessarily mean physical violence. Rather she describes it as a relationship marked by some or all of the follow-ing parental behaviours: high degrees of anger and distrust, incidents of verbal abuse, intermittent physical aggression, ongoing difficulty in com-municating about the children's care, ongoing difficulty in co-operating, and sabotage of children's relationship with the other parent. These behaviours continue post separation, often coupled with high rates of litigation and relitigation, covert and overt hostility, an ongoing negative attitude about ex-spouse, avoidance, and unsubstantiated allegations about the ex-partner's behaviour.

Sixth, the child appears to be completely void of guilt or remorse regarding feelings of the lost parent. Gardner (1992) believes that the lack of guilt here is not simply explained by cognitive immaturity (often the case of very young children), but a statement of the degree to which children can be programmed to such points of cruelty that they are totally oblivious to the effects of their sadism on innocent victims.

Seventh, there is clear presence of borrowed scenarios. The litanies the child produces have a rehearsed, coached quality to them and often include expressions and phrases of the loved parent: 'She would be telling us what to say and I remember repeating it. For the most part, it was cursing. Some-times, she would make me say that he was a womanizer' (Interviewee, quoted in Baker, 2006, p. 77).

Eighth, finally, there is an obvious spread of the animosity towards the hated parent's extended family: 'His mother called me a brat.' Grand-parents, aunts, uncles and cousins are tarred with the same brush as the child argues that all they do is try to get him or her to 'like' the alienated parent: 'I hate them all because they are like my father.' (See e.g. Gardner,

1992, and Kopetski, 1998a, 1998b, for detailed descriptions of these symptoms.)

SEVERE CASES OF PARENTAL ALIENATION SYNDROME

Based on his in-depth experience, gained through extensive work with alienating families, Gardner (1991, 1999, 2003) has condensed the above typology into three broad categories or levels according to their severity: severe; mild; moderate. Researchers in the field have been guided by this taxonomy. The section that follows summarizes Gardner's description of severe parental alienation syndrome.

In cases of severe parental alienation syndrome, alienators are often described as experiencing some form of psychopathology (Baker, 2006; Gardner, 1991, 1992, 1999; King, 2002; Kopetski, 1998a; Warshak, 2000). They are described as hysterical or panic-stricken. These researchers describe alienators as desperate individuals who will resort to any conceivable trick (legal, illegal or backhanded) to destroy the child's relationship with the father, typically by obstructing contact. Such parents are said to be envenomed towards their ex-spouses or ex-partners. In many cases they are said to be paranoid. Baker (2006), however, describes them as having a narcissistic personality, as grandiose, extremely egocentric and void of interest in or sympathy for others. In terms of the motivation, the alienating parent is claimed to hold no value at all for the other parent; the hatred and disdain are overt. She will do anything to keep the child apart from the target parent. In extreme cases, children are enmeshed with the alienating parent such that they uphold and internalize the parent's wishes, emotions and hatred to the extent that they parrot them until they eventually come to believe that they are their own. In other words, children share fully the loved parent's devaluation of the other parent: they too believe that the target parent is a villain and scum of the earth. At this stage, children even deny ever having had positive feelings for the target parent.

Nonetheless, Baker's (2006) recent study, which involved 40 adult participants (15 men and 25 women) aged between 19 and 67 years (M = 40.5) who actively participated in parental alienation, found that the alienation is not always completely internalized, as Gardner (1991) earlier suggested. At the severe stage, many alienating parents entertain the overt belief that the target parent presents an actual risk of harm to the children. They present this belief as concrete knowledge that if the children should spend time with the target parent they would be physically or emotionally harmed (Gardner, 1991; Kopetski, 1998a, 1998b; Warshak, 2000).

OBSERVABLE ALIENATING PARENT–CHILD DYNAMICS

Kopetski (1998a, 1998b) has outlined some of the parent–child interactions that are observable when a child has been engaged in the process of parental alienation. They include the following:

- The parent communicates to the child a distorted (mainly unfavourable) perception of the target parent. The child then begins to show signs of puzzlement (or genealogical bewilderment), but progresses towards identification with the alienating parent, culminating in assuming ownership of the negatively distorted perception of the alienated parent. The child comes to accept the perception as a fact – the 'independent thinker' phenomenon.
- A child old enough to assert an opinion adamantly refuses any form of contact with the parent to be alienated. A younger child either experiences or is described by the alienating parent as exhibiting uncharacteristic emotional and/or behavioural disturbance or anger on separation from the alienating parent or on return from contact with the other parent, though often not during the visit itself.
- The parent attempts to control and deviously severs the child's relationship with the other parent through such manoeuvres as removing the child from physical proximity to the target parent (taking the child several hundred miles away) and/or engaging in repeated litigation aimed at enforcing exclusion, indefinite supervision or curtailment of contact.
- She often defends her claim to elimination of the other parent from the child's life by assaulting that parent's character, for example, by depicting him as a person of immoral and/or irresponsible, dangerous and unpredictable disposition, and alleging that the child needs protection from him. Sometimes, with the (unwitting) help of professionals involved, she may appeal to convenient psycho-social developmental theories (notably attachment theory) that may suggest damaging and lasting consequences for the child of separation from a primary carer (i.e. the alienating parent). It is sometimes justified by appeals to 'children's rights', such as the child's right to be believed literally and without question, or the right to refuse a relationship with an unwanted parent.
- The other parent's contact with the child is often discussed by the alienating parent as a reward or punishment for the target parent.
- The child's need for a relationship with two parents is belittled; to the alienating parent, the essential question is which one of the parents will remain in the child's life.

Besides these subtle (and sometimes not so subtle) techniques of manipulation employed by the alienating parent, she uses also other methods. They include: denying the existence of the target parent; branding the child as delicate and thus requiring the alienating parent's vigilance and continuous protection; creating an allegiance between the child and her in a battle with the alienated parent, and turning mundane differences into 'good/bad' or 'right/wrong' solutions; generalizing from specifics to global meanings; accusing the other parent of bullying, putting the child in the middle; attacking the target parent's character or lifestyle; telling the child the 'truth' about past events ('your father wanted you aborted'); communications or actions designed to provoke fear or anxiety in the child; intimidation, threats, or being merely overly indulgent or extremely permissive.

As the literature indicates, in most instances, alienating parents are able to achieve their purpose. Some of them will go to any lengths to ensure that the target parent is not only physically absent but, more importantly, that the children forget that they ever had a father. For example, Dunne and Hedrick (1994) describe a case where a mother repeatedly referred to her husband's 'abandonment of the family' and conducted a 'burial ceremony' during which she and the children said 'goodbye' by symbolically burying him so that the 'new family' which no longer included him could move forward. In Chapter 3, we saw a similar case in which a mother tried to obliterate every trace of happy memory that her children had of their father, including his name. In such extreme cases, portrayal of the alienating parent suggests that she would be pleased if the alienated parent were to evaporate from the face of the earth. Such alienators basically believe that absolutely nothing would be lost to the children under such circumstances (Dunne and Hedrick, 1994). It must be pointed out that parents who induce parental alienation in their children are so overwhelmed by their own negative emotions that often they are oblivious to the psychologically detrimental effects of the progressive erosion of the child's bond with the target parent. A parent who participated in one of the present author's own studies was shocked, during an interview with her, at the realization of what she had been doing to her own children.

EFFECTS ON THE CHILD

Given the extant voluminous literature on psycho-social development and child psychopathology, we hardly require new research evidence to convince us that children ideally need emotional support, comfort and warmth provided in the context of secure, safe, reliable relationships with at least one and preferably two parents for psychological growth. However, emotional dependency is not the whole story for children. Kopetski (1998a, 1998b) has pointed out that children's limited experience and perceptual abilities force them to be dependent not only emotionally but also cognitively on one or more significant adults. That is to say, children rely on adults for an understanding of both the physical and social worlds, and so are heavily influenced and moulded by adults in their immediate social milieu. Because children naturally trust fully the perceptions of parents, they normally participate in any perceptual distortion or delusion they share (Kopetski, 1998a).

Still, parenting is augmented by a whole variety of resources, by the totality of the child's eco-system, or undermined by participants in that system (Bronfenbrenner, 1979, 1992, 1999). This provides the child with a variety of potential relationships with many people, besides their birth parents. These relationships provide the child with important and valuable resources. Thus, it stands to reason that if children are given unhindered access to these different people (or systems), they are unlikely to rely solely on their parents to foster and nourish their social, emotional and psychological growth and development. These systems serve to rectify parental inadequacies or failures.

Kopetski is right to suggest that it is not individual parental mistakes that harm the development of children, but rather the exclusion of these different people from the developing child's life or world which places them at risk of becoming an emotional or psychological clone (of their parents). Such children are likely to repeat parental mistakes rather than learning from them. Kopetski (1998b) believes that a child who has access to multiple relationships with people who can help in different ways, and learns to process a variety of experiences, has a more positive outlook towards the future than those denied the opportunity of such experiences. According to her, the most important mitigating factors against sharing a distorted perception are a relationship with a different person who offers different data and interpretation. Sadly, the child of an alienating parent is often deprived of that relationship and therefore its potentially neutralizing or corrective influence.

The crucial question is: what specifically are the effects of parental alienation syndrome on the child's emotional, social, psychological functioning, identity development and mental health and, by extension, on the parties involved? General examples of the short-term consequences for the adults involved include:

- The alienator experiences 'sweet revenge' (sadistic pleasure) and the thrill of 'victory', though a pyrrhic victory in the long term.
- The target parent experiences the anguish of the loss of a child or children.
- One set of grandparents, relatives and friends is similarly affected by being dismissed.

Cartwright (1993) regards the consequences for the child as far more serious. He likens the loss experienced by the child and the magnitude of it to the death of a parent and the lost parent's relatives and friends, all in one fell swoop. Baker (2006) conducted a qualitative retrospective study involving a sample of 40 adults who experienced parental alienation as children. The results revealed seven major areas of impact:

- low self-esteem/self-hatred
- depression
- drug and alcohol abuse
- lack of trust
- alienation from own children
- divorce
- employment difficulties.

In childhood and adolescence these effects combined amount to a formidable developmental challenge. Cartwright (1993) summarizes the medium- and long-term consequences for the child under these headings: emotional and psychological; social; identity (or self-concept); mental health.

Emotional and psychological effects

As gleaned from the pertinent clinical literature, the psychological symptoms of emotional distress are seen in virtually all separated children, those of divorce being no exception. The distress usually abates when the parents are able to establish a workable routine in the child's life, such that they are permitted unobstructed, direct, frequent and predictable contact with the non-resident parent and other people (e.g. Furstenberg *et al.*, 1985). This enables the child to utilize their inner resources to cope with and exploit the strengths and limitations of the parents and other significant people in the same way as children do in ordinary families. Where such a situation prevails, the importance and impact of the separation recedes.

The psychological distress that the children otherwise experience largely stems from the malignant emotional environment in which they find themselves. The most common symptoms displayed by children in such an environment include sleep disturbances, regression in achievement of regulation of bodily functions – such as enuresis and encopresis (soiling) – academic or intellectual achievement, and behavioural and emotional difficulties, such as a lack of impulse control or emotional lability (Carr, 1999). It has also been suggested that parental alienation is a damaging and emotionally painful experience for children which if left to run its course results in and precipitates mental health problems. Thus, Lodge (1998), agreeing with others (e.g. Gardner, 1991, 1999, 2001; Owusu-Bempah, 1995), equates it with emotional abuse.

Effects on identity

Divorcing or separating parents frequently try to destroy or undermine their children's warm relationship with the other parent. In situations where the parent's efforts are marked by bizarre, severe and cyclical vilification, the children run the risk of estrangement from the alienated parent (Cartwright,

1993; Waldron and Joanis, 1996). Most researchers and child welfare professionals agree that in parental alienation the child's emotional development is stunted. Vestal (1999) for instance, claims that when a child's relationship with the target parent is abruptly brought to an end, the child's emotional development is arrested. The alienating parent's programming creates confusion in the child as a result of internalizing distorted beliefs and perceptions. In an extensive longitudinal study Clawar and Rivlin (1991) found that 40 per cent of the children developed self-hatred and guilt because they were used as an ally in the war against the rejected parent. According to Kopetski (1998a, 1998b), this is mainly due to the fact that the child's inner world is dominated by the rejection of the target parent.

In normal family circumstances, the child develops identity through a process of identification with both parents, a process that begins very early in the child's life (Erikson, 1968). Thus, the rejection of the despised parent, in terms of socio-genealogical connectedness, is a rejection of half of the child, resulting in self-loathing, fear of rejection, depression and often suicidal ideation. Clawar and Rivlin (1991) claim that these developments often are a surprise to the alienating parent and others because while the child remains alienated they may often appear mature, assertive, and self-confident. According to these investigators, this is a clear sign that the child has accepted and internalized the vile rage of the alienating parent as part of their self-concept. This, Clawar and Rivlin have argued, often combines with intense guilt over the harm done to the target parent to become a chronic feeling state. Namely, sadness and longing often accompany these and other feelings. This is consistent with the findings of Waldron and Joanis (1996) of high rates of low self-esteem, if not outright self-hatred; in their sample 68 per cent of their participants directly referenced negative self-feelings. Similarly, Baker (2005) found amongst her participants that the first source of low self-esteem was the internalization of the hatred of the target parent.

Because Baker's participants believed that the 'bad' parent was part of them (genetically as well as through an early relationship), they felt that they must be bad too. The alienating parent's rejection of the target parent was experienced as a rejection of that part of themselves that was the target parent:

> When you have somebody like my mother who is constantly sitting there telling you this person who is your dad and is part of you is such a bad person and he is going to do all these terrible things and it is like if he is so bad and I am part of him then doesn't that sort of make me like that too?
>
> (Baker, 2005, pp. 293–294)

Self-hatred also seemed to result from the alienating parents' communication to their children that the target parent did not love or want them. More than one of Baker's participants told of how an alienating parent actually saved the child from an intended abortion; one woman recalled her father describing the procedure in detail and providing graphic illustrations of aborted foetuses. One man is reported to have recalled his mother telling him that his father wanted to throw him in the river. These vivid and horrifying images planted themselves into the mind of the child as a fundamental truth (especially because the stories were repeated) about the target parent's feelings about the child.

Social effects

Besides child and adolescent behavioural problems commonly associated with parental divorce, research suggests that alienated adolescents unleash themselves from parental or adult authority sooner than other children. Alienated children of all ages show more problems with impulse control than normal, and many of them demonstrate less ability to empathize with others (except in the case of a chosen parent) than normal for the child's age (Baker, 2006; Gardner, 1991, 1999; Kopetski, 1998b). When the parental alienation syndrome includes gross distortions of reality, Kopetski argues, the child's reality-testing abilities become compromised and they acquire a licence to turn other aspects of life topsy-turvy, particularly social relations. The child's unhealthy relationship with the alienated parent often generalizes with age so that they continue to relate to others according to their distorted perception of them rather than to the reality. The child's interpersonal functioning is equally affected. Frequently, the child may become socially withdrawn, regress in social situations or be seen by others as immature (Baker, 2006; Waldron and Joanis, 1996).

In adulthood, summarizing the effects of parental alienation syndrome on the child, Waldron and Joanis (1996) aver that this syndrome is never benign; it is malevolent and intense. The degree of the severity, however, varies according to the extent of the brainwashing, the amount of time the child spends enmeshed with the alienating parent, the age of the child, the amount and quality of the support which people in the child's life provide, and the degree to which the child 'believes' the delusion. They claim that the effects run across all areas of functioning. They affirm that a dominant emotion for the child is loss, although this may not show up right away; that the effects of the loss of the parent on other aspects of adjustment are pervasive. As other separated children, alienated children have been found to underachieve academically, to have increased chance of psychological disturbance, lower self-esteem, cognitive deficiencies, high impulse control problems, school adjustment problems, higher fear and anxiety (particularly about abandonment), greater dependency, and so forth. There are also generally negative effects on sibling relationships. Roseby and Johnston (1998) have reported that, by latency, affected children present as fragmented within themselves and relationships with others. They reinforce Cartwright's summary in arguing that mental health and legal professionals must use the insight into children's responses in order to help parents reappraise their situation so that they may resolve their post-divorce disputes in the interest of their children.

Effects on mental health

Finally, the alienating parent and the child must modify their beliefs about and behaviour towards the target parent, else the child is very likely to lose one parent or the other and so will face, for the rest of life, the problems that accompany parental loss. Namely, that loss will have serious consequences for the child, especially if help is not available to them to deal with the resultant feelings of guilt, sadness and grief. According to Kopetski (1998b), for example, younger children will be vulnerable to the unmitigated pathology of the alienating parent. Walsh and Bone (1997) have observed that these children tend to become despondent, withdrawn and develop psychopathic manipulative characteristics which may be carried into adulthood. Similarly, Johnson and co-researchers (1985) and Roseby and Johnston (1998) have suggested that excessive alienation often causes or triggers mental illness in the child. These researchers have reported that one response of latency children (6–12 years) to parental conflict is to act in a diffusely disturbed manner, such as exhibiting anxiety, tension, depression and psychosomatic illness. Hence, they suggest that consideration must be given to the question of what happens in the long run to children who are alienated. Such an analysis must take into account whether the problems caused by alienation wounds will heal with time or scar the child's personality for life.

Cartwright (1993) has likewise noted that alienation can become so powerful as to precipitate other forms of mental and emotional illness with resultant maladaptive behaviour. Cartwright reports an instance in which an alienated son tried to poison his father by slipping air freshener into his stomach medicine. Childcare professionals need to be aware of this and able to identify children who are going through this process at an early stage, so that they may provide them and their parents with appropriate help and support. Professional involvement is essential, since leaving a child in such a pathological environment is most damaging and the child may frequently become anxious, isolated and depressed. In time, if proper intervention is not forthcoming, evidence suggests that the child will develop a deep and profound sense of self-hatred and shame for condemning the other parent, or even attempting patricide (Baker, 2006; Cartwright, 1993; Kopetski, 1998a, 1998b; Warshak, 2000).

The effects of parental alienation syndrome on the child are often carried into adulthood. In a qualitative study involving 38 adults who experienced PAS in their childhood, the majority (70 per cent) of the participants reported suffering from significant episodes of depression in their adult lives (Baker, 2005). They believed that their depression was rooted in early feelings of being unloved by the target parent and from the actual extended separation from the parent. One male participant explained his experience with depression: 'I feel like I have a hole in my soul. And it is not something you can physically point to and say here it is but you know it is there' (Baker, 2005, p. 296). About one third of the participants reported having serious problems with drugs and/or alcohol at some point in their lives. Some recognized that they were drawn to substance abuse as a way to escape the feelings of pain and loss they felt as young children. The following type of comments were common throughout the interviews: 'It was very painful and I started taking a lot of drugs at that time to try to block it out, not feel it.' One young man reported: 'My drug abuse had gotten pretty bad and I had to get out of there or I was going to die and I knew it. I was slowly destroying myself' (Baker, 2005, p. 297).

In many cases, the alienating parents were emotionally abusive in their attempts to subjugate the child's independent thoughts and feelings to their will. One response to this abuse was to seek solace in alcohol and drugs. For many, the realization that the alienating parent had manipulated them also led to pain, guilt and resentment. Baker believes that the emergence of these intense negative feelings coincided with attainment of late adolescence/ early adulthood, a time when there tends to be increased access to and experimentation with drugs and alcohol.

The enduring effects of parental alienation on the participants included a lack of trust in themselves and others. Sixteen of the participants spoke about their difficulty in trusting themselves and/or other people. Many of the women who were alienated from their fathers reported not trusting that a man would be able to love them. They assumed that if their father (their first male love) could not love them enough to stay involved in their lives, then they could not expect any man to find them worthy of love and commitment. One young woman succinctly summarized these feelings: 'If my father can't love me who will?' (Baker, 2005, p. 298) Another woman is reported to have narrated that she continually created conflict in her romantic relationships in order to gauge how much the man could take before he eventually rejected her. When they finally did leave, she concluded that of course it would happen; it confirmed that all men would eventually leave her, as her father did. She explained:

> It all stems from my parents' separation and I think also because I wasn't allowed to have a fruitful relationship with my father after he left. That really scarred me in my relationships with men. I keep thinking they are going to leave and I have to test them until they leave. As a result I am divorced and I find it really difficult to trust men.
>
> (Baker, 2005, p. 298)

A substantial proportion (50 per cent) of Baker's participants who were parents at the time of the study were experiencing what their own alienated parents endured – they were alienated from their children. They seemed to be repeating their early experiences of loss, rejection and feeling unloved. Not only were they unloved by a parent, but they were unloved and rejected by their own children as well. Several of the male participants remarked that they had married women similar in personality traits to their mothers (who were the alienators). To them, this is what love from a woman felt like and it was all they knew. When their marriages soured, the men became non-resident parents and subjected to the same type of rejection as their fathers. Other effects of the parental alienation mentioned by a few of the participants included problems with identity (low self-esteem) and not having a sense of belonging or roots, choosing not to have children to avoid being rejected by them, low achievement and anger and bitterness over the time lost with the alienated parent. Baker concluded that, at the time of the interview, all of the participants were aware that they had been manipulated to turn against the target parent. Although that was a painful realization, Baker sees it as the beginning of reclaiming the parent they lost and the part of themselves which loved and cherished that parent and that part of themselves: 'One participant reported that the moment he met his father for the first time in 40 years he could feel the hole in his soul closing' (p. 301).

THE IMPLICATIONS OF SOCIO-GENEALOGICAL CONNECTEDNESS

To recapitulate, parental alienation syndrome results from one parent's efforts to eliminate the other from their child's life. When the alienator has successfully inculcated the syndrome into the child, the 'bad' parent, the alienated parent, is loathed and verbally maligned, whereas the 'good' parent, the alienator, is idolized by the child. In this situation, one parent who previously had a good relationship with the child becomes the object of hate and degradation due to the alienating parent's conscious and unconscious manipulation of their minds. The alienator utilizes a variety of methods, including brainwashing or indoctrination, threat induction, as well as unconscious means, to achieve this end. To be effective, however, these techniques must combine with the child's and/or alienated parent's characteristics or contributions. A pernicious hallmark of the syndrome is the false allegation or accusation of child abuse by the child or the alienating parent against the alienated parent. The literature suggests this often happens when the alienated parent perseveres to have a relationship with the child and the alienating parent is bent on driving him away.

Parental alienation can be induced in very young children as well as those in their early teens, irrespective of the quality of the child's previous relationship with the target parent. Research indicates that children in the 7 to 12 age group whose parents are involved in high-conflict divorce are particularly vulnerable to forming strong alignments with one parent. It can involve all children in the family constellation or only one of the children. Gardner (1985, 1991) originally postulated that parental alienation is peculiar to child-custody disputes. However, more recent evidence (Baker, 2006; Cart-wright, 1993; Gardner, 2001) indicates that it can also occur in non-divorced families. It has been found that the alienator is not always the parent; it can be induced and fostered by the alienating parent's relatives.

As the literature reviewed in this chapter clearly shows, as in other forms of childhood separation, protracted alienation of the child can trigger or even cause other forms of mental health problems in the child besides the syndrome itself. It shows that its long-term consequences for the child are similar to those of adoption and donor insemination. In other words, the long-term effects of parental alienation syndrome parallel those associated with childhood separation and loss generally. The medium- and long-term difficulties commonly experienced by adopted persons and children of donor insemination include behavioural, emotional, psychiatric, identity, relationship and mental health problems. Clinical evidence indicates that alienated children share these and other problems with groups of separated children. Namely, intrinsic to their psycho-social developmental difficulties is a lack of a sense of socio-genealogical connectedness. Indeed, the fully alienated child may simply be described as experiencing 'genealogical bewilderment'. Their psychological and identity difficulties, especially, are further compounded by the fact that their disconnection from one side of their heritage, their biological, cultural and social heritage, is deliberately or unwittingly engineered and induced by a third party, by the very adults, the alienator and those around her, who profess to love the child and have their best interests at heart, by adults on whom the child relies to serve and protect their interests. Instead, these same adults feed the child with grossly negative, distorted and perniciously damaging information about the other (50 per cent) side of their total being. For example, Baker's (2005) participants attributed their feeling of low self-esteem to the fact that they were made to believe that they were bad because the 'bad' parent, the father who was in every way a substantial part of them, was despicable. This demonstrates clearly that in later years, alienated children often eventually come to realize and acknowledge the fact that they were poisoned against the other parent unjustifiably.

It cannot be stressed strongly enough that inducing parental alienation syndrome into a child (ultimately an innocent victim) or contributing to the process is a vicious, malevolent thing to do. It is inimical to the child's developmental outcomes, especially their identity development and mental health. Gardner (2001) expresses the lasting and gnawing psychological anguish of losing a parent or child through parental alienation in these sobering words:

> I consider losing a child because of PAS to be more painful and psychologically devastating than the death of a child. Death is final and there is absolutely no hope for reconciliation. Most bereaved parents ultimately resign themselves to this natural painful reality. The PAS child is still alive and may even be in the vicinity. Yet, there is little, if any contact

feasible. Therefore, resignation to the loss is much more difficult for the PAS alienated than for the parent whose child has died. For some alienated parents the continuous heartache is similar to living death.

(Gardner, 2001, pp. 101–102)

Substitute 'child' for 'parent' in the above scenario and it is nigh impossible not to empathize with a child who later realizes that they have been manipulated into such a virtually irredeemable situation by the people in whom they placed all their trust. From the child's perspective, Ward and Harvey (1993) are bold enough to assert: 'To have to choose between parents is, in itself damaging to the child, and, if the end result is the exclusion of a parent from the child's life, the injury is irreparable' (p. 2). One of Baker's interviewees endorses, somehow, Ward and Harvey's insight:

> ... I don't know whether he believed we really felt that way or not because we were saying things to him. I am hoping in my heart he knew but it must have hurt any way.
>
> (Interviewee, quoted in Baker, 2006, p. 77)

The consequences of parental alienation, a clear form of childhood separation, for the child's development and general well-being have been stressed throughout this book. We now know that it is not just adoption, divorce, donor insemination or spatial separation but severance of social-genealogical roots which poses a risk to developmental outcomes for children. Thus, to gain a deeper understanding of children's psycho-social developmental needs, any such analysis must take into account the child's need for socio-genealogical connectedness.

8 Research, policy and practice implications

It has been stressed throughout this book that Bowlby's notion of human attachment has almost supplanted other major theoretical explanations of children's psycho-social developmental needs. As such, it has heavily influenced childcare policy and practice throughout much of the world. Bowlby continued to modify his original ideas until his death in 1990. Other theorists and researchers, notably Mary Ainsworth (1967, 1989), Ainsworth and Bell (1970), Ainsworth and colleagues (1971), Robertson and Robertson (1971), Schaffer and Emerson (1964), Rutter (1981), to mention a few, joined him in refining those ideas. In spite of these efforts, it is his original ideas, especially those concerning monotrophy and maternal deprivation, which endure amongst childcare professionals, family lawyers and psychiatrists. The notion of maternal deprivation is frequently evoked in professional discourse and case conferences, particularly those concerning child custody and adoption and fostering. In these situations, professionals tend to give little or no consideration to other relevant or alternative theories or explanations. In other words, many practitioners seem to be unaware of or tend to ignore the fact that attachment theory as a whole rests on the assumption that human beings innately strive for connection with others, especially with their kith and kin. This final chapter discusses the theoretical, policy and practice implications of socio-genealogical connectedness in relation to separated children, as defined in this book.

CROSS-COUNTRY ADOPTION

One of the major concerns frequently expressed by theorists and childcare professionals as well as many others about adopted children relates to their identity. In cross-country adoption, for instance, several studies (besides those reviewed in previous chapters) have demonstrated the ill-fated consequences of the practice for the children's national, cultural, ethnic and personal identity. Some 20 years ago, Ngabonziza (1988) argued:

> The fundamental objection to inter-country adoption, even if the practice is well regulated, is that children adopted from Third World countries

will lose access to their own culture and their roots, and will have a confused identity. In addition, they will be exposed to racism, an evil which they will not meet in their country. The Western belief that a comfortable middle class home more than offsets loss of culture and positive identity, and exposure to racism, is seen as one more example of racism and colonialism at work.

(Quoted in Tizard, 1991, p. 746)

The following studies provide cases in point. One of these was carried out in Denmark (Rørbech, 1990). According to Tizard's (1991) extensive review of the pertinent literature, it is the largest study to raise issues of identity. The participants (*n* = 455) aged 18–25, had been adopted mainly from Asia, two-thirds (66.7 per cent) of them at the age of 3 or more. The study reported that of the 455 respondents hardly any of them could remember their native language, although one-third (33 per cent) could remember people and incidents, often violent, from their lives before arriving in Denmark. Concerning national, cultural and ethnic identity, almost all (90 per cent) perceived themselves to be mostly Danish, irrespective of their age of arrival in Denmark; whilst only 32 (7 per cent) wished they had remained in their own country. Two-thirds, on the other hand, denied any emotional or psychological attachment to their country of origin and the same proportion refused information about their family of origin. Tizard construes this as a sign of the respondents' alienation from their origins. Other respondents were ambivalent about their country of origin, Korea. Nonetheless, some of these found certain elements of Korean culture, such as music, appealing. One of these, a 25-year-old female, stated that she loved Korean music and often listened to it; she listened to Danish music too, but not with the same emotional intensity.

An earlier study in Germany (Kühl, 1985), using a postal questionnaire, posed similar questions to a sample of 202 cross-country adopted persons; their average age at adoption was 6 years. At the time of the study, their age ranged from 13 to 18, with just over 50 (25 per cent) over the age of 18. Unlike the Danish study, a third of the sample stated that they were fairly or very interested in their country of origin, and two-thirds expressed a wish to visit it. However, in terms of nationality or national identity, the majority expressed allegiance to Germany. Studies from other countries have reported similar findings. For example, in a US study (Feigelman and Silverman, 1983; see Tizard, 1991, for a review summary), fewer adopted Korean adolescents than younger children were found to be interested in their country of origin and proud of their racial group.

However much cross-country adopted individuals regard themselves as Americans, Finnish, Danish, Dutch, German or British, they do so at a psychological cost. Twenty-six per cent of the sample in Feigelman and Silverman's (1983) study were said sometimes to have felt uncomfortable about their appearance, and 20 per cent were said to feel ashamed of their origins. In Norway, some of Dalen and Saetersdal's (1987) young adult interviewees adopted from Vietnam by Norwegian families reported that they were made anxious by the fact that their identity was questioned. They would have preferred to conceal their racial and cultural background and to believe themselves to be native Norwegians. The Danish study reported similar findings: 21 per cent reported that they were aware that they were different from other people in general and 13 per cent felt uncomfortable about that. Most of the respondents wanted to distance themselves from the Vietnamese boat refugees. The study also noted that the cross-country adopted individuals wished to distance themselves from immigrants and two-thirds thought there should be stricter immigration policy to curb the flow of refugees and asylum seekers into Denmark (Rørbech, 1990). Obviously, these attitudes involve their denying a part of themselves. The report highlighted that some of the young people were aware of the danger and were making efforts to ward it off or minimize its effects.

Overall, the findings of the above studies, as summarized by Tizard (1991), suggest a feeling of socio-genealogical disconnectedness or discontinuity amongst a majority of the samples with their ethnic, religious, cultural and linguistic backgrounds. They also show a failure on the parents' part to assist their cross-country adopted children to 'preserve his or her identity, including nationality, name and family relations', contrary to the UN Convention on the Rights of the Child. In short, socio-genealogical disconnectedness is an inherent feature of cross-country adoption, with all its harmful psychological implications.

Efforts by some adoptive parents to foster their children's sense of continuity with their origins must be recognized; but such efforts often tend to be tokenistic (Carsten and Juliá, 2000). For instance, Tizard (1991), in her extensive review of the literature, has noted that, initially, many adoptive parents enthusiastically try to convey something of the children's culture – food, music, stories, and so forth to them. These attempts, however, tend to peter out because of the child's lack of interest. She attributes the parents' failure to preserve the children's family relations, cultural and national identity to their desire, reinforced by their peers and school, to think of themselves as American, Swedish, German, and so on; they do not welcome reminders that they are different. It is a difficult balance for the parents to maintain, especially in an all-white community. Nevertheless, her explanation may easily be construed as apologetic. Caring parents do not stop teaching their children good manners just because the child prefers to emulate the uncouth behaviour of their schoolmates; nor do they stop emphasizing to them the benefits of a balanced diet simply because they prefer burgers, like their mates do.

Even when such efforts are sustained, conveying culture indirectly through music, stories and food, they are inadequate to maintain the children's continuity with their origins. For instance, children and adolescents all over the world know the story of Robin Hood, eat at McDonald's, and listen to rap music. It would be difficult to convince anyone that these children, wherever they are and regardless of their 'racial' origin, nationality, culture or ethnicity, have an English, Euro-American or African-American identity. In short, to enable these parents to fulfil their duty, as prescribed by the UN Convention on the Rights of the Child, requires effective and sustained local policy and professional support.

In England and Wales, under the Adoption and Children Act 2002, in line with the recommendation of the Houghton Committee (1972), adopted people who have attained the age of 18 are entitled to a copy of their original birth certificate. This reflects the view which is now widely accepted and taken account of in adoption practice that an adopted child, if he or she is to develop a proper sense of identity, needs to know they were adopted and should be given information about their origins. Until then, the person's access to such information or any identifying information is severely restricted. Although the Act recognizes the adopted person's and, by extension, other separated children's need for biographical information, from the standpoint of socio-genealogical connectedness it does not go far enough. Rather, this information must be made available to the child from the moment of adoption. This, of course, would necessitate unambiguous guidelines from central government to enable courts and adoption agencies to ensure that all relevant and available information has been gathered, and that the adoptive parents are genuinely committed to feeding it to the child 'like babyfood'.

Post-adoption measures should also include ascertaining not only that the child is being provided with the information, but also that the parents do make every possible effort to update this information. Every child needs socio-genealogical information in order to establish a sense of psychological wholeness:

> Even a photo might help; everyone remarks on how similar you are to your father but in fact it is the mannerisms and not the physical characteristics they refer to. I often ask myself; who do I look like? If I had some description of my original parents it might help me to recognise myself.
>
> (Respondent, quoted in Triseliotis, 1973)

The UN Convention on the Rights of the Child sanctions cross-country adoption in cases where a child cannot be looked after by their biological family to be an acceptable way to care for a child. However, there is the proviso that 'due regard shall be paid to the desirability of continuity in a child's upbringing and to the child's ethnic, religious, cultural and linguistic background' (Article 20). Implicitly, then, the Convention acknowledges these as a human need. Hence, it confers on the child the right to 'preserve his or her identity, including nationality, name and family relations' (Article 8). From socio-genealogical connectedness perspective the practice of cross-country adoption violates the child's fundamental right in this important respect. Indeed, from this perspective it is inimical to the child's overall well-being in that it entails the severance of the child's socio-genealogical linkage.

To rectify this situation, whatever requirements apply to domestic adoption today must equally apply to cross-country adoption. However, in cross-country adoption extra efforts are needed on the part of all concerned parties to ensure the availability and provision of full and adequate biographical information to the child. Current international and national guidelines, policies and practices fail the child in this important respect: for example, by leaving a child until they are aged 18 or over to pursue such essential information. Besides its serious implications for identity formation during adolescence, in cross-country adoption the child's (or even adult's) access to socio-genealogical information is very often further impeded for various reasons; these include unregistered births, infant and child kidnapping, smuggling and trafficking. Even where such basic information as a birth certificate exists, the document is likely to have been tampered with or completely falsified, including the child's name and birthplace. It is therefore imperative that adoption agencies assure themselves 100 per cent of the adequacy and accuracy of such information before the child is placed.

Tizard (1991) has rightly suggested that, whilst children's needs are in most respects very well met by cross-country adoption, a permanent and satisfactory home in their country of origin would save them from having to cope with problems of identity and other difficulties resulting from adoption. She points out that the Third World countries such as Russia, China, Korea, Romania, Guatemala, India, from where the children come are poor but, with the exception of Ethiopia, they are not amongst the 25 poorest countries of the world. She argues, notwithstanding, that if such a home cannot be found then in almost all respects their development is likely to be more satisfactory if adopted abroad than if abandoned in their country of origin. It is difficult to subscribe to this argument. It is hard to envision how, given domestic and international political, institutional and individual will, a child cannot be found a home in their own country. In other words, given the economic and other essential resources and support, a child can be expected to develop as satisfactorily, if not better, at home if adopted by their kith and kin than they can in an alien country.

We lack the will to help these children unless they become our own possession. That is, as Hollingsworth (2003) has argued, children generally become available for cross-country adoption as a result of social structures that most people consider unjust. One is very much inclined toward Hollingsworth's position that by pretending to address these unjust social structures simply by adopting the children, especially when the adoption fulfils a desire of those who are infertile to parent, western families may be benefiting from the injustices. Many others have advanced similar arguments. For example, Triseliotis (2000) argued that a substantial part of cross-country adoption has forsaken its humanitarian principles. Instead, it has become a trade in children with scant regard paid to children's rights as set out in the UN Convention on the Rights of the Child. Arrangements under such terms do not necessarily preclude cross-country adoption in toto, but rather the concern here is that to be truly beneficial to the child it must be as open as possible and where feasible should include contact:

> ... The [child] needs to know about his origins – about his parents, for instance, the type of people they were, their appearance, any special qualities or gifts they may have had ... for the proper development of a sense of identity and in order that he and his adoptive parents may have a fuller understanding of him as an individual with his own unique combination of characteristics both inherited and acquired from his upbringing and environment.
>
> (Houghton Committee Report, quoted in Triseliotis, 1973, p. 3)

DIVORCE AND PARENTAL ALIENATION SYNDROME

The literature reviewed in previous chapters indicates the large numbers of children caught in divorce. We have seen the ease with which one or the other parent or other adults in a child's life can manipulate a child in such a situation to turn against the non-resident parent. This section summarizes research regarding ways in which this state of affairs may be avoided; it considers the kind of policy and practice necessary to achieve this.

Child custody

The 'best-interest-of-the-child standard' has traditionally been at the heart of child-custody decisions in western societies. This principle, bolstered by attachment theory, continues to be applied by courts and childcare professionals. In other words, there is an enduring presumption that the children's best interests are served by living with their mother. Bauserman (2002) has noted that the tradition of awarding custody to mothers following divorce is entrenched in western societies; so much so that until recently a father was awarded custody only under exceptional circumstance, for instance, if the mother proved exceptionally unfit to fulfil her maternal role. In recent years, however, interest in father custody has spawned considerable research. This is mirrored by burgeoning research (e.g. Bianchi and Setzer, 1986; Eggbeen *et al.*, 1996; Furstenberg and Cherlin, 1991; Garasky and Meyer, 1996; Johnson *et al.*, 1995; Stewart, 1999; Stewart-Clarke and Hayward, 1996; Warshak, 1986, 2000). This interest, combined with the increasing rate of divorce, may account for the rise in custody disputes. Given that parental alienation syndrome is an inherent feature of child-custody disputes, the important task is to consider effective ways to ensure its avoidance or to mitigate its effects on the developmental outcomes for the children involved. A helpful solution lies in well-informed, research-guided custody or residence arrangements.

Joint parental custody

From the socio-genealogical connectedness perspective, joint custody, legal or physical, would be the ideal arrangement for children of divorce. Yet not everyone sees either type of joint custody as an ideal arrangement for children in parental divorce or separation. For example, researchers and practitioners (including lawyers) who subscribe to the school of thought of Goldstein *et al.* (1973) argue that its negative aspects outstrip its benefits. The kernel of their argument is that joint custody disrupts emotional short-term and long-term stability in a child's life, and can lead to harm by exposing children to ongoing parental conflict. They consider that joint physical custody is especially destabilizing for the children because, on top of inter-parental conflict, it causes excessive disruption in the children's lives since they must oscillate between two separate households which are very often located in separate communities (e.g. Johnston *et al.*, 1989). In contrast, other researchers (e.g. Bender, 1994; Warshak, 1992) support it on the grounds that, among other things, it facilitates continuity with both parents; that is, it enables the children to maintain relationships with both parents, which in turn enhances the children's general well-being. Thus, they claim that joint custody must be the norm in most cases at least in order to preserve relationships between the child and both parents and to enhance the child's welfare after divorce.

Trust social scientists to complicate further an intrinsically complex issue. Although actual research examining the association between type of custody and children's adjustment has been limited, their findings are mixed. Whereas some writers conclude that joint custody has a positive impact on children (e.g. Bauserman, 2002; Bender, 1994; Emery, 1988; Gunnoe and Braver, 2001; Kelly, 1988; Stewart-Clarke and Hayward, 1996; Warshak, 1986, 1992, 2000), others argue that the benefits of joint custody, especially joint physical custody, have not been supported by research. For example, other researchers have reported that whether children live in joint or sole custody is unrelated to their behavioural, emotional or social adjustment; rather, children's adjustment is predicted by their age and gender, parental emotional functioning at the time of divorce, and inter-parental conflict one year after the divorce (Buchanan *et al.*, 1996; Johnston *et al.*, 1989; Kline *et al.*, 1989).

Buchanan and co-researchers (1996), in a study which involved 1500 adolescents, have classified factors affecting children's post-divorce adjustment into three categories: (a) loss of a parent; (b) inter-parental conflict; (c) diminished parenting (in which the quality of parenting from the custodial parent deteriorates, typically during the first two years after divorce). From their results, they are of the opinion that the type of custody arrangement may be less important in influencing children's adjustment than the quality of family relationships after the divorce. Namely, custody arrangements do not necessarily affect the quality of these relationships. Likewise, Maccoby and colleagues (1990) found that parents sharing custody reported greater co-operative communication, but found that custody arrangements neither systematically increased nor decreased conflict between former spouses.

Heads or tails?

In the USA, Gunnoe and Braver (2001) have argued that with over one million children experiencing parental divorce each year and the projection that over 30 per cent of children born to married parents will experience marital dissolution before their sixteenth birthday, there is an urgent need for psychologists to provide policymakers as well as parents with quality research on typical outcomes associated with various divorce provisions. Gunnoe and Braver, pursuing this rationale, used prospective longitudinal design to examine the two most common types of legal child-custody arrangements, sole versus joint custody, and their associated outcomes in various domains, including parental adjustment, inter-parental conflict, parent–child relationships, parental compliance with child support orders and children's adjustment. They compared a random sample of 254 recently separated (not yet divorced) families on 71 pre-divorce variables likely to differentiate between families awarded joint versus sole maternal custody. They identified 20 such factors. They further controlled these factors in subsequent comparisons of 52 sole maternal and 26 joint legal custody families two years post-divorce. These variables included such sample characteristics as age, level of education attained, ethnicity and religion. Summarizing their findings, Gunnoe and Braver suggested that families with joint custody had more father–child contact; lower maternal satisfaction with custody arrangements; more rapid maternal remarrying; and fewer child adjustment problems. Moreover, these effects did not appear to be moderated by level of pre-decree parental conflict. Regarding non-resident parent–child relationship, the results of the study reinforced the general belief that a good relationship with their non-custodial parent can be a major support to children who have experienced a divorce (e.g. Bisnaire *et al.*, 1990; Guidubaldi *et al.*, 1987; MacKinnon, 1989). They maintained that joint custody reduces the children's fears of abandonment and loss of love, and confirms the idea that they are not caught up in their parents' dispute; in other words, they do not have to take sides. Gunnoe and Braver stressed that in most maternal custody families, continuing contact between children and their non-custodial father plays an important role in children's, particularly boys', positive adjustment. For girls, a positive relationship with the non-resident mother was associated with competence in peer relationships.

Although other studies either support (e.g. King, 1994; Healy *et al.*, 1990) or refute this claim (e.g. Johnston *et al.*, 1989), it is supported by the findings of socio-genealogical connectedness studies (Owusu-Bempah, 1995; Owusu-Bempah and Howitt, 1997, 2000a). As in many other studies (e.g. Barn, 1993; Bianchi and Setzer, 1986; Furstenberg and Windquist-Nord, 1985; Warshak, 1986, 1992, 2000), in most mother-custody families the father's visits with his children tail off over time. Indeed Furstenberg *et al.* (1983) reported that even those of their sample who maintained contact with their children often played the mere role of 'friend' as opposed to assuming parental responsibility or being an active co-parent.

Gunnoe and Braver also assessed the quality of the relationship between non-custodial parents and their children through interviews with custodial and non-custodial parents and children. Custodial mothers reported a progressive deterioration in the father–child relationship after divorce. Compared with custodial mothers, their non-custodial counterparts reported the least conflict and most enjoyment in their relationship with their children. Gunnoe and Braver implicitly recognized parental alienation syndrome as a factor in these custodial arrangement differences. They argued that the child's identification with the same-sex parent is an important component of personality development and this identification may be more difficult to sustain when the parent is less available. They also pointed out that a resident parent's denigration of the ex-spouse can create ambivalence in the child's identification with the non-resident parent. With qualifications, they concluded from their findings:

> Our results suggest that while mothers clearly prefer sole custody [to themselves], the awarding of joint custody serves to preserve father–child relationships, facilitates mother remarrying, and deter some child adjustment problems. While we must always be mindful that there are families with characteristics that demand other types of custody arrangements, the interest of many families would appear to be served, or at least not harmed, by judicial presumption in favour of joint legal custody.
>
> (Gunnoe and Braver, 2001, p. 38)

Previously, Braver and O'Connell (1998) had availed us with their insight:

> If each parent is empowered by joint legal custody and is allowed involvement in the full variety of child rearing activities, few parents or children will be deprived. A parent overly concerned that he should see his child exactly the same amount of time as his ex-spouse becomes more of an accountant than a parent. Furthermore, this strict accounting of time can also set the stage for many future arguments ... In short, insisting upon strict equality of time spent with the child may be in the weaker parent's interest but it is rarely in the child's.
>
> (Quoted in Lye, 1999, p. 24)

One of the most recent studies carried out in an effort to adjudicate the debate surrounding sole custody versus joint custody is that of Bauserman's (2002) meta-analysis of studies on these custody arrangements. The analysis involved a total of 33 studies, 11 published and 22 unpublished studies. These studies which compared joint custody children with children in intact families dated from 1982 to 1999. Their combined sample size was 1846 sole custody and 814 joint custody children (total $N = 2660$). Bauserman hypothesized that joint custody children and intact family children did not differ in overall adjustment. Analysis of the results of these studies revealed children in joint custody to be better adjusted across multiple types of measures than children in sole (primarily maternal) custody. This difference was found regardless of type of custody (legal or physical) and remained robust and significant even when various categorical and continuous qualities of the research studies as moderators were tested. This finding is consistent with the argument made by some researchers, the pro-joint custody proponents, that joint custody is beneficial because it provides the child with ongoing contact with both parents. This lends support to Warshak's (1986) conclusion from his analyses that a preference for maternal custody is unwarranted.

Bauserman argues that the results of his study do not support claims by critics of joint custody that joint custody children are likely to be exposed to more conflict or to be at greater risk of adjustment problems due to their having to adjust to two households or feeling 'torn' between parents. Namely, joint custody arrangements do not appear, on average, to be harmful to any aspect of children's well-being, and may in fact be beneficial. Bauserman emphasizes that this suggests that courts should not discourage parents from attempting joint custody. He cautions, though, that it is important to recognize that the results clearly do not support joint custody as preferable to or even equal to sole custody in all situations. For instance, when one parent is clearly abusive or neglectful, a sole custody arrangement may be the best solution. Similarly, if one parent suffers from serious mental health or adjustment difficulties, a child may be harmed by continued exposure to such an environment.

Sole custody: father vs mother

The studies described above contradict other researchers' claims that joint custody arrangements, compared to children in intact families, have favourable, negative or no significant impact on children's adjustment after parental divorce. We need, therefore, to examine the issue further in order to determine the type of custody which promotes the children's welfare. In other words, we need to compare children's functioning in paternal versus maternal custody with regard to their identity, emotional and social development as well as their relationships with their parents. We must remember, however, that in only about one in ten (10 per cent) divorced/separated families do children reside primarily with their father. For this reason, studies comparing children's functioning in father-custody and mother-custody households have been sparse.

Warshak (1986) has grouped studies comparing the developmental outcomes of paternal custody for the children into three categories: (a) studies which look at father custody through the eyes of the parents; (b) studies which focus principally on the children's personality traits; (c) studies which assess parent and child functioning using several types of measures. (See Warshak, 1986, for a detailed review and discussion; for a more recent review and summary, see Lye, 1999.) Warshak's study revealed more favourable outcomes in children living with the same-sex parent than in children living with the opposite-sex parent. Same-sex custody children were more socially competent than children in opposite-sex custody, particularly in interactions with their resident parent: for example, they were rated more mature and co-operative and higher in self-esteem. Paternal custody girls were more likely than maternal custody girls to express separation anxiety, but this difference was not present for boys. In their projective stories, the children were much more likely to indicate a preference for custody with the parent of the same sex. Also, paternal custody girls, more than boys, expressed a wish for more visits with their mother; mother-custody boys, more than girls, expressed a wish for more contact with their father (Warshak, 1986).

The reporting of contradictory findings continues in more recent studies. For example, Guttman and Lazar (1998) found that the sex of the resident parent mattered very little for the social functioning of the children in their study. Stewart-Clarke and Hayward (1996) found in their study with a self-selected sample that paternal custody was better than maternal custody for children's well-being (especially for boys). Buchanan and co-researchers (1996) discovered in their comprehensive research only minor differences on average in adolescent adjustment in maternal, paternal or joint custody. Sitting on the fence as it were, Emery (1988) suggested that sole custody, in comparison with joint custody, may have unintended negative effects on the non-custodial parent. Emery (1988) argued that because both parents have custody while married, sole custody arrangements do not give custody to one parent so much as take it away from the other.

The legal and social systems

Many researchers (e.g. Baker, 2006; Cartwright, 1993; Vassiliou and Cartwright, 2001) of parental alienation syndrome have noted that, given the opportunity, alienated parents will go to great lengths to avoid experiencing alienation again. They continue to hope for a reunion with their children in the future. Most of them believe that persisting to maintain or re-establish contact with their children, for example, by sending letters and seasonal gifts and cards, increases the possibility of reconciliation with their children. Unfortunately for many of these parents, as we saw earlier, their cards, letters and gifts never 'arrive'. This section considers the role of the legal and social systems, childcare and mental health professionals in aggravating and perpetuating parental alienation syndrome. It also considers the role they may play either to avoid it or at least to ameliorate its effects.

In spite of its prevalence, pervasiveness and severe psychologically damaging consequences, parental alienation syndrome appears to be a very little known concept outside North America. Survey of the literature for this chapter yielded only two publications (in English) within the European Union. One of these was by an author in England (King, 2002) and the other by a group of researchers in the Netherlands (Spruijt *et al.*, 2005). The Dutch studies involved a total sample of 138, comprising divorce experts, lawyers, psychiatrists, psychologists and social workers and divorced non-resident parents. The extent of parental alienation was classified as mild or moderate. Of the respondents 58 per cent thought that parental alienation syndrome either did not or rarely did occur in the Netherlands, and 42 per cent thought it did occur. These results indicate a lack of awareness in the European Union even amongst professionals who encounter it in their daily work with children and families of the phenomenon and its pervasiveness. This is unlike the USA where a number of studies have reported its prevalence and commonplaceness. For instance, in a longitudinal study of 700 high-conflict divorce cases followed over 12 years, Bone and Walsh (1999) concluded that elements of parental alienation were present in the vast majority of the samples.

Several fingers point to the legal system for contributing to and exacerbating parental alienation syndrome, and consequently the damage it causes its victims (e.g. Cartwright, 1993; Gardner, 1991, 2001, 2003; King, 2002; Kopetski, 1998a, 1998b). These investigators and practitioners argue that the prolonged involvement of lawyers and the courts contributes not only to the development of the syndrome but also to its protraction and increase in severity. They claim that the adversarial system renders itself easily to being manipulated or exploited by one or both parents, and failing to find a solution. They make the observation that frequently in custody disputes a deadlock is reached whereby the parent who currently has custody of the children retains sole control of them, despite the fact that the other parent is capable of and willing to be actively involved in their parenting.

The simplest solution to this problem would be to avoid court involvement completely. However, it appears that most practitioners (outside North America) are ignorant of this phenomenon. The resistance of those who are aware fades when the temptation to attribute parental alienation syndrome to brainwashing beckons. This is understandable because the child disobeys even a court order for contact with the alienated parent; instead she or he expresses hostility, hatred and disdain towards him. The father then hastily accuses the mother of brainwashing; the mother promptly denies and resorts to counter-recrimination, oftentimes in the form of child abuse and/or neglect (Gardner, 1999; Johnston *et al.*, 2005). In no time, this creates a vicious circle. In other words, because of the child's witting or unwitting role in parental alienation, it is very often considered by one parent to be the result of parental alienation, indoctrination, and the other to be the result of bona fide abuse or neglect. In such a situation, one can only sympathize with the courts for exercising caution since a hasty decision can, in certain cases, easily result in even more detrimental consequences for the child.

To help courts and practitioners separate 'the wheat from the chaff', Gardner (1991) has provided a series of legal and therapeutic measures. His recommendations to the courts include:

- imposing court-ordered increased contact between the alienated parent and the child, or curtailment of the alienated or alienating parent's contact with the child
- transfer of primary custody from the resident alienating parent
- court-ordered therapy
- imposing bond or fines, community service, probation, house arrest
- in extreme cases, custodial sentence for the alienating parent.

Gardner (2001) followed up 99 cases in which he made recommendations to the courts. In all, his recommendations were implemented by the courts in 22 of those cases. At follow-up, alienation had ceased or significantly reduced in all (100 per cent) of the 22 cases. In the remaining 77 cases, only in 7 of them (9 per cent) had alienation reduced in any significant manner. On the basis of these findings, Gardner boldly concluded:

> The study provides confirmation of my longstanding observation that the most potent therapeutic measure that one can utilize for PAS children is reduction of their access to the alienating parent. In some cases the reduction requires custodial transfer. In others, reduction of the alien-ator's access time may prove effective. And only the courts have the power to such reduction of access.
>
> (Gardner, 2001, p. 100)

Gardner is emphatic that in order to effectively combat parental alienation syndrome the parent–child bond, whatever its strength, must be exploited to the maximum. He is convinced that the bonding which the child has with the alienated parent is potentially the most powerful preventive of parental alienation syndrome, and a very powerful antidote to parental alienation symptomatology in many cases. In his opinion, formed through extensive experience, traditional therapy is of little if any value for the vast majority of alienating families. In fact, he is convinced that for most it makes them worse, because traditional therapists usually do just the opposite to what alienated children need.

Alternative to legal sanctions: mental health professionals

There are alternatives to legal sanctions, one of them being appropriate therapy. Warshak (2000) sees one of the central goals of therapy with chil-dren in alienating families as to help them to recognize and accept that they do not have to choose one, to appreciate that they have two parents and not one parent. To the point, therapists should try to help them to appreciate the benefits of avoiding an exclusive alliance with one parent, and work with the parents at the same time not to sabotage the children's loyalty to them. Achieving this objective is no simple task. That is, even though alienated children are frequently referred to mental health professionals, Kopetski (1998b) argues that they do not always receive appropriate help. She suggests that in order to be helpful psychotherapy must be based upon accurate diagnosis. She acknowledges, however, that alienating parents habitually counteract accurate assessment of the children's needs because they have decided on their own diagnosis long before they enter therapy with their children. Thus, they are adamant, according to Kopetski, when there is even the slightest intimation that the child's symptoms could be due to anything other than what they have assigned. They fiercely object to any such insinuation as utterly preposterous. The alienating parent will select or co-operate only with a therapist whose expertise falls in the area of assessing or treating the problem the parent has already 'diagnosed'. Kopetski fears that such therapists may even deliberately limit their assessment to comply with the contract, to satisfy the parent. She believes that therapists who have the ability and interest in providing thorough and objective assessments can be helpful. She notes, however, that conclusions and interventions which do not match the opinion of the alienating parent are often sabotaged, and the therapists who have them are discharged or not consulted in the first place.

Ward and Harvey (1993) have outlined three principles regarding child development that must guide professional work with alienating families:

1   All litigation concerning children can affect their health, growth and development negatively; the greater the acrimony and the greater part that the children need or are asked to play in the litigation, the greater the potential for harm.
2   It is psychologically harmful to children to be deprived of a healthy relationship with one parent.
3   With the exception of abuse, there is no good reason why children should not want to spend optimum time with each of their parents, and even with abuse, most children still want to maintain some relationship with the abusive parent.

Ward and Harvey put the onus on concerned adults, the parents, the professionals and the courts, to ensure that such contact is possible under auspicious circumstances. They see part of the therapist's role in facilitating this as identifying the reason for a child's rejection of their parent, and to determine whether or not it is the product of a process of parental alienation syndrome. According to these investigators, this psychological evaluation, to be used as the integral part of the therapeutic plan, must go beyond the identification process. It must be directly oriented toward the motives of all family members, the defence factors or functions of parental alienation syndrome in the family, and the specific techniques and patterns involved.

On these principles, and also because of the difficulties often encountered in therapeutic work with alienating families, Gardner (1998) has recommended therapeutic intervention in all instances of parental alienation syndrome, regardless of its severity, whether a case is assessed as mild, moderate or extreme. The aims of such intervention, as outlined by Gardner, should include: (a) making the alienating parent aware of the changes in his or her perception of the child and child development, as well as the reasons underlying these changes; (b) furnishing the parent with relevant (educational) information; (c) making the link between these factors and events occurring in his or her life. Gardner defines successful therapeutic intervention of parental alienation syndrome, whether its goals have been achieved, as the maintenance of some contact between the alienated parent and the child. Furthermore, he recommends a preventive psychological measure for custodial parents. He suggests this measure principally because, following a bitter custody case, the parent in whose favour a decision has been made may need a certain kind of psychological help in order to prevent or minimize the possibility of her vindictiveness which is very likely to worsen the development of the problems to which children have already been subjected.

To back up such intervention, Walsh and Bone (1997) advocate for a strict policy of not criticizing parents in the presence of the children; they regard this as a critically important first step. In this endeavour, they see mental health professionals as having a central role. These professionals can, for example, encourage divorcing parents to refrain from open hostility and criticism. Walsh and Bone rightly emphasize that respect and admiration for both parents is important for the child's healthy emotional development. They suggest that therapeutic intervention must, therefore, include helping the parents to acknowledge the importance and value of giving an accurate picture of the other parent's 'assets and liabilities', and of answering the child's questions in simple, unambiguous language with honesty tapered by discretion, and refrain from brutal honesty, or providing them with negatively distorted information about the other parent.

The evidence examined so far indicates clearly that the syndrome is seriously harmful to both children and parents. It indicates also that parental alienation cases pose a particularly difficult challenge to lawyers and mental health professionals attempting to help families negotiate divorce. To meet this challenge effectively, Johnston (2003) stresses the need for therapeutic interventions which are family focused and include all parties involved in the process – the child and both the aligned and rejected parents.

Parental alienation syndrome mainly involves purging the child's memory of any enjoyable relationship with the alienated parent and replacing it with negative feelings. The alienating parent, using both overt and subtle means, achieves this by cyclically feeding the child with nothing but the most damaging information about the other parent. The degree of the severity, however, depends on the extent of the brainwashing, the amount of time the child spends enmeshed with the alienating parent, the age of the child, and the degree to which the child believes the damaging information. Socio-genealogical connectedness predicts that the greater and more favourable the knowledge children possess about their birth parents, the deeper their sense of connectedness and, therefore, the better adjusted they are. Intervention based upon socio-genealogical connectedness would, therefore, involve the following:

- re-establishing contact between the child and the alienated parent
- reducing the time the child is enmeshed with the alienating parent
- providing the child with counter-information about the alienated parent, in order to neutralize the negative feelings she or he harbours towards that parent; and to facilitate the child's incorporation of the positive aspects of that parent
- the alienated parent spending more time and engaging in enjoyable leisure activities with the child, especially spending holidays together
- educating both parents about the damaging psychological and emotional effects of PAS on the child and on themselves.

Achieving this important goal obviously calls for collaborative work between mental health and legal professionals. The necessity for a family-focused and professionally collaborative approach is demonstrated by the evidence that all family members, the courts and social workers wittingly and/or unwittingly contribute in various ways to the development and maintenance of parental alienation syndrome (e.g. Cartwright, 1993; Gardner, 1991, 1999, 2001; Johnston, 2003; Kopetski, 1998a). Thus, it is essential that the courts and professionals recognize and support healthy family systems. To this end, Ward and Harvey (1993) have suggested that lawyers, courts and childcare professionals work together by combining their knowledge and expertise. It is, therefore, important for the courts and professionals to recognize and support healthy family systems, and not to aggravate an already explosive situation further:

> Lawyers are available and have access to the legal process, but do not have a system of understanding. Attorneys can easily become part of a divorce impasse system, aggravating an already inflamed system. Mental health professionals must have a systems understanding and are available but do not have the power of the court or ready access to the legal process. A partnership is essential.
>
> (Ward and Harvey, 1993, p. 17)

Participation and protection of the child in custody decisions is particularly essential (Kaltenborn, 2001; Kaltenborn and Lempp, 1998). Kaltenborn (2001) has argued that, to be complete, this partnership must include the ultimate victims of divorce and parental alienation, the children. He argues that although children's views, wishes and rights receive increasing attention in the social sciences and in legal statements, their participation and protection in custody decision-making is still a difficult and controversial topic, often discussed passionately in legal reforms. He points out that in the USA, for instance, evidence shows that the reality for many children, to a variable degree in each state, differs from legal statements. He cites Skolnick's (1998) claim regarding the minor role of the child in the courtroom and quotes a family court judge addressing this issue with the words: 'The single biggest failing in our system today is that the voice of the child is not heard. That goes for adoption cases and custody' (Skolnick, 1998, quoted in Kaltenborn, 2001, p. 84).

Consideration of Kaltenborn's and Ward and Harvey's suggestions may go some way towards addressing the question: 'Heads or tails?' Namely, the success of custody decisions depends on consideration of the children's needs and preferences. Hence, the participation of the child in custody decision-making is essential and should be guaranteed by appropriate substantive and procedural laws and court practice. Kaltenborn warns that while we accept that children are active and competent participants in legal custody disputes, they can also be misused by parents or other adults for their own interests and may suffer as a result of inappropriate custody arrangements. He recommends, therefore, that the results of custody and adjustment studies be communicated more widely to judges, lawyers, social workers, counsellors and other mental health professionals involved in divorce counselling and litigation, as well as divorce researchers. Such communication could lead to better informed policy decisions based on research evidence and better informed decision-making in individual cases.

DONOR INSEMINATION

> The inability to know one's genetic origin leaves a void that deprives one of a sense of wholeness.
>
> (Respondent, quoted in Baran and Pannor, 1993, p. 85)

Despite the parallel experiences of adopted children and the offspring of donor insemination, there is still a reluctance to accept the importance of socio-genealogical information to the identity and mental health of children resulting from the practice. Like most things in life, we can easily find justification for actions we want to take. By the same token, we can, in most cases, easily conjure up excuses for our inactions. Namely, little doubt is expressed when it comes to the importance of socio-genealogical knowledge (or parental contact) for the developmental outcomes for adopted children and those separated from their parent through divorce. Yet, with regard to donor-insemination children, we frequently encounter excuses in the form of questions, hypotheses or statements such as: 'What really is best for a child when it comes to disclosure versus non-disclosure?' 'We have no controlled studies comparing children who have been told with children who have not.' Research on contact and openness in donor insemination is still too limited, anecdotal and imprecise (i.e. 'unscientific'). These reservations are in disregard of the compelling and often disturbing evidence from those affected themselves about disclosure versus non-disclosure (e.g. Baran and Pannor, 1993; Blyth, 2002; Blyth *et al.*, 2001; Ehrenshaft, 2005; Ethics Committee of the American Society for Reproductive Medicine, 2004; Turner and Coyle, 2000). McWhinnie (2000) has noted that researchers tend to concern themselves with such questions as: Does secrecy in DI families matter? Does the fact that the perceived father is not the biological father impact adversely on the child or on the father's relationship with the child? Does the cover-up situation present particular psychological problems and/or ethical dilemmas that the parents, and more particularly the children, have to deal with? Does that rebound on the child and affect his or her well-being, both during the growing-up years and later in adulthood?

Research concerning the identity and mental health implications of donor insemination aside, if we extrapolate the results and findings of research in the adoption field and divorce, then the answer to each of the above questions is in the affirmative. McWhinnie (2000) has reported a series of studies involving families created by in vitro fertilization and donor insemination which support this conclusion. Overall, the research suggests that for families where donated gametes are used, the psychological and ethical issues for the children and their parents are stark, and that they also last a lifetime. Endorsing Baran and Pannor's (1993) suggestions, she recommends that more consideration be given to these implications at the very beginning of 'treatment'. She recommends also that the whole question of children's need to have factual information about their origins be addressed. Furthermore, she argues that without such an approach, we are acquiescing in ignoring the rights and needs of dependent, vulnerable children and that they are being used instrumentally to fulfil the needs and wishes of adults. Other studies (e.g. Blyth, 2002; Blyth *et al.*, 2001; Landau, 1998; Owusu-Bempah, 1993, 1995; Owusu-Bempah and Howitt, 1997, 2000a; Warnock, 1987) support McWhinnie's further claim that not having or making available to them information about their donor father or donor mother is flying in the face of the spirit of Articles 7 and 8 of the United Nations Convention on the Rights of the Child. The relevant phrase in Article 7 is 'as far as possible the right to know . . . his or her parent'. Article 8 states: 'the right of the child to preserve his or her identity'. The central question to be addressed, therefore, is when and how much openness is necessary. This is, of course, a matter not just for the parents and researchers but equally for policymakers and childcare professionals.

Within the community of researchers and clinicians, it is now commonsense that the lack of knowledge of one's genetic origins that is implicit in donor anonymity has psycho-social implications, since our genetic heritage is part and parcel of our identity. This is evinced by research and clinical experience showing that, like adopted persons, increasing numbers of children born as a result of donor insemination have been seeking out their biological parents in order to find out more about who they are. Such research indicates that searching is not just triggered by uncertainty about whether there are genetic problems in the background, it is more for a feeling of psychological and mental stability. As we saw earlier, those who enquire about their origins fare better if they are given the information than if they are left in the dark. In short, both research and professional experience from the adoption field, accumulated over the last 80 years (since the Adoption Act 1926 in England and Wales), should serve as a beacon to guide research, policy and practice regarding the socio-genealogical needs of children conceived through donor insemination, and also to respect their rights and promote their mental health.

What, when and how much to tell?

To recapitulate Korntzer's (1971) analogy, in ordinary families socio-genealogical information is fed to the child like 'babyfood'; the timing, amount and manner of its provision to the offspring of gamete donation should not be different. In other words, what, when and how much background information one provides to any child, regardless of the method of their conception, should largely be determined not so much by the child's chronological age but rather by the degree and extent of their hunger or need for it. So, telling a child merely that they are a donor child is not sufficient to fulfil their socio-genealogical need at any stage; as full information as possible is required and it is the parent's duty to fulfil this basic human urge. However, in the UK, for instance, research shows that the degree of openness varies with the status of the recipients: in heterosexual couples, the very fact of donor insemination is usually accompanied by secrecy and deception; in lesbian couples and families of lone parents by choice, on the other hand, the fact of the insemination is generally revealed to the child, but the donor's identity is unknown to all concerned (Blyth *et al.*, 2001; McWhinnie, 2000). Whatever the status of the parents, a child in a donor-insemination family is born into a situation of either false or missing paternal identity.

Recent research in Sweden (Gottlieb *et al.*, 2000), the first country to grant donor offspring legal access to the identity of their donor, supports findings of studies concerning the parents' reticence or unwillingness to inform their children of their origins. The study also shows that legislative mandate alone is insufficient to ensure that the children will ever learn the identity of their donor or, indeed, discover the true nature of their conception, because a large proportion of parents of donor offspring in the study indicated their unwillingness to tell their children about their origins. Such reluctance has been consistently highlighted in studies undertaken in different countries and different eras, as we saw in Chapter 6. These studies suggest that only those parents who have come to terms with their own infertility, who can fully and candidly accept that donation or indeed adoption is a bona fide method of establishing a family, can deal adequately with 'telling' (Snowden and Snowden, 1993). Even then, they need to accept that 'telling' is not enough; they must also appreciate that biographical information is the raw material from which identity is developed, and forms the basis of their own identity. In short, it is clear from research and professional experience that parents do need not only professional guidance and help to address these issues, but also, as in adoption, a degree of formal guidelines and enforcement of the rights of the child.

Policy

In the UK, following the recommendations of a Committee of Inquiry chaired by Mrs (Baroness) Mary Warnock, the government published the Human Fertilization and Embryology Bill in 1989 which was enacted in 1990. The Committee's remit was to consider, inter alia, the then current and potential developments in medicine and science related to human fertilization and embryology, policies and safeguards to be applied, including consideration of the social, ethical and legal implications of these developments. Lost in these terms of reference are the psychological implications of these developments and their application. Issues of rights to personal biographical information and identity, necessary for the establishment of a sense of socio-genealogical connectedness, were completely eschewed both in the Bill and the Act itself. Concerned researchers and practitioners have pointed out that, in the interests of the child born as a result of gamete donation, this situation must be fully rectified. In Blyth's (2002) words: 'Unless we believe that donor-conceived people should be satisfied with simply having been given the opportunity of life, it is evident that the status quo fails to do justice to their rights' (p. 190).

In line with the UN Convention on the Rights of the Child, most national governments have accepted the primacy of the rights of *all* children, regardless of ethnicity, gender, religion, class, and so forth. These rights include the right to identity and socio-genealogical information. In the UK, for instance, the Adoption and Children Act 2002 incorporates a basic assumption that adopted people will be informed of their origins and that adoptive parents should be assisted to provide their adopted child with information about their background. All that is required is for this policy to be extended fully to include children conceived through gamete donation, to grant them the right to learn the identity of their donor, to respect their right to fulfil their socio-genealogical need. Similarly, Daniels and Taylor (1993) have questioned the principle and practice of secrecy in donor insemination and have urged parents, professionals and policy makers to re-examine their views about the need for maintaining secrecy in this area. The above suggestions are evocative of the assertion by Snowden and colleagues (1983):

> If we really believe that it is the child who is our primary concern, then the whole issue of keeping that child in ignorance of his or her true origins and of setting up procedures to ensure that such ignorance is maintained needs to be examined carefully.
>
> (p. 79)

Taking a leaf out of Snowden *et al.*'s book as it were, the Warnock Committee implicitly upheld a child's right to and need for complete socio-genealogical information:

> The child is being used as a means to the parents' ends, namely to have, or seem to have a 'normal' family; and I do not think that using one person as a means to another's ends can ever be right, unless the person has consented to be so used . . . I cannot argue that children who are told their origins, if they are [DI] children are necessarily happier, or better off in any way that can be estimated. But I do believe that if they are not told, they are being wrongly treated.
>
> (Quoted in Daniels and Taylor, 1993, p. 160)

This duty and the Act's requirements on treatment centres clearly indicate the popular belief inherent in the Act that a failure to meet a child's need for socio-genealogical knowledge, due to anonymity and secrecy about their origins, may have adverse consequences for the child. The Act in its present form, however, is weak in ensuring that these conditions are fulfilled. Even in countries such as Sweden, Switzerland and the Netherlands which have legally abolished donor anonymity, there is evidence to suggest that a large proportion of donors remain anonymous. For example, recent research in Sweden (Gottlieb *et al.*, 2000), the first country to grant donor offspring legal access to the identity of their donor, indicates that a change in legislation is of itself insufficient to ensure that the children will invariably learn the identity of their donor or, indeed, discover the true nature of their conception. Howe and Feast (2000) have argued that in the UK the development of adoption contact registers offers guidance for practice, not only in relation to the statutory Register of Information established by the Human Fertilization and Embryology Act, but also for the establishment of a voluntary Donor Offspring Contact Register. Such a register will, however, remain ineffectual for as long as donors hold the right to decide whether or not they will provide the necessary information. In short, in the best interests of the offspring and to respect their rights, the decision regarding contact must be with the child and not the donor or the parents. In the words of an English judge:

> It is to my mind entirely understandable that AID children . . . should wish to know about their origins and in particular to learn what they can about their biological father or, in the case of egg donation, their biological mother. The extent to which this matters will vary from

individual to individual. In some cases ... the information will be of massive importance. I do not find this at all surprising bearing in mind the lessons that have been learned from adoption. A human being is a human being whatever the circumstances of his conception and an AID child ... is entitled to establish a picture of his identity as much as anyone else.

(Quoted in Blyth, 2002, p. 185)

FUTURE DIRECTIONS

Miller (1999) has noted that no one approach to understanding child development is going to sweep the board, to render earlier ones obsolete. She suggests rather that the success of any new approach is to be judged by the extent to which it can be integrated with previous ones. It is legitimate, therefore, to ask where the potential contributions of socio-genealogical connectedness are likely to lie. Following Miller's suggestion, the most exciting advances are likely to emerge from eclecticism, a marriage between perspectives or approaches in the field. She suggests attachment theory as an example. She rightly points out that Bowlby integrated his psychoanalytic background with ethology and systems theory, as well as incorporating elements from other areas of psychology. For instance, Ainsworth added the insights of a developmental psychologist as well as the strange situation technique. Socio-genealogical connectedness may thus be regarded as an eclectic approach to psycho-social development, an integration of attachment theory and related concepts, such as the notion of the self-concept and eco-system perspective, rather than an alternative to them. Namely, it crosses and crisscrosses the innate cultural, social and individual levels of complexity; it takes into account the exogenous forces or factors which interact to shape the developing child and ultimately his or her personality or identity.

Miller has suggested that a theory serves two principal functions: to stimulate and to interpret data. In this context, traditional learning theory, with its emphasis on drive reduction, guided the selection of the original variables in 1960. In later years, as new theories emerged, investigators interpreted the data first in terms of Skinnerian operant learning (early 1970s), then social learning (mid-1970s), and finally cognitive theory (mid-1980s). Thus, in these four phases of learning-theory development, investigators sought the causes of aggression in frustration (drive reduction), reinforcement of aggression (Skinner), aggressive model (social learning), and finally the child's attitudes and interpretation of potential instigators of aggression (or cognition; Miller, 1999). It is hoped that the notion of socio-genealogical connectedness will provoke thought and point to new ways of interpreting data concerning the socio-psychological developmental needs of separated children of the world. Regarding parental alienation syndrome, adoption and gamete donation, for example, it has already pointed to new ways of understanding and helping affected children and their families. Still, one would expect the present thesis to raise more theoretical, policy and practice questions than it answers.

Bibliography

Abramsom, A. (1990). Ethics and technological advances: contributions of social work practice. *Social Work in Health Care*, 15 (2), 5–17.

Ainsworth, M. (1967). *Infancy in Uganda: Infant Care and the Growth of Love*. Baltimore: Johns Hopkins University Press.

Ainsworth, M. (1989). Attachments beyond infancy. *The American Psychologist*, 44, 709–716.

Ainsworth, M. and Bell, S. (1970). Attachment, exploration and separation: illustrated by the behavior of one-year-olds in a strange situation. *Child Development*, 41, 49–67.

Ainsworth, M., Bell, S. M. and Stayton, D. J. (1971). Individual differences in Strange-Situation behaviour of one-year-olds. In H. H. Schaffer (ed.). *The Origins of Human Social Relations*. London: Academic Press, pp. 17–52.

Ainsworth, M. and Eichberg, C. (1991). Effects on infant–mother attachment of mother's unresolved loss of an attachment figure, or traumatic experience. In C. M. Parkes, J. Stevenson-Hinde and P. Marris (eds). *Attachment Across the Life Cycle*. London: Routledge.

Akin-Ogundeji, O. (1991). Asserting psychology in Africa. *The Psychologist: Bulletin of the British Psychological Society*, 4, 3–4.

Allison, P. D. and Furstenberg, F. F. (1989). How marital dissolution affects children: variations by age and sex. *Developmental Psychology*, 25, 540–549.

Amato, P. R. (1987). Family process in one-parent, step-parent, and intact families: the child's point of view. *Journal of Marriage and the Family*, 49, 327–337.

—— (1991). Parental absence during childhood and depression in later life. *Sociological Quarterly*, 32 (4), 543–556.

—— (1993). Children's adjustment to divorce: theories, hypotheses, and empirical support. *Journal of Marriage and the Family*, 55, 23–38.

—— (1996). Explaining the intergenerational transmission of divorce. *Journal of Marriage and the Family*, 58, 628–640.

—— (1999). Parental involvement and children's behavior problems. *Journal of Marriage and the Family*, 61, 375–384.

—— (2000). The consequences of divorce for adults and children. *Journal of Marriage and Family*, 62, 1269–1287.

—— (2001). Children of divorce in the 1990s: an update of the Amato and Keith (1991) meta-analysis. *Journal of Family Psychology*, 15, 355–370.

Amato, P. R. and Booth, A. (1991). The consequences of parental divorce and marital unhappiness for adult well-being. *Social Forces*, 69, 895–914.

Amato, P. R. and Gilbreth, J. G. (1999). Nonresident fathers and children's well-being: a meta-analysis. *Journal of Marriage and the Family*, 61, 557–573.

Amato, P. R. and Keith, B. (1991a). Parental divorce and the well-being of children: a meta-analysis. *Psychological Bulletin*, 110, 26–46.

—— (1991b). Parental divorce and adult well-being. *Journal of Marriage and the Family*, 53, 43–58.

Amato, P. R. and Ochiltree, G. (1987). Child and adolescent competence in intact, one-parent, and step-families: an Australian study. *Journal of Divorce*, 10, 75–96.

Amato, P. R., Loomis, L. S. and Booth, W. A. (1995). Parental divorce, marital conflict and offspring well-being during early adulthood. *Social Forces*, 73, 895–915.

American Psychiatric Association (APA, 1994). *Diagnostic and Statistical Manual of Mental Disorders, DSM-IV.* Washington, DC: APA.

Anthony, E. J. (1974). Children at risk from divorce: a review. In E. J. Anthony (ed.). *The Child and his Family: Children at Psychiatric Risk*. New York: Wiley.

Auer, G. J. (1983). Contact with the absent parent after separation or divorce. *International Journal of Family Psychiatry*, 4, 95–140.

Austin, R. L. (1978). Race, father-absence, and female delinquency. *Criminology: An Interdisciplinary Journal*, 15, 487–504.

Bach, G. (1946). Father fantasies and father-typing in father separated children. *Child Development*, 17, 63–80.

Bagley, C., Young, L. and Scully, A. (1993). *International and Transracial Adoptions*. Aldershot: Avebury.

Baker, A. J. L. (2006). Patterns of parental alienation syndrome: a qualitative study of adults who were alienated from a parent as a child. *American Journal of Family Therapy*, 34, 63–78.

Baker, M. J. L. (2005). Long-term effects of parental alienation on adult children. *American Journal of Family Therapy*, 33, 298–302.

Baldwin, J. A. (1979). Theory and research concerning the notion of black self-hatred: a review and interpretation. *Journal of Black Psychology*, 5, 51–77.

Bandura, A. (1992). Social cognitive theory. In R. Vasta (ed.). *Six Theories of Child Development: Revised Formulations and Current Issues*. London: Jessica Kingsley Publishers, pp. 1–60.

Baran, A. and Pannor, R. (1993). *Lethal secrets: the psychology of donor insemination – problems and solutions*. New York: Amistad.

Baran, A., Pannor, R. and Sorosky, A. (1975). Secret adoption records: the dilemma of our adoptees. *Psychology Today*, 9, 38–42.

Barn, R. (1993). *Black Children in the Public Care System: Child Care Policy and Practice*. London: Batford.

Bauserman, R. (2002). Child adjustment in joint-custody versus sole-custody arrangements: a meta-analytical review. *Journal of Family Psychology*, 16, 91–102.

Beaston, J. and Taryan, S. (2002). Predisposition to depression: the role of attachment. *Australian and New Zealand Journal of Psychiatry*, 37, 219–225.

Bender, W. N. (1994). Joint custody: the option of choice. *Journal of Divorce and Remarriage*, 21, 115–131.

Berry, J. W. (1983). The sociogenesis of social sciences: an analysis of the cultural relativity of social psychology. In B. Brian (ed.). *The Sociogenesis of Language and Human Conduct*. New York: Plenum.

Bharat, S. (1988). Children of single-parents in a slum community. *Indian Journal of Social Work*, 49, 367–376.

Bianchi, S. M. (1995). The changing demographic and socio-economic characteristics of single-parent families. In S. Hanson, M. Heims, D. Julian and M. Sussman (eds). *Single-Parent Families: Diversity, Myths, and Realities*. New York: Haworth Press, pp. 71–98.

Bianchi, S. M. and Setzer, J. A. (1986). Life without father: children of divorce. *American Demographics*, 8, 43–49.

Bilson, A. and Baker, R. (1992–93). Siblings of children in care or accommodation: a neglected area in practice. *Practice*, 6, 307–328.

Bisnaire, L. M., Firestone, P. and Rynard, D. (1990). Factors associated with academic achievement in children following parent separation. *American Journal of Orthopsychiatry*, 60, 67–76.

Blechman, E. A. (1982). Are children with one-parent at psychological risk? A methodological review. *Journal of Marriage and the Family*, 44, 179–195.

Bloom, P. (1957). Artificial insemination. *Eugenics Review*, 48, 205–207.

Blyth, E. (1999). The social work role in assisted conception. *British Journal of Social Work*, 29, 727–740.

—— (2000). Sharing genetic origins information in third party assisted conception: a case for Victorian family values? *Children and Society*, 14, 11–22.

—— (2002). Information on genetic origins information in donor-assisted conception: is knowing who you are a human rights issue? *Human Fertility*, 5, 185–192.

—— (2004). Anonymity in donor-assisted conception and the UN Convention on the Rights of the Child. *International Journal of Children's Rights*, 12, 89–104.

Blyth, E., Crawshaw, M., Hasse, J. and Spiers J. (2001). Implications of adoption for donor offspring following donor-assisted conception. *Child and Family Social Work*, 6, 295–304.

Blyth, E. and Farrand, A. (2004). Anonymity in donor-assisted conception and the UN Convention on the Rights of the Child. *International Journal of Children's Rights*, 12, 89–104.

Bone, J. M. and Walsh, M. R. (1999). Parental alienation syndrome: how to detect it and what to do about it. *Florida Bar Journal*, 73, 44–48.

Bonnerjea, L. (1994). Disaster, family tracing and children's rights: some questions about the best interests of separated children. *Disasters*, 18, 277–283.

Bowlby, J. (1944). Forty-four juvenile thieves: their characteristics and home-life. *International Journal of Psychoanalysis*, 25, 19–53.

—— (1951). *Maternal Care and Mental Health*. Geneva: World Health Organization.

—— (1969). *Attachment and Loss: I. Attachment*. London: Hogarth Press

—— (1973). *Attachment and Loss: II. Separation Anxiety and Anger*. London: Hogarth Press.

—— (1980). *Attachment and Loss: III. Loss, Sadness and Depression*. New York: Basic Books.

—— (1988). *A Secure Base: Clinical Application of Attachment Theory*. London: Routledge.

Bradshaw, J. and Millar, J. (1987). The living standard of lone-parent families. *Quarterly Journal of Social Affairs*, 3, 233–252.

—— (1991). *Lone-Parent Families in the UK: DSSs Report No. 6*. London: HMSO.

Brady, C.P., Bray, J. H. and Zeeb, L. (1986). Behaviour problems of clinic children:

relation to parental marital status, age and sex of child. *American Journal of Orthopsychiatry*, 56, 399–412.

Braver, L. and O'Connell, D. (1998). *Divorced Dads: Shattering the Myths*. New York: Tarcher/Putman.

Bream, V. and Buchanan, A. (2003). Distress among children whose separated or divorced parents cannot agree arrangements for them. *British Journal of Social Work*, 33, 227–238.

Bretherton, I. (1985). Attachment theory: retrospect and prospect. In I. Bretherton and E. Waters (eds). *Growing Points of Attachment Theory and Research*. Monograph of the Society for Research in Child Development, 50, pp. 3–38.

—— (1991). The roots and growing points of attachment theory. In C. M. Parkes, J. Stevenson-Hinde and P. Marris (eds). *Attachment Across the Life Cycle*. London: Routledge, pp. 9–32.

Bretherton, I. and Munholland, K. A. (1999). Internal working models in attachment relationships: a construct revisited. In J. Cassidy and P. R. Shavers (eds). *Handbook of Attachment: Theory, Research, and Clinical Applications*. New York: The Guilford Press, pp. 89–111.

Brewaeys, A., Devroey, P., Helmerhorst, F., Van Hall, E. and Ponjaert, I. (1995). Lesbian mothers who conceive after donor insemination. *Human Reproduction*, 10, 2731–2735.

Brinich, P. and Shelley, C. (2002). *The Self and Personality Structure*. Maidenhead: Open University Press.

Brodzinsky, D. M. (1987). Adjustment to adoption: a psychological perspective. *Clinical Psychology Review*, 8, 27–32.

—— (1990). Stress and coping model of adoption adjustment. In D. M. Brodzinsky and M. D. Schechter (eds). *The Psychology of Adoption*. Oxford: Oxford University Press, pp. 3–24.

Brodzinsky, D. M. and Schechter, M. D. (eds). (1990). *The Psychology of Adoption*. Oxford: Oxford University Press.

Brodzinsky, D. M., Schechter, M. D. and Henig, R. M. (1992). *Being Adopted*. New York: Doubleday

Bronfenbrenner, U. (1979a). *The Ecology of Human Development: Experiments by Nature and Design*. Cambridge, MA: Harvard University Press.

—— (1979b). Context of child-rearing, *American Psychologist*, 34, 847.

—— (1992). Ecological systems theory. In R. Vasta (ed.). *Child Development: Revised Formulations and Current Issues*. London: Jessica Kingsley Publishers.

Brown, J. V. (1966). The measurement of family activities and relationships: a methodological study, *Human Relations*, 19, 241–263.

Brown, J. (1989). *Why Don't They Go to Work? Mothers on Benefit*. London: HMSO.

Buchanan, C. M., Maccoby, E. E. and Dornbusch, S. M. (1996). *Adolescents after Divorce*. Cambridge, MA: Harvard University Press.

Burns, A. and Dunlop, R. (2002). Parental marital quality and family conflict: longitudinal effects on adolescents from divorcing. *Journal of Divorce and Remarriage*, 37, 57–74.

Burns, A. and Scott, C. (1994). *Mother-Headed Families and Why They Have Increased*. Mahwah, NJ: Lawrence Erlbaum Associates Inc.

Burns, R. B. (1979). *The Self Concept: In Theory, Measurement, Development and Behaviour*. London: Longman.

Butler, B. (1989). Adoption an indigenous approach. *Adoption and Fostering*, 13 (2), 27–31.

Byng-Hall, J. (1991). The application of attachment theory to understanding and treatment in therapy. In C. M. Parkes, J. Stevenson-Hinde and P. Marris (eds). *Attachment Across the Life Cycle*. London: Routledge.

Byrne, J. B., O'Connor, T., Marvin, R. S. and Whelan, W. F. (2005). Practitioner review: the contribution of attachment theory to child custody assessments. *Journal of Child Psychology and Psychiatry*, 46 (2), 115–127.

Camara, K. A. and Resnick, G. (1988). Interparental conflict and cooperation: factors moderating children's post-divorce adjustment. In E. M. Hetherington and J. D. Arasteh (eds). *Impact of Divorce, Single Parenting, and Stepparenting on Children*. Hillsdale, NJ: Lawrence Erlbaum Associates, Inc.

Cantos, A. L., Gries, L.T. and Slis, V. (1997). Behavioral correlates of parental visiting during family foster care. *Child Welfare*, 76 (2), 309–329.

Carr, A. (1999). *The Handbook of Child and Adolescent Clinical Psychology: A Contextual Approach*. London: Routledge.

Carsten, C. and Juliá, M. (2000). Ethnoracial awareness in intercountry adoption: US experiences. *International Social Work*, 43, 61–73.

Cartwright, G. F. (1993). Expanding the parameters of parental alienation syndrome. *American Journal of Family Therapy*, 21, 205–215.

Cassidy, J. (1999). The nature of the child's ties. In J. Cassidy and P. R. Shavers (eds.). *Handbook of Attachment: Theory, Research, and Clinical Applications*. New York: Guilford Press, pp. 3–20.

Chase, P. L., Cherlin, A. J. and Kiernan, K. E. (1995). Long-term effects of parental divorce on the mental health of young adults: a developmental perspective. *Child Development*, 66, 1614–1634.

Chase-Landsdale, P. L., Cherlin, A. C. and Kiernan, K. (1995). The long-term effects of parental divorce on the mental health of young adults: a developmental perspective. *Child Development*, 66, 1614–1634.

Chennels, P. (1988). *Explaining Adoption to your Adopted Child*. London: BAAF.

Cherlin, A. J., Furstenberg, F. F., Chase-Lansdale, P. L., Kiernan, K. E., Robins, P. K., Morrison, D. and Teiler, J. G. (1991). Longitudinal studies of effects of divorce on children in Great Britain and the United States. *Science*, 252, 1386–1389.

Children's Society (2002). *British Public Back Change in Law to Give Children Right to their Identity*. London: Children's Society.

Clarke, L. (1996). Demographic change and the family situation of children. In J. Brannen and M. O'Brien (eds). *Children in Families*. London: Falmer Press.

Claudia, F. (2002). Politics of adoption: child rights in the Brazilian setting. *Law and Policy*, 24, 119–227.

Clawar, S. S. and Rivlin, B. V. (1991). *Children Held Hostage: Dealing with Programmed and Brainwashed Children*. Chicago, IL: American Bar Association.

Cleaver, H. (2000). *Fostering Family Contact*. London: The Stationery Office.

Cook, R., Goloomok, S., Bish, A. and Murray, C. (1995). Disclosure of donor insemination: parental attitudes. *American Journal of Orthopsychiatry*, 65 (94), 549–559.

Cooley, C. H. (1902). *Human Nature and Social Order*. New York: Scribner.

Courtney, A. (2000). Loss and grief in adoption: the impact of contact. *Adoption and Fostering*, 24, 33–44.

Dalen, M. and Saetersdal, B. (1987). Transracial adoption in Norway. *Adoption and Fostering*, 11, 41–46.

Daniels, K. R. and Taylor, K. (1993). Secrecy and openness on donor insemination. *Politics and Life Sciences*, August, 155–169.

David, E. and New, C. (1985). *For the Children's Sake*. Harmondsworth: Penguin.

Dennis, M. and Erdos. (1992). *Families without Fatherhood*. London: IEA Health and Welfare Unit.

Derdeyn, A. P. (1977). Child abuse and neglect: the rights of parents and the needs of their children. *American Journal of Orthopsychiatry*, 47, 377–387.

Diehl, M., Coyle, N. and Labouvie-Vief, G. (1996). Age and sex differences in strategies of coping and defense across the life span. *Psychology and Aging*, 11 (1), 127–139.

Dollard, J. and Miller, N. E. (1950). *Personality and Psychotherapy*. New York: McGraw-Hill.

Dornbusch, S. M., Carlsmith, J. M., Bushwall, S. J. *et al.* (1985). Single parents, extended households, and the control of adolescents. *Child Development*, 56, 326–341.

Downey, D. B., Ainsworth-Darnell, J. W. and Dufur, M. K. (1998). Sex of parent and children's well-being in single-parent households. *Journal of Marriage and the Family*, 60, 878–893.

Downey, D. B. and Powell, B. (1993). Do children in single-parent households fare better living with same-sex parents? *Journal of Marriage and the Family*, 55, 55–71.

Dunn, J. (1996). *Young Children's Close Relationships: Beyond Attachment*. Newbury Park, CA: Sage.

Dunne, J. and Hedrick, M. (1994). The parental alienation syndrome. *Journal of Divorce and Marriage*, 21, 21–38.

Durkin, K. (1995). *Developmental Social Psychology: From Infancy to Old Age*. Oxford: Blackwell.

Eagle, R. S. (1994). The separation experience of children in long-term care: theory research, and implications for practice. *American Journal of Orthopsychiatry*, 64, 421–434.

Edwards, A. (1966). *Experimental Design in Psychological Research*. New York: Holt, Rinehart and Winston.

Eggbeen, D. J., Synder, A. and Manning, W. (1996). Children in single father households in demographic perspective. *Journal of Household Issues*, 17, 441–465.

Ehrenshaft, D. (2005). *Mommies, Daddies, Donors, Surrogates*. New York: Guilford Press.

Elliot, B. J. and Richards, P. M. (1991). Children and divorce: educational performance and behaviour before and after parental separation. *International Journal of Law and the Family*, 5, 285–276.

Eme, R. F. and Kavannaugh, L. (1995). Sex differences in conduct disorder. *Journal of Child Clinical Psychology*, 24, 406–426.

Emery, R. E. (1982). Interparental conflict and the children of discord and divorce. *Psychological Bulletin*, 92, 310–330.

—— (1988). *Marriage, Divorce, and Children's Adjustment*. Newbury Park, CA: Sage.

Emery, R. E. and Coiro, M. J. (1995). Divorce: consequences for children. *Paediatrics Review*, 16 (8), 306–310.

Enriquez, V. G. (1993). Filipino psychology. In U. Kim and J. W. Berry (eds). *Indigenous Psychologies: Research and Experience in Cultural Context*. London: Sage, pp. 152–169.

Epstein, S. (1976). Anxiety, arousal and self-concept. Cited by G. J. Auer (1983) Contact with the absent parent after divorce: a therapeutic resource. *International Journal of Family Psychiatry*, 4, 105.

Erikson, E. (1950). *Childhood and Society*. New York: Norton.

—— (1968/1980). *Identity: Youth and Crisis*. New York: Norton.

Erikson, J. M. (1997). *Erik H. Erikson: the Life Cycle Completed*. New York: Norton.

Ethics Committee of the American Society for Reproductive Medicine. (2004). Informing offspring of their conception by gamete donation. *Fertility and Sterility*, 81, 527–531.

http.//europa.eu.int/en/comm/eurostat/compres/en/9798/6309798a.htm (accessed 18/04/2005).

EuroStat (Statistical Office of the European Community) (1996). *Demographic Statistics.* Luxembourg: EuroStat.

Evans, J. J. and Bloom, B. L. (1996). The effects of parental divorce among college undergraduates. *Journal of Divorce and Remarriage*, 26 (1/2), 69–91.

Fahlberg, V. (1991). *A Child's Journey Through Placement*. London: BAAF.

Feigelman, W. and Silverman, A. R. (1983). *Chosen Children: New Patterns of Adoptive Relationships*. New York: Praeger.

Felner, R. D., Stolberg, A. and Cowen, E. L. (1975). Crisis events and school mental health referral patterns of young children. *Journal of Consulting and Clinical Psychology*, 43, 305–310.

Fincham, F. D. and Osborne, L. N. (1993). Marital conflict and children: retrospect and prospect. *Clinical Psychology Review*, 13, 75–88.

Flugel, J. C. (1921). *The Psychoanalytic Study of the Family*. London: Hogarth Press.

Fonseca, F. (2002). Politics of adoption: child rights in the Brazilian setting. *Law and Policy*, 24, 199–227.

Foster, R. P. (1998). The clinician's cultural transference: the psychodynamics of culturally competent practice. *Clinical Social Work Journal*, 26 (3), 253–270.

Fox, N. A., Kimmerly, N. L. and Schafer, W. D. (1991). Attachment to mother/attachment to father: a meta-analysis. *Child Development*, 62, 210–225.

Freud, A. and Burlingham, D. T. (1944). *Infants Without Families: The Case For and Against Residential Nurseries*. New York: International Universities Press.

Freud, S. (1916/1963). *Introductory Lectures on Psychoanalysis. SE*, Vols 15 and 16. London: Hogarth Press.

—— (1969). *An Outline of Psychoanalysis*. New York: Norton.

Freundlich, M. (1998). Supply and demand: the forces shaping the future of infant adoption. *Adoption Quarterly*, 2, 13–46.

Furstenberg, F. F. and Cherlin, F. F. (1991). *Divided Families: What Happens to Children When Parents Part*. Cambridge, MA: Harvard University Press.

Furstenberg, F. F., Nord, C. W., Peterson, J. L. and Zill, N. (1983). The life course of children of divorce: marital disruption and parental contact. *American Sociological Review*, 48, 656–668.

Furstenberg, F. F. and Windquist-Nord, C. W. (1985). Parenting apart: patterns of childrearing after marital disruption. *Journal of Marriage and the Family*, 47, 893–904.

Gaber, I. and Aldrige, J. (1994). *Culture, Identity and Transracial Adoption: In the Best Interest of the Child*. London: Free Association Press.

Garasky, S. and Meyer, D. R. (1996). Reconsidering the increase in father-only families. *Demography*, 33, 385–393.

Gardner, R. A. (1985). Recent trends in divorce and custody litigation. *Academy Forum*, 33, 517–523.

—— (1987). *The Parental Alienation Syndrome and the Differentiation between Fabricated and Genuine Sexual Abuse*. Cresskill, NJ: Creative Therapeutics.

—— (1991). Legal and psychotherapeutic approaches to the three types of parental alienation syndrome families: when psychiatry and the law join forces. *Court Review*, 28, 14–21.

—— (1992). *Parental Alienation Syndrome*. Cresskill, NJ: Creative Therapeutics.

—— (1998). *The Parental Alienation Syndrome, 2nd edn*. Cresskill, NJ: Creative therapeutics.

—— (1999). Differentiating between parental alienation and bona fide abuse-neglect. *American Journal of Family Therapy*, 27, 97–107.

—— (2001). Should courts order PAS children to visit/reside with the alienated parent? A follow-up study. *American Journal of Forensic Psychology*, 19 (3), 61–106.

—— (2003). The judiciary's role in the etiology, symptom development, and treatment of the parental alienation syndrome (PAS). *American Journal of Forensic Psychology*, 21, 39–64.

Gbadegsin, S. (1998). Individual, community, and the moral order. In P. H. Coetzee and A. P. J. Roux (eds). *The African Philosophy Reader*. London: Routledge, pp. 292–305.

George, C. and Solomon, J. (1999). Attachment and caregiving: the caregiving behavioral system. In J. Cassidy and P. R. Shavers (eds). *Handbook of Attachment: Theory, Research, and Clinical Applications*. New York: Guilford Press, pp. 649–670.

Gerbner, G., Ross, C. J. and Ainsworth, M. (1989). Attachment beyond infancy. *American Psychologist*, 44, 709–716.

Gibson, H. B. (1969). Early delinquency in relation to broke homes. *Journal of Child Psychology and Psychiatry*, 10, 195–204.

Giddens, A. (1991). *Modernity and self-identity: self and society in the late modern Age*. Cambridge: Polity Press.

Giwa-Osagie, O. F. (2002). Assisted technologies: with particular reference to sub-Saharan Africa. In E. Vayena, P. J. Rowe and P. D. Griffin (eds). *Current Practices and Controversies in Assisted Reproduction*. Geneva: WHO, pp. 22–30.

Glenn, N. D. and Kramer, K. B. (1985). The psychological well-being of adult children of divorce. *Journal of Marriage and the Family*, 47, 905–912.

—— (1987). The marriages and divorces of the children of divorce. *Journal of Marriage and the Family*, 49, 811–825.

Glueck, S. and Glueck, E. T. (1950). *Unravelling Juvenile Delinquency*. New York: Commonwealth Fund.

—— (1962). *Family Environment and Delinquency*. New York: Routledge and Kegan Paul.

Goldfarb, W. (1943). The effects of early institutional care on adolescent personality. *Journal of Experimental Education*, 12, 106–129.

Goldstein, J., Freud, A. and Solnit, A. J. (1973). *Beyond the Best Interest of the Child*. New York: Free Press.

Golombok, S., Brewaeys, A., Cook, R., Giavassi, M. T., Crosiganani, P. G. and Dexeus, S. (1996). The European study of assisted reproduction families: family functioning and child development. *Human Reproduction*, 11, 2324–3113.

Golombok, S., Brewaeys, A., Giavazzi, M., Guerra, D., MacCullum, F. and Rust, J. (2002a). The European study of assisted conception families: the transition to adolescence. *Human Reproduction*, 17, 830–840.

Golombok, S., Cook, R., Bish, A. and Murray, C. (1995). Families created by the new reproductive technologies: quality of parenting and social and emotional development of the children. *Child Development*, 64, 285–288.

Golombok, S., MacCullum, F., Goodman, E. and Tutter, M. (2002b). Families with children conceived by donor insemination: a follow-up at age twelve. *Child Development*, 73, 952–968.

Golombok, S., Murray, A., Brisden, P. and Abdalla, H. (1999). Social versus biological parenting: family functioning and the socioemotional development of children conceived by egg or sperm donation, *Child Psychology and Psychiatry*, 40, 519–527.

Goode, W. J. (1992). World changes in divorce patterns. In L. J. Weitzman and M. Maclean (eds). *Economic Consequences of Divorce*. Oxford: Clarendon Press, pp. 1–49.

Gottlieb, C., Lalos, O. and Lindblad, F. (2000). Disclosure of donor insemination to the child: the impact of Swedish legislation on couple's attitudes. *Human Reproduction*, 15, 2052–2056.

Greenberg, M. T. (1999). Attachment and psychopathology in childhood. In J. Cassidy and P. R. Shavers (eds). *Handbook of Attachment: Theory, Research, and Clinical Applications*. New York: Guilford Press, pp. 469–496.

Grief, G. L. (1997). *Out of Touch: When Parents and Children Lose Contact After Divorce*. Oxford: Oxford University Press.

Grigsby, K. (1994). Maintaining attachment relationships among children in care. *Families in Society*, 75, 269–276.

Grotevant, H. D. (1987). Toward a process model of identity formation. *Journal of Adolescent Research*, 2, 203–222.

—— (1997). Coming to terms with adoption: the construction of identity from adolescence into adulthood. *Adoption Quarterly*, 1, 3–27.

Grych, J. H. and Fincham, F. D. (1992). Intervention for children of divorce: toward greater integration of research and action. *Psychological Bulletin*, 111, 434–454.

Guidubaldi, J., Perry, J. D. and Nastasi, B. K. (1987). Growing up in a divorced family: initial and long-term perspectives on children's adjustment. *Applied Social Psychology Annual*, 7, 202–237.

Gunnoe, M. L. and Braver, S. L. (2001). The effects of joint legal custody on mothers, fathers, and children controlling for factors that predispose a sole maternal versus joint legal award. *Law and Human Behavior*, 25, 25–43.

Guttman, J. and Lazar, A. (1998). Mother's or father's custody: does it matter for social adjustment? *Educational Psychology*, 18, 225–234.

Haimes, E. and Timms, N. (1985). *Adoption, Identity and Social Policy: The Search For Distant Relatives*. Aldershot: Gower.

Haimes, E. and Weiner, K. (2000). Everybody's got a dad . . .: Issues for lesbian families in the management of donor insemination. *Sociology of Health and Illness*, 22, 477–499.

Hall, G. S. (1904). *Adolescence*. New York: Appleton.

Hamilton, R. (2002). Donor-conceived adults challenge the ethics of anonymity. *Journal of Fertility Counselling*, 9, 33–34.

Harlow, H. F. (1962). The development of affectional patterns in infant monkeys. In B. M. Foss (ed.). *Development of Infant Behaviour*, vol. 1. London: Methuen, pp. 75–88.

Harlow, H. F. and Harlow, M. K. (1965). The affectional systems. In A. D. Schrier, H. F. Harlow and F. Stollnitz (eds). *Behaviour of Non-Human Primates*, vol. 2. London: Academic Press, pp. 287–334.

Harris, T. and Bifulco, A. (1991). Loss of parent in childhood, attachment style, and depression in adulthood. In C. M. Parkes, J. Stevenson-Hinde and P. Marris (eds). *Attachment Across the Life Cycle*. London: Routledge, pp. 234–267.

Hartman, A. and Laird, J. (1990). Family treatment after adoption: common themes. In D. M. Brodzinsky and D. Schechter (eds). *The Psychology of Adoption*. Oxford: Oxford University Press.

Haskey, J. (1989). One-parent families and their children in Great Britain: numbers and characteristics. *Population Trends*, 55, 27–33.

—— (1990). Children in families broken by divorce. *Population Trends*, 61, 34–42.

—— (1997). *Children Who Experience Divorce in their Family: Population Trends*. London: Office for National Statistics, pp. 5–11.

Healy, J., Malley, J. and Stewart, A. (1990). Children and their fathers after parental separation. *American Journal of Orthopsychiatry*, 60, 531–543.

Hess, R. D. and Camara, K. A. (1979). Post-divorce family relationships as mediating factors in the consequences of divorce for children. *Journal of Social Issues*, 35, 79–96.

Hetherington, E. M. (1972). Effects of father absence on personality development in adolescent daughters. *Developmental Psychology*, 7, 313–326.

—— (1973). Girls without fathers. *Psychology Today*, February, 47–52.

—— (1989). Coping with transitions: winners, losers, and survivors. *Child Development*, 60, 1–14.

Hetherington, E. M. and Arasteh, J. D. (eds). (1988). *Impact of Divorce, Single Parenting, and Stepparenting on Children*. Mahwah, NJ: Lawrence Erlbaum Associates, Inc.

Hetherington, E. M., Bridges, M. and Isabella, G. M. (1998). What matters? What does not: five perspectives on the association between marital transition and children's adjustment. *American Psychologist*, 53, 167–184.

Hetherington, E. M., Cox, M. and Cox, R. (1982). Effects of divorce on parents and children. In N. J. Lamb (ed.). *Nontraditional Families*. Hillsdale, NJ: Lawrence Erlbaum Association, Inc., pp. 233–288.

Hetherington, E. M., Cox, M. and Cox, R. (1985). Long-term effects of divorce and remarriage on the adjustment of children. *Journal of the American Academy of Child Psychiatry*, 24, 518–530.

Hinde, R. A. (1979). *Towards Understanding Relationships*. London: Academic Press.

—— (1992). Ethological and relationships approaches. In R. Vasta (ed.). *Six Theories of Child development: Revised Formulations and Current Issues*. London: Jessica Kingsley Publishers, pp. 251–285.

Holbrook, S. (1996). Social workers' attitudes towards participants' rights in adoption and new reproductive technologies. *Health and Social Work*, 21, 257–266.

Holdstock, L. T. (2000). *Re-examining Psychology: Critical Perspectives and African Insights*. London: Routledge.

Hollingsworth, L. D. (2003). International adoption among families in the United States: consideration of social justice. *Social Work*, 48, 209–217.

Holmes, J. (1993). *John Bowlby and Attachment Theory*. London: Routledge.

Horton, R. (1967). African traditional thought and western science. *Africa*, 37, 50–71.

Hountonji, P. J. and Zegeye, A. (1989). *Religion, Magic and Witchcraft: Structures of Belief in Everyday Life*. Oxford: Hans Zeller.

Howe, D. (1995). *Attachment Theory for Social Work Practice*. London: Macmillan.

Howe, D. and Feast, J. (2000). *Adoption, Search and Reunion: The Long-term Experiences of Adopted Adults*. London: Children's Society.

Howitt, D. and Cramer, D. (1997). *An Introduction to Statistics for Psychology*. London: Prentice Hall.

Howitt, D. and Owusu-Bempah, J. (1994). *The Racism of Psychology*. Hemel Hempstead: Harvester Wheatsheaf.

Hurlock, E. B. (1955). *Adolescent Development*. New York: McGraw Hill.

Hoyt, L. A., Cowen, E. L., Pedro-Carol, J. L. and Alpert-Gillis, L. J. (1990). Anxiety and depression in young children of divorce. *Journal of Clinical Child Psychology*, 19 (1), 26–32.

Humphrey, M. and Humphrey, H. (1988). *Families With a Difference: Varieties of Surrogate Parenthood*. London: Routledge.

Hunter, M., Salter-Ling, N. and Glover, L. (2000). Donor insemination: telling children about their origins. *Child Psychology and Psychiatry Review*, 5, 157–163.

Imbimbo, P. V. (1995). Sex differences in the identity formation of college students from divorced families. *Journal of Youth and Adolescence*, 24 (6), 745–761.

Ingersoll, B. D. (1997). Psychiatric disorders among adopted children: a review and commentary. *Adoption Quarterly*, 1, 57–73.

Inhorn, M. C. (2006). Middle Eastern men's discourses of adoption and gamete donation. *Medical Anthropology Quarterly*, 20, 94–120.

Jacobson, D. (1978). The impact of marital separation/divorce on child adjustment. *Journal of Divorce*, 1, 341–360.

James, W. (1890). *The Principles of Psychology*. New York: Holt.

Johnson, J., Campbell, L. and Mayers, S. (1985). Latency children in post separation and divorce disputes. *Journal of the American Academy of Child Psychiatry*, 24, 536–574.

Johnson, P., Wilkinson, W. K. and McNeil, K. (1995). The impact of parental divorce on the attainment of the developmental tasks of young adulthood. *Contemporary Family Therapy*, 17, 249–264.

Johnston, J., Lee, S., Olesen, N. C. and Walters, M. J. (2005). Allegations and substantiations of abuse in custody-disputing families. *Family Court Review*, 43, 283–294.

Johnston, J. R. (1994). High-conflict divorce. *Children and Divorce*, 4 (1), 165–182.

—— (2003). Parental alignment and rejection: an empirical study of alienation in children of divorce. *Journal of the American Academy of the Law and Psychiatry*, 31, 158–170.

Johnston, J. R., Gonzales, R. and Campbell, L. G. (1987). Ongoing post divorce conflict and child disturbance. *Journal of Abnormal Child Psychology*, 15 (4), 493–509.

Johnston, J. R., Kline, M. and Tschann, J. M. (1989). Ongoing post divorce conflict: effects on children of joint custody and frequent access. *American Journal of Orthopsychiatry*, 59, 576–592.

Kagitcibasi, C. (1984). Socialization in traditional society: a challenge to psychology. *International Journal of Psychology*, 19, 145–157.

Kakar, S. (1979). (ed.). *Identity in Adulthood*. Oxford: Oxford University Press.

Kaltenborn, K. F. (2001). Children and young people's experience in various residential arrangements: a longitudinal study to evaluate criteria for custody and residence decision making. *British Journal of Social Work*, 31, 81–117.

Kaltenborn, K. F. and Lempp, R. (1998). The welfare of the child in custody disputes after parental separation or divorce. *International Journal of Law, Policy and the Family*, 12, 74–106.

Kaltner, N., Kloner, A., Schreier, S. and Okla, A. (1989). Predictors of children's post-divorce adjustment. *American Journal of Orthopsychiatry*, 59, 605–620.

Kaplan, L. J. (1995). *Lost Children: Separation and Loss Between Children and Parents*. London: Harper Collins.

Kelly, J. B. (1988). Longer-term adjustment in children of divorce: converging findings and implications for practice. *Journal of Family Psychology*, 2, 119–140.

—— (2000). Children's adjustment in conflicted marriage and divorce: a decade of research. *Journal of the American Academy of Child and Adolescent Psychiatry*, 39, 963–973.

Kessler, R. C. and Magee, W. J. (1993). Childhood adversity and adult depression: basic patterns of association in a U.S. national survey. *Psychological Medicine*, 23, 679–690.

Kiernan, K. E. and Wicks, M. (1992). The impact of family disruption in childhood on transitions made in young adult life. *Population Studies*, 46, 213–234.

King, M. (2002). An autopoietic approach to 'parental alienation syndrome'. *Journal of Forensic Psychiatry*, 13, 609–635.

King, V. (1994). Nonresident father involvement and child well-being: can dads make a difference? *Journal of Family Issues*, 15, 78–96.

Kline, M., Tschann, J. M., Johnston, J. R. and Wallerstein, J. (1989). Children's adjustment in joint and sole physical custody families. *Developmental Psychology*, 25, 430–438.

Kopetski, L. M. (1998a). Identifying cases of parent alienation syndrome – Part I. *Colorado Lawyer*, 27, 63–66.

—— (1998b). Identifying cases of parent alienation syndrome – Part II. *Colorado Lawyer*, 27, 65–68.

Korntzer, M. (1971). The adopted adolescent and the sense of identity. *Child Adoption*, 66, 43–48.

Kreamer, G. (1992). A psychobiological theory of attachment. *Behavioural and Brain Sciences*, 15, 493–541.

Kroger, J. (1989). *Identity in Adolescence: The Balance between Self and Other*. London: Routledge.

Kurtz, L. (1994). Psychological coping resources in elementary school-age children of divorce. *American Journal of Orthopsychiatry*, 64, 554–562.

Laing, R. D. (1965). *The Divided Self*. Harmondsworth: Penguin.

Lamb, M. E. (ed.). (1976). *The Role of the Father in Child Development*. New York: Wiley.

Landau, R. (1998). Secrecy, anonymity, and deception in donor insemination: a genetic, psycho-social and ethical critique. *Social Work in Health Care*, 28, 75–89.

Landrine, H. (1992) Clinical implications of cultural differences: the referential versus the indexical self. *Clinical Psychology Review*, 12, 401–441.

Lengua, L. J., Wolchik, S. A. and Braver, S. L. (1995). Understanding children's divorce adjustment from an ecological perspective. *Journal of Divorce and Remarriage*, 22, 25–53.

Levy, D. (1992). Review of parental alienation syndrome: a guide for mental health and legal professionals. *American Journal of Family Therapy*, 20, 276–277.

Li, L. G. and Lu, G. X. (2005). How medical ethical principles are applied in treatment with artificial insemination by donors (AID) in humans: effective practice at the Reproductive and Genetic Hospital of CITIC-Xiangya. *Journal of Medical Ethics*, 31, 333–337.

Lifton, B. (1994). *Journey of the Adopted Self: A Quest for Wholeness*. New York: Basic Books.

Lindbald, F., Hjern, A. and Vinnerljung, B. (2003). Intercountry adopted children as adults: a Swedish cohort study. *American Journal of Orthopsychiatry*, 73, 190–202.

Littner, N. (1975). The importance of the natural parent to the child in placement. *Child Welfare*, 54, 175–181.

Lodge, P. (1998). The cheque's in the post: alienation revisited. http://www.deltabravo.net/custody/pas-lodge.htm

Lorenz, K. (1935). Der Kumpan in der Umwelt des Vogels (Instinctive Behaviour). *Journal Ornithologie*, 83, 137–213.

Lowenstein, J. S. and Koopman, E. J. (1978). A comparison of self-esteem between boys living with single-parent mothers and single-parent fathers. *Journal of Divorce*, 2, 195–208.

Lowenstein, L. F. (1998). Parent alienation syndrome: a two step approach toward a resolution. *Contemporary Family Therapy*, 20, 505–520.

Lycett, E., Daniels, K. R., Curson, R. and Golombok, S. (2005). School-aged children of donor insemination: a study of parents' disclosure patterns. *Human Reproduction*, 20, 810–819.

Lyddon, W. J. (1995). Attachment theory: a metaperspective for counseling psychology. *Counseling Psychologist*, 23, 479–483.

Lye, D. N. (1999). *What the Experts Say: Scholarly Research on Post-Divorce Parenting and Child Well-Being*. Chapter 4. Washington: Washington State Gender and Justice Commission and Domestic Relations Commission.

Maccoby, E. E., Depner, C. E. and Mnookin, R. H. (1990). Coparenting in the second year after divorce. *Journal of Marriage and the Family*, 52, 141–155.

Maccoby, E. E. and Mnookin, R. H. (1992). *Dividing the Child: Social and Legal Dilemmas of Custody*. Cambridge, MA: Harvard University Press.

MacKinnon, C. E. (1989). An observational investigation of sibling interactions in married and divorced families. *Developmental Psychology*, 25, 36–44.

McCord, J. W., McCord, W. and Thurber, E. (1962). Some effects of parental absence on male children. *Journal of Abnormal and Social Psychology*, 64, 361–369.

McLanahan, S. S. (1985). Family structure and the reproduction of poverty. *American Journal of Sociology*, 90, 873–901.

McLanahan, S. S. and Bumpass, L. (1988). Intergenerational consequences of family disruption. *American Journal of Sociology*, 94, 130–152.

McMillen, J. C. (1992). Attachment theory and clinical social work. *Clinical Social Work Journal*, 20, 205–218.

McWey, L. (2000). I promise to act better if you let me see my family: attachment theory and foster care visitation. *Journal of Family Social Work*, 5, 91–105.

McWhinnie, A. (1996) Outcome for families created by assisted conception programmes. *Journal of Assisted Reproduction Genetics*, 13, 363–365.

—— (2000). Children from assisted reproductive technique: the psychological issues and ethical dilemmas. *Early Child Development and Care*, 163, 13–23.

Main, M. (1999). Attachment theory: eighteen points with suggestions for future studies. In J. Cassidy and P. R. Shavers (eds). *Handbook of Attachment: Theory, Research, and Clinical Applications*. New York: Guilford Press, pp. 845–887.

Mbiti, J. S. (1969). *African Religions and Philosophy*. London: Heinemann.

Mead, G. H. (1934). *Mind, Self and Society*. Chicago: Chicago University Press.

Melzak, S. (1992). The secret of children who have experienced emotional abuse. In V. P. Varma (ed.). *The Secret life of Vulnerable Children*. London: Routledge, pp. 75–100.

Millar, J. (1989). *Poverty and the Lone-Parent Family*. Avebury: Gower.

Miller, P. H. (1999). *Theories of Developmental Psychology* (3rd edn). New York: Freeman Worth.

Milner, D. (1975). *Children and Race*. Harmondsworth: Penguin.

Mishen, J. M. (1984). Trauma of parental loss through divorce, death and illness. *Child and Adolescent Social Work Journal*, 1, 74–88.

Mitchell, N. K. (1983). Adolescents' experiences of parental separation and divorce. *Journal of Adolescence*, 19, 356–361.

Moyo, E. (1979). Big Mother and Little Mother in Matabeleland. In Bristol Women's Studies Group. *Half The Sky: An Introduction to Women's Studies*. London: Virago.

Ngabonziza, D. (1988). Inter-country adoption: in whose best interest? *Adoption and Fostering*, 12, 35–40.

Oakley, A. (1981). *Subject Women*. Oxford: Martin Robertson.

Office for National Statistics (2000). *1999 Mid-year Population Estimates*. London: ONS.

Office for National Statistics (2005a). *Population Trends 121*. London: ONS.

Office for National Statistics (2005b). *Social Trends*. London: ONS.

Offord, D. R. (1982). Family backgrounds of male and female delinquents. In J. Gunn and D. P. Farrington (eds). *Abnormal Offenders, Delinquency and the Criminal Justice System*. New York: Wiley, pp. 129–151.

Owusu-Bempah, J. (1993). *Parental information and children's behaviour.* Unpublished study. School of Social Work, University of Leicester, UK.

Owusu-Bempah, J. and Howitt, D. (1997). Socio-genealogical connectedness, attachment theory, and childcare practice. *Child and Family Social Work*, 2, 199–207.

—— (1999). Even their soul is defective. *The Psychologist*, 12 (3), 126–130.

—— (2000a). Socio-genealogical connectedness: on the role of gender and same-gender parenting in mitigating the effects of parental divorce. *Child and Family Social Work*, 5, 107–116.

—— (2000b). *Psychology Beyond Western Perspectives*. Oxford: BPS/Blackwell.

Owusu-Bempah, K. (1994). Race, self-identity and social work. *British Journal of Social Work*, 24, 123–136.

—— (1995). Information about the absent parent as a factor in the well-being of children of single-parent families. *International Social Work*, 38, 253–275.

—— (2006). Socio-genealogical connectedness: knowledge and identity. In J. Aldgate, D. Jones, W. Rose and C. Jeffery (eds). *The Developing World of the Child*. London: Jessica Kingsley Publishers, pp. 112–121.

Palmer, S. E. (1990). Group treatment of fostered children to reduce separation conflicts associated with placement breakdown. *Child Welfare*, 69 (3), 227–238.

Pannor, R., Sorosky, A. and Baran, A. (1974). Opening the sealed record in adoption: the human need for continuity. *Journal of Jewish Communal Service*, 51, 188–196.

Parkes, C. M. and Stevenson-Hinde, J. (eds). *Attachment Across the Life Cycle*. London: Routledge.

Parosaari, U. and Laippala, A. H. (1996). Parental divorce and depression in young adulthood: adolescents' closeness to parents and self-esteem as mediating factors. *Acta Psychiatric Scandinavica*, 93, 20–26.

Peretti, P. O. and Divitorrio, A. (1992). Effects of loss of father through divorce on personality of the preschool child. *Journal of Instructional Psychology*, 19, 269–273.

Peterson, J. L. and Zill, N. (1986). Marital disruption, parent–child relationships, and behaviour problems in children. *Journal of Marriage and the Family*, 48, 95–307.

Poussin, G. and MartinLebrun, E. (2002). A French study of children's self-esteem after parental separation. *International Journal of Law, Policy and the Family*, 16, 313–326.

Powell, B. and Downey, D. B. (1997). Living in single-parent households: an investigation of the same-sex hypothesis. *American Sociological Review*, 62, 521–539.

Price, J. L. and Poiske, K. S. (1994). Parental alienation syndrome: a developmental analysis of vulnerable population. *Journal of Psychological Nursing*, 32, 9–12.

Pringle, M. L. K. and Bossio, V. (1960). Early prolonged separation and emotional adjustment, *Journal of Child Psychology and Psychiatry*, 1, 37–48.

Pringle, M. L. K. and Clifford, L. (1962). Conditions associated with emotional adjustment among children in care. *Educational Review*, 14, 112–123.

Rand, D. C. (1997). The spectrum of parental alienation syndrome (Part II). *American Journal of Forensic Psychology*, 15, 39–92.

Raphael, B., Cubis, J., Dunne, M. *et al.* (1990). The impact of parental loss on adolescents' psychological characteristics. *Adolescence*, 25, 689–700.

Ressler, E., Boothby, N. and Steinbock, D. (1988). *Unaccompanied Children: Care and Protection in Wars, Natural Disasters and Refugee Movements*. Oxford: Oxford University Press.

Ringbäck, W. G., Hjern, A., Haglund, B. *et al.* (2003). Mortality, severe morbidity, and injury in children with single parents in Sweden: a population-based study. *Lancet*, 361, 289–295.

Robertson, J. and Robertson, J. (1971). Young children in brief separation: a fresh look. *Psychoanalytic Study of the Child*, 26, 264–315.

Roche, H. and Perlesz, M. (2000). A legitimate choice and voice: the experience of adult adoptees who have chosen to search for their biological families. *Adoption and Fostering*, 24, 8–19.

Rogers, B. and Pryor, J. (1998). *Divorce and Separation: The Outcomes for Children*. York: Joseph Rowntree Foundation.

Rogers, K. N. (2004). A theoretical review of risk and protective factors related to post-divorce adjustment in young children. *Journal of Divorce and Remarriage*, 40, 135–147.

Roland, A. (1988). *In Search of Self in India and Japan: Towards a Cross-Cultural Psychology*. Princeton: Princeton University Press.

Roll, J. (1992). *Lone-Parent families in the European Community: The 1992 Report to the European Commission*. London: European Family and Social Policy Unit.

Rørbech, M. (1990). *Denmark – My Country: The Conditions of 18–25-year-old Foreign Born Adoptees in Denmark*. Copenhagen: Danish National Institute of Social Research, booklet no. 30.

Roseby, V. and Johnston, J. R. (1998). Children of Armageddon: common developmental threat in high-conflict divorcing families. *Child and Adolescent Psychiatric Clinics of North America*, 7 (2), 295–309.

Ross, C. E. and Mirowsky, J. (1999). Parental divorce, life-course disruption, and adult depression. *Journal of Marriage and the Family*, 61, 1034–1045.

Rumball, A. and Adair, V. (1999). Telling the story: parents' scripts for donor offspring. *Human Reproduction*, 14, 1392–1399.

Rutter, M. (1981/1991). *Maternal Deprivation Reassessed* (2nd edn). Harmondsworth: Penguin.

—— (1994). Family discord and conduct disorder: cause, consequences, or correlate? *Journal of Family Psychology*, 8, 170–186.

—— (1995). Clinical implications of attachment concepts: retrospect and prospect. *Journal of Child Psychology and Psychiatry*, 36, 549–571.

—— (1999). Resilience concepts and findings: implications for family therapy. *Journal of Family Therapy*, 21, 119–144.

Rutter, M. and O'Connor, T. G. (1999). Implications of attachment theory for child care policies. In J. Cassidy and P. R. Shavers (eds). *Handbook of Attachment: Theory, Research, and Clinical Implications*. New York: Guilford Press, pp. 823–844.

Sachdev, P. (1992). Adoption reunion and after: a study of the search process and experience of adoptees. *Child Welfare*, 71, 53–68.

Samuelson, M. A. K. (1997). Social networks of children in single-parent families: differences according to sex, age, socioeconomic status and housing type and their associations with behavioural disturbances. *Social Networks*, 19, 113–127.

Savage, O. M. N. (1995). Secrecy still the best policy: donor insemination in Cameroon. *Politics and the Life Sciences*, 14, 87–88.

Sawyer, H. (1970). *God: Ancestor or Creator?* London: Longman.

Scarr, S. (1985). Cultural lenses on mothers and children. In L. Friedrich-Cofer (ed.). *Human Nature and Public Policy*, New York: Praeger.

Schaffer, H. R. (1971). *The Growth of Sociability*. Harmondsworth: Penguin.

Schaffer, H. R. and Emerson, P. E. (1964). The development of social attachments in infancy. *Monographs of the Society for Research in Child Development*, 29, 1–77.

Schechter, M. D. and Bertocci, D. (1990). The meaning of the search. In D. M. Brodzinsky and M. D. Schechter (eds). *The Psychology of Adoption*. Oxford: Oxford University Press, pp. 62–90.

Sergrin, C., Taylor, E. and Atlman, J. (2005). Social cognitive mediators and relational outcomes associated with parental divorce. *Journal of Social and Personal Relationships*, 23, 361–377.

Shants, H. J. (1964). Genealogical bewilderment in children with substitute parents. *British Journal of Medical Psychology*, 37, 133–141.

Shenfield, F. (1997). Privacy versus disclosure in gamete donation: a clash of interest, of duties or an exercise in responsibility. *Journal of Assisted Reproduction Genetics*, 14, 371–373.

Simmons, G., Gumpter, J. and Rothman, B. (1973). Natural parents as partners in child care placement. *Social Casework*, 54, 224–232.

Simons, R. L., Lin, K. H., Gordon, L. C., Conger, R. D. and Lorenz, F. O. (1999). Explaining the higher incidence of adjustment problems among children of divorce compared with those in two-parent families. *Journal of Marriage and the Family*, 61, 1020–1033.

Skolnick, A. (1998). Solomon's children: the new biologism, psychological parent-hood, attachment theory, and the best interest standard. In A. Skolnick and S. D. Sugarman (eds.). *All Our Families: New Policies for a New Century*. New York: Oxford University Press.

Smith, A. B. and Gollop, M. M. (2001). What children think separating parents should know. *New Zealand Journal of Psychology*, 30, 23–39.

Snowden, R., Mitchell, G. D. and Snowden, E. M. (1983). *Artificial Reproduction: A Social Investigation*. London: Allen and Unwin.

Snowden, R. and Snowden, E. (1993). *The Gift of a Child: A Guide to Donor Insemination*. Exeter: Exeter University Press.

Sogolo, G. S. (1989). Doctrinal opposition and religious conversion: the African experience. *Ibadan Journal of Religious Studies*, 21, 119–130.

Sorosky, A. D., Baran, A. and Pannor, R. (1975). Identity conflicts in adoptees. *American Journal of Orthopsychiatry*, 45, 18–27.

Southworth, S. and Schwarz, J. C. (1987). Post-divorce contact relationship with father and heterosexual trust in female college students. *American Journal of Orthopsychiatry*, 57, 371–382.

Spencer, N. (2005). Does material disadvantage explain the increased risk of adverse health, educational, and behavioural outcomes among children in lone parent households in Britain? A cross sectional study. *Journal of Epidemiology and Community Health*, 59, 152–157.

Spitz, R. A. (1945). Hospitalism: an inquiry into the genesis of psychiatry conditions in early childhood. *Psychoanalytic Study of the Child*, 1, 53–74.

Spruijt, E., Eikelenboom, B., Harmeling, J., Stokkers, R. and Kormos, H. (2005). Parental alienation syndrome (PAS) in the Netherlands. *American Journal of Family Therapy*, 33, 303–317.

Sroufe, L. A., Carlson, E. A., Levy, A. K. and Egeland, B. (1999). Implications of attachment theory for developmental psychopathology. *Developmental Psychopathology*, 11, 1–13.

Stayton, D. J. and Ainsworth, M. (1973). Individual differences in infant response to brief, everyday separations as related to other infant and maternal behaviors. *Developmental Psychology*, 9, 213–215.

Stevens, R. (1983). *Erik Erikson*. Milton Keynes: Open University Press.

Stewart, S. D. (1999). Nonresident mothers' and fathers' social contact with children. *Journal of Marrriage and Family*, 61, 894–907.

Stewart-Clarke, K. A. and Hayward, C. (1996). Advantages of father custody and contact for the psychological well-being of children of school-age. *Journal of Applied Developmental Psychology*, 17, 239–270.

Stolberg, A. L., Camplair, C., Currier K. and Wells, M. J. (1987). Individual, familial and environmental determinants of children's post-divorce adjustment and maladjustment. *Journal of Divorce*, 11 (1), 51–70.

Stonequist, E. (1937). *The Marginal Man: A Study in Personality and Culture Conflict*. New York: Russel and Russel.

Studer, J. (1993). Comparison of the self-concepts of adolescents from intact, maternal custodial, and paternal custodial families. *Journal of Divorce and Remarriage*, 19, 219–227.

Taylor, C. (1989). *Source of the Self*. Cambridge: Cambridge University Press.

Teffo, L. J. and Roux, P. J. (1998). Metaphysical thinking in Africa. In P. H. Coetzee and A. P. J. Roux (eds). *The African Philosophy Reader*. London: Routledge.

Tennant, C. (1988). Parental loss in childhood: its effect in adult life. *Archives of General Psychiatry*, 45, 1045–1050.

Tessman, L. H. (1978). *Children of Parting Parents*. New York: Jason Aronson.

Thompson, R. A. (2000). The legacy of early attachments. *Child Development*, 71, 145–152.

Tizard, B. (1991). Inter-country adoption: a review of the evidence. *Journal of Child Psychology and Psychiatry*, 32, 743–756.

Tizard, B. and Phoenix, A. (1989). Black identity and transracial adoption. *New Community*, 15, 427–438.

Triandis, H. C. (1995). *Individualism and Collectivism*. Boulder: Westview Press.

Triseliotis, J. (1973): *In Search of Origins: The Experiences of Adopted People*. London: Routledge and Kegan Paul.

—— (1983). Identity and security in long-term fostering and adoption. *Adoption and Fostering*, 7 (1), 22–31.

—— (1985). Adoption with contact. *Adoption and Fostering*, 9, 4.

—— (2000). Intercountry adoption: global trade or gift? *Adoption and Fostering*, 24, 45–54.

Triseliotis, J. and Hill, M. (1990). Contrasting adoption, foster care, and residential rearing. In D. M Brodzinsky and M. D. Schecter (eds). *The Psychology of Adoption*. Oxford: Oxford University Press, pp. 107–120.

Triseliotis, J., Shireman, J. and Hundleby, M (1997). *Adoption: Theory, Policy and Practice*. London: Cassell

Turner, A. J. and Coyle, A. (2000). What does it mean to be a donor offspring. The identity experiences of adults conceived by donor insemination and the implications for counselling and therapy. *Human Reproduction*, 15, 2041–2051.

Turner, C. (1993). A call for openness in donor insemination. *Politics and the Life Sciences*, 12, 197–199.

Underwood, P. and Kamien, M. (1984). Health care needs of the children of single mothers in a Perth suburb. *Australian Paediatric Journal*, 21, 203–204.

Valsiner, J. (2000). *Culture and Human Development*. London: Sage.

Vassiliou, D. and Cartwright, G. F. (2001). The lost parents' perspective on parental alienation syndrome. *American Journal of Family Therapy*, 29, 181–191.

Vercollone, C. F., Moss, H. and Moss, R. (1997). *Helping the Stork: The Choices and Challenges of Donor Insemination*. London: Macmillan.

Vesta, R. (ed.). (1992). *Child Development: Revised Formulations and Current Issues*. London: Jessica Kingsley Publishers.

Vestal, A. (1999). Mediation and parental alienation syndrome: considerations for an intervention model. *Family and Conciliation Court Review*, 37 (4), 487–503.

Waddington, C. H. (1957). *The Strategy of the Genes*. London: Allen and Unwin.

Wadsworth, M. E. J. (1976). Delinquency, pulse rate and early emotional deprivation. *British Journal of Criminology*, 16, 245–256.

Wadsworth, J., Burnell, I., Taylor, B. and Butler, T. (1985). The influence of family type on children's behaviour and development at five years. *Journal of Child Psychology and Psychiatry*, 26, 245–254.

Walby, C. and Symons, B. (1990). *Who am I? Identity, Adoption and Human Fertilisation*. London: British Agencies for Adoption and Fostering.

Waldron, K. H. and Joanis, D. E. (1996). Understanding collaboratively treating parental alienation syndrome. *American Journal of Family Law*, 10, 121–133.

Walker, I. and Broderick, P. (1999). The psychology of assisted reproduction – or psychology assisting its reproduction? *Australian Psychologist*, 34, 38–44.

Wallerstein, J. and Kelly, J. (1980). *Surviving the Break-up: How Parents and Children Cope with Divorce*. London: Grant McIntyre.

Wallerstein, J. S. (1991). The long-term effects of divorce on children: a review. *Journal of the American Academy of Child and Adolescent Psychiatry*, 30, 349–360.

Walsh, M. R. and Bone, J. M. (1997). PAS: an age-old custody problem. *Florida Bar Journal*, June, 93–96.

Ward, P. and Harvey, J. C. (1993). Family wars: the alienation of children. *New Hampshire Bar Journal*, 34 (1), 2 (http://www.fact.on.ca/Info/pas/ward02.htm).

Warnock, M. (1984). *Report of the Committee of Inquiry into Human Fertilisation and Embryology*. London: HMSO.

—— (1987). The good of the child. *Bioethics*, 1, 141–155.

Warshak, R. A. (1986). Father-custody and child development: a review and analysis of psychological research. *Behavioral Sciences and Law*, 4, 185–202.

—— (1992). *The Custody Revolution: The Father Factor and the Motherhood Mystique*. New York: Poseidon.

—— (2000). Remarriage as a trigger of parental alienation syndrome. *American Journal of Family Therapy*, 28, 229–241.

Warshak, R. A. and Stantrock, J. W. (1983). The impact of divorce in father-custody and mother-custody homes: the child's perspective. In L. A. Kurdek (ed.). *Children and Divorce*. San Francisco: Jossey-Bass.

Wellisch, E. (1952). Children without genealogy: a problem of adoption. *Mental Health*, 13, 1.

Westhues, A. and Cohen, J. (998). Ethnic and racial identity of internationally adopted adolescents and young adults: some issues in relation to children's rights. *Adoption Quarterly*, 4, 33–55.

White, L. K., Brinkerhoff, D. and Booth, A. (1985). The effect of marital disruption on children's attachment to parents. *Journal of Family Issues*, 6, 5–22.

Whiting, B. B. and Edwards, C. P. (1988). *Children of Different Worlds: The Formation of Social Behaviour*. Cambridge, MA: Harvard University Press.

Wiredu, K. (1998). The moral foundations of an African Culture. In P. H. Coetzee and A. P. J. Roux (eds). *The African Philosophy Reader*. London: Routledge, pp. 306–316.

Witte, de M. (2001). *Long Live the Dead! Changing Funeral Celebrations in Asante, Ghana*. Amsterdam: Aksant.

World Health Organization (WHO, 1992). *International Statistical Classification of Diseases and Related Health Problems, ICD-1D*. Geneva: WHO.

Zaslow, M. J. (1988). Sex differences in children's response to parental divorce: 1. Research methodology and postdivorce family forms. *American Journal of Orthopsychiatry*, 58, 355–378.

—— (1989). Sex differences in children's response to parental divorce: 2. Samples, variable, ages and sources: *American Journal of Orthopsychiatry*, 59, 118–141.

Zimiles, H. and Lee, V. E. (1991). Adolescent family structure and educational progress. *Developmental Psychology*, 27, 314–320.

Author index

Subject index